NOBODY
AN AMERICAN TRAGEDY

By Brandon Nobles

———————————

I'd like to thank:
My *editor*, Katie Chiles,
without whose whip this work would still be incomplete.
Her editorial analysis and suggestions over the course of the first
draft proved invaluable.
My copy editor, Josh Baier, for correcting my typos, shouting at
me when my writing sucked, and for mocking my characters and
threatening my life, often, for no apparent reason.
My brothers, my sisters, my family, and friends:
Thanks for the adoption, the food, the money,
and the support.
Consider this an IOU with your name on it.
And for *both* of my fans,
this one's on the house.

Author's note:

Due to the nature of a novel regarding slavery, it is expected, and unfortunate, that, to render realistically the inexplicable hatred of our fellow man for the pigment of their skin (there are far better reasons to hate people) there are slanderous, offensive, and racist words and attitudes in this book. These attitudes and prejudices are not shared by the author; they are the views of the characters within the story. Astute readers will note, however, that the issue of race is a non-factor in the development of this narrative as Nobody, the anonymous people who die without being known, is without color, without opinion, and without the notoriety to have opinions taken seriously. And, with that said, I've one more thing to say: don't get pissed off at me because there are racist characters in the world I'm writing about.

Brandon Nobles, 2008,
Whitmire, South Carolina.

1. *Galilee's Eulogy*

Neddy was a slave who lived in South Carolina long ago. His family worked for many years on a lovely Hill called Rose.

Rose Hill was a large, off-white colonial mansion where near a hundred slaves once worked before Lincoln's proclamation set them free—before the miserable maniac Booth closed the drapes on *Lincoln's show*, no bow, no audience, bloodstained opera glasses, empty seats speak silence now, and *they all loved the show.*

At the Rose the ghosts of those dead choirs sang and sang— the wind the chorus, rain refrain, and Nobody knew their name.

A long row of run down wooden cabins lined the end of the dusty driveway, mansion to the left, the meadow to the right.

Twisted elms and pecan trees stood out front, a canopy of interconnected limbs and broken twigs, pinecombs scattered on the ground; and near the field a nature trail, the carpet of leaves for lackadaisical walks. They were all made by the slaves, a thousand hours, several days, ten minute breaks under the shade, all for the Master and his guests: church groups and their kids came every Easter to hide and dye the eggs. Even the slaves got the day off. Alexander, Alex as known to his guests, was quite the host indeed: mint juleps, snifters of brandy, wine glass iridescent lights and bourbon on the rocks.

Neddy's mother stood with her hands behind her back against the wall, nothing to do, head down blank face vacant, staring at her feet.

Neddy's mother's name was Frannie. Frannie's mother, Ava, was eight months pregnant when she got on the ship, a ship with white curtains in the wind, from one world to another. Some slaves—old slaves, they couldn't row. They had to go, went over the side, into the ocean by a laughing crowd, "Now don't y'all eat 'em all at once! Wouldn't want to spoil your supper, boys. Besides, we need a few ourselves."

Frannie's father Samuel died the following winter from pneumonia. Her mother Ava went quite mad, a shrieking fury all the night screaming at people who weren't there, on the edge of the bed, rocking back and forth and mumbling. Due to her condition she was considered unfit to work. So the Master Alexander in his mercy dragged her by the hair behind the barn, threw her to the ground, and shot her in the head before she

4

even made a sound. Blood scattered on white roses when she fell.

The slaves heard the echo of the gun and mumbled, oh God, dear God. The startled starlings fled the bush. The tired slaves worked on, black bags under their eyes a defeated hopeless look. And when they heard the shot, they worked as though they heard it not. There was nothing they could do and if they tried the same would happen to them.

Neddy's father's name was Ray. He made the trip from the old world to the new with his father and his uncle and his little brother too.

Ray's mother died giving birth to his younger brother.

His uncle hanged himself.

His brother, Neddy's uncle, was named Nate. Nate and Ray were the oldest slaves still working at Rose Hill.

They had no last names, no hope, but in the end it was the same: when a slave died on the hill, regardless of the cause, it was the responsibility of the family to dig the hole, wrap the body in linen and chisel the name into the headstone their sad song, a joyful epigraph:

Work is never finished,
Master got me working...
Some day Master set me free.

Neddy's father plowed the fields and shucked corn in the barn. His mother had to sew and cook and clean. His uncle did a bit of this, a bit of that, planting flowers, tending a tomato garden by the veranda. Neddy once had a sister by the name of Galilee— named for a church down the road—for whom he wrote a eulogy.

When she fell into the well while playing hide and seek—her tearful face he could not see, but heard—as though it were some mockingbird.

"Somebody help me, please!" she cried—for several days and then she died, slumped over, face down in the pond, blood clotting in her once fair eyes, down her chin, the blood like tiny rivers by her body.

Other shameless crying slaves begged and pleaded with the Master.

"Master help..."

"I'm busy."

"Oh dear God help her please... She's just a little girl!"

"For the sake of God do something!"

Master yelled at them to leave and then refused, spitting at the weeping nobody's with their black eye sockets burnt-out wide, closed the door, the slaves walked into the rain dejected, slumping shoulders, pouting lips.

Rain, rain, go away...

Again the next day when they asked the dreadful Master, "Help!"

He looked around and laughed and laughed.

"Let them help themselves. Who helps us? They do. We can't help ourselves. Neither than can they. We're all equal in the end, you know. You think God sees us in different colors?"

When she was dead, another beautiful flower too early plucked, the Master, at last, decided to get the frail girl's body out of his drinking water.

The masked sad Master sighed, the unhidden Master said, "Bury her behind the shed."

The day her face went underground, Neddy spoke, sad faces round.

His sister liked the songs he wrote, so he wrote a song for her, a song to sing, her eulogy, trembling hands, monotone words— he read in quiet by the jasmine covered grave.

Three other slaves and nameless grey watched her go into the grave with not a thing to say or do, twitching lips those bubbling eyes with tears of blue crawl out in wrinkles drawn by time.

"Sister, dear, how well I know, how much you meant to me. You were beautiful and saw what was beautiful in the world, the trees, the flowers, those yellow jasmines you picked for me. I felt that way for you, as though you were my flower, and I wish I could see you one more time, holding one of those flowers for me.

"And now another flower in the field *has* laid its head, back onto the garden where once it lay in bed."

A preacher read a solemn prayer. Neddy bowed his head.

When Galilee was a little girl, how bright then was all the world; she knew, at ten, *it* would begin, her servitude unfurled. She would become a slave. No more walks, no late night talks, just that far-off vacant gaze.

When she was young she often sung, walking in the gardens with the Master's wife, and often ate inside at night. None of the other slaves got warm food, or custom dresses, fancy clothes— and they dressed her, Galilee, in a thousand outfits and she posed...

Neddy didn't understand their concern for Galilee, or why they didn't treat all of the slaves that way. Neddy had cold bowls of grits and molded bread for breakfast every day, the sour taste of tears, unwelcome Heaven over head; a hole in the mud where they screamed trapped, walking in quicksand desperate circles until swallowed by the Earth.

They won't see the shore tonight...not with the lighthouse out; ships are crashing, people screaming heads on fire faces dive into the ink black sea.

They saw the stars as iron bars above them in the sky—the sight of Heaven blurred—that often overhead passed by to blot out all the stars, leaving them like jailbirds looking up, singing songs about a place for which they longed, whose door for them was always shut, and locked, the key long thrown away.

That growing hole was always there, forever at the Rose, where on the hills, where men once tilled, a thousand jasmines flowed with listless wind and to no end.

When you're a slave you work and strive yet never have a thing. All your tears and prayers won't consolation bring. That's how the Master wished for it to be. That is how it was.

Neddy was a slave who worked inside the ivy maze, behind the house in endless patterns of intersecting hedges, false directions. Neddy in comfort walked alone into the maze though overgrown—*I'll figure it out,* he thought.

He trimmed the bushes, trimmed the hedges, and often lost his way. He did his best, day after day, to avoid the other slaves; he could not look them in the eye.

After a day, and hard at work, on stained cobblestone he walked alone; quiet, in his way, in silence passed a lonely grave. He turned his head. He would not look, a silent requiem for Galilee sang. He stared at the ground as he walked without sound. Tired at home he lay.

His home was bare; nobody there. His sister's empty bed was made. His mother must've been he thought in Master's kitchen where, every night by lantern light a hot meal she prepared.

When Neddy slept in his poor house he often dreamed he was a louse.

In that dream, how small he seemed; trapped on a free man's head. Around he went, by God's hand sent; a light shone overhead. It rained and rained, less lice remained, and those who did yelled, "No!" as they were swallowed by the memory hole.

The lice who didn't oft would shout at fingers that with just a hat could blot the sunlight out. Tense fingers crawled the scalp about ten times every day. When they were gone he was alone. One louse still remained.

And Nobody was his name.

Neddy the slave, Nobody the louse, lay on the bare floor of his house. In his mind he strayed. He saw a thousand vacant, forlorn faces, different people, different races, wild-eyed and staring plain—on a *stairwell to nowhere* walking again.

He'd stand at the bottom of the white stairwell, worried, eyes wide, the bitter taste of sweat, the frightened animal looked at the sky.

Steps receded into clouds and step by step he walked into the sky. When he made it to the top another step was added, another and another, more, the unending walk to no where.

He turned around, and looked back down, and no longer saw the ground—where once he saw his home—his family and friends—there was, instead, nothing but those dread white stairs, descending in the billows of the clouds.

By the stairway in his dreams he saw a grave with no last name. His sister's ghost sat on a gravestone by the rose white steps. She wore a sky blue dress of lace.

"Hello?" Neddy halfway asked.

She wouldn't look—eyes to the side—downcast a drooping frown.

"Hello!" he screamed, her face unflinching, mannequin like and terrifying, blank unwavering eyes as white as snow, a stagnant glow.

"Hello!" the hollow word in monotone echoed back. She would not look his way. She pulled petals from a rose and one by one they fell. Each petal plucked made Neddy's chest go numb and twinge, then dry heave, roll around a while in leaves—the burning, electricity of panic, nervous system set on fire, flooded adrenaline alight, fight or flight or run into the night.

Galilee hummed a haunting jingle in the dark:

'And now another flower in the field has laid its head, back onto the garden where once it lay in bed.'

"Hello?"

She's dead. She can't hear.

She'll always hear me.

Then why won't she look at you? There are better lice than you for her to talk to. You just stood there and listened to her scream, Somebody help! Dear God, help me please!

Oh God help us all...

2. The Quietus in the Crowd

Neddy tossed and turned and tried to sleep but wept. Tears fell on the floor un-swept. Shapes pressed against his tight closed eyes and in his mind he heard sublime his sister's lilting lullabies, flowers of the field, now in the shape of words and waves and birds and graves.

And round and round it goes.

Neddy watched her run under the sky, above them Heaven flying by, Neddy himself not far behind. He chased her in the dark. Her white dress wafted in the wind. He chased and chased but never caught.

Neddy would follow her childlike laughter to the edge of the world and back.

The slaves never talked about their memories, not in Neddy's house. Neddy wondered if the other slaves thought back when by themselves, alone, or when they tossed and turned and tried to sleep, damp cot on the floor and counting sheep, one, two, three, four, five, six...

Slaves who worked and lived on the Hill rarely talked about memories and never talked about their lives.

They walked around in quiet looking down, a forever branded downcast frown. When they thought about their life—their childhood or the old world—they'd scream and shout and cry; they'd mumble 'til the Master with his loaded gun came by.

They went to sleep at the same time every night. They woke up at the same time every morning. They worked for twelve hours every day under the sun.

Their memories were no different than their present lives, some worse, memory nothing but a sorrowful hole the days went down. Memories don't help when you watch a baby drown sink in the ground once vibrant now lifeless dead.

They made the children cry at night. People screamed at the walls and pulled out their hair until the Master came and dragged them to the woods. The horrible metal squeal again, smoking chamber, another nameless nobody slave slumps over in the dust, bullet wound the brain leaks out, the blood spread like black flowers in the dirt.

Whenever the working or the sleeping slaves heard the sound of Master's gun they knew another life was gone.

When they thought about their memories, their young lives, the flowers of the field shaded in the thick bush of the sun, they lost their minds.

Neddy went to sleep to the sound of the terrible indecipherable screams of the slaves in the cabin next to his, fingers in his ears and, "And now another flower in the field has laid it's head..."

Some slave cried out every night, about this and about that, more. Neddy couldn't sleep until a slave cried out. And even then he struggled, sometimes for hours, tossing, turning, painful images flitting by the eye.

Slaves weren't given much: a metal barrel full of coal, heat in the center of their cabin, kept them warm when winter came, dingy green and rain stained cots spread on the floor.

Each cabin had five plates, five spoons, five cups, and those damp cots on the floor. The slaves who could read, like Neddy's father Ray, were given Bibles.

Each night Ray read a different Bible story aloud.

Neddy pretended to be asleep beside his mother, clinging to her legs so soft, *what warmth...*

Neddy's father seemed to never lose his mind. He was overworked and mistreated and degraded, but it didn't seem to matter.

He seemed content with his lot in life but suffered the lives of others, sad faces of children with bricks on their backs, those melancholy years—young slaves dead in accidents or fights, Master's gun behind the barn—the kids who worked like worker bees all in service to the Queen.

Ray suffered the heat on the children's back, their sigh, their sweat, a small hand to their brow would shield them from the golden sun, the match behind the jar who burned all the days away, a future slavery the cards to play, poker chips on the table, no matching bet was laid, and still they lost to lose again.

The Master never got an unkind word from Ray, no disapproving sigh, no complaints, just courteous, "Yes, sir," and "No, sir."

They enslaved his body but they did not have his mind.

He hummed until he fell asleep but he never screamed. His eyes were sharp and always focused, seeing all, deducing, calculating and understanding.

He didn't talk that much, often the *quietus* in the crowd, but he listened and what little he did say was just enough, thoughtful and provocative.

None of the insults, or the beatings, convinced Ray he was a slave. He did what they said because that was his choice.

Every day he went to work on time. He would work as long as they asked him. Ray was liked by all who knew him—a well respected man on the flower covered Hill.

Neddy got home from work two hours before his father. Neddy couldn't sleep until daddy walked through the door. Every night he planned to say, but couldn't:

How was your day? Too childish... *Feelin' okay, daddy?* No, what a ridiculous question to ask a slave, a slave with sagging eyes and a beard like Moses. The *other side* of Neddy's mind chimed in:

Your father is a slave, just another worker bee. How do you think his day was? Same old story, sweating in the heat under the sun for that old baboon on the hill. Did you hear him holler? I bet you'd like to make the Master squeal. Wouldn't you? Just think about it. No. Think about it...

Neddy pretended to be asleep when the wooden door creaked opened after midnight, a cold draft flowing in. Neddy was pretending to be asleep on the floor so his father would pick him up, to feel like a child again, held by strong and caring arms. His father covered him up snug and tight and tucked him in with a knowing smile.

Ray smiled at Neddy's make-believe dreams, knowing his son's eyes looked different when he was asleep; his face was less strained, relaxed, a little smile on little lips. Ray smiled at the tenderness of his son's affections proud.

Ray stopped at the threshold of the kitchen and took his boots off.

"Whew," he said. "I think I need some new socks."

Neddy suppressed a laugh.

Pots and pans clanged together, cabinets opened, and the sound of a breaking plate rang out. The noise startled Neddy. He sat up straight and breathless gasping.

"It's alright, son," Ray said. "I dropped a plate. Want something to eat, some grits, maybe?"

"No, daddy," Neddy said, looking away. "I already ate..."

Ray smiled.

He never looks me in the eye when he lies.

Ray fixed two bowls of grits and returned to the living room.

"Eat some more," he said. "I don't want to eat alone."

Neddy ate his grits resigned, prodding with the spoon, turning it over, looking at it, delaying the nasty taste of the grits.

"It don't have to taste good," Ray said, "as long as you can live off it. We'll have some fish sometime soon. Daddy's going fishing again tonight."

"Don't forget your rod and reel this time," Neddy said.

Ray smiled, his mind returning to *that night,* "I won't forget again. I'll never forget again."

Ray finished his dinner and returned the plates to the kitchen. He walked into the main room, stretched, yawned, and sat down in a brass iron chair.

Ray grabbed his old timer carving knife and whittled away at a thick chunk of elm the shavings falling to the floor as he cut and pruned away at the block of wood until it began to the take the shape of a kneeling angel. He sat it on a stack of rags in the corner. He stared at Galilee's empty bed for a moment, a tired sigh, old bones moved across the floor.

Ray washed the dishes and returned to the living room. He leaned against the wall opposite Neddy. He undressed and lay down. Neddy slept on the cot with his mother. His dead sister's bed was made up nice and pretty, but Neddy had dreadful dreams when he slept in Galilee's bed. Neddy had awful dreams when he slept with his mother, too, but he felt safe with her beside him, his cold feet and toes against the warmth of naked legs. The comfort of her bosom reminded him of being a baby still clinging to her chest. He thought of those days and smiled but longed, those worry free days again...

The last time Neddy slept in Galilee's bed was two weeks before his father's *retirement.* Retirement was simple; when you're too old to work, you can wait around to die.

Every slave was allowed to live out their days without work after their sixtieth birthday. And his father's was coming up soon.

Ray set in the chair on the other side of the room, like a shadow, reading from the Book:

He who lives in the secret place of the highest scarf will abide under the shadow of the Almighty.

His father's comforting voice, steady and consistent, articulate and eloquent; perhaps, Neddy thought, I could be like daddy someday... go fishing, gamble...play *that game* he liked, a game that always made Neddy's mother cry, some foreign game of chance.

His father turned the page:

In whom we have redemption through his blood, the forgiveness of the sins that scar, according to the riches of his grace...

And Neddy peaceful looked asleep and was.

3. *To the End of the World*

In the dream he walked with Galilee through the woods. He was afraid at first, until she took his hand to guide him. The children walked slow hand in hand down the dusty road.

They picked yellow jasmines and whistled with the birds for hours until Galilee said she was thirsty.

They walked to the other side of the manor to get water from the bird feeder by the maze. Halfway there she could not walk, exhausted. Neddy said he'd hold her feet so she could get a sip of water from the well. The well was in the woods, set in brick and stone, not far from the trail.

The hole was deeper in the dream than it was in life, more terrifying, an endless tunnel of black forever.

Neddy held Galilee's feet and lowered her into the well. Her wrinkled dress slid down her back. Neddy was startled by the sight of his sister naked and let go embarrassed. The water splashed when she hit the surface.

She yelled for help.

"I'll find daddy," Neddy said. *Daddy's always there...*

Neddy ran home, nobody there. He ran toward the Master's house and climbed the cement steps. He looked through the window.

The Master sat by the fireplace, in a rocking chair, under an ornate chandelier, relaxing in his living room drinking tea.

"Oh God, help me please!"

"Go away," the Master said. "I'm busy."

He sipped at his glass of tea.

Neddy ran around the house in screaming circles, crusted fingers in his ears, *la, la, la...*

Neddy watched his father's head disappear into the maze, into the grey fog of the hedge until he was gone.

Neddy followed into the archway to the maze. He called out as he walked, random directions, "Daddy! Daddy help!"

The echoes of his words returned.

Neddy was lost in the maze again, so far from the well in life, a long walk from where he stood, but there he found the well again.

"Help!" Neddy shouted. "Somebody help *me* please!"

He looked into the well when it appeared and could not see her face, just the shadow's shape. Her face was a silhouette cast by the moon against the water.

"Help!" she called out.

"I can't!" he cried. "Help me, please!"

He stood at the edge of the well, breathing heavy, above the shadow of his sister, yelling unintelligible murmurs between tears and gasps.

"Neddy?" she muttered between the gasps and sobs. "Please help me. I'm scared."

Neddy shouted, screaming, confusion, anguish, indecipherable mutterings of despair, calling out to a world with only two slaves in it, both in crisis, both trapped in their position, unable to do a thing but scream.

His sister's face changed to his own and he stumbled, face first headlong, until he hit the frigid water in the well, black as ink and sink white puddles *mama's milk* gathered under the moon.

The desperate slave, still trapped inside, screamed and screamed until he cried.

Neddy woke up sweating, screaming, "Help!"

"It was just a dream," he heard, his father's voice. "You're alright, son. You're safe."

I'm not alright, Neddy thought. *I'll never be alright...*

Well, life... It's a crap shoot, a Game of Chance *you know. What can you do?*

Tragedy comes for all of you, for your mother and your father, as it did with Galilee and for you it will come too.

Tragedy has no empathy. And in the end the hours take the nameless slaves like smoke away—and they turn into the shadows on the hill but wander on through mazes still...

Tragedy had arrived, entered without knocking, a ticket in his hand with Ray's name written on it, another body to collect.

4. *The Broken Angel*

Ray was with a friend and in the rain, and once a thousand bricks were laid, Ray stood on the ladder, bricks in hand, his friend applying mortar, laying bricks, one after another.

The spectral grey shade slave was startled by a bird and Ray, unable to see through the slanting rain, slipped and fell and dropped the bricks. A fragment of a cement block struck Ray just above the ear. He lost his footing, slipped and fell, hit the wheelbarrow, shattering ribs, bruising a lung.

Ray awoke a few days later, amnesia, white memory fog cobwebs, didn't know his name, what he was, delirious raving talking to his dead parents and friends wide-eyed sweating in the bed. He couldn't remember his name, so, at last, he made up a new name for himself: "Old man," he'd say. "That's who I am. Ray? I don't know a Ray...a ray, fragment of light and me...I'm just a black old man."

The room kept spinning, he said, and would faint, wake delirious in the middle of the silent night, sweating and yelling incoherent slobbering sentences at people who were not there, got out of bed, walked in circles, breathing heavy walking on the suspicious inclined floors. Vertigo, that spin, appeared, and Ray collapsed. He remained in bed for a month before he showed signs of coherency and life again.

We'll make it to the top, he thought. *Move on old man, move on...*

Move on, old man, move on...

Bit by bit Ray regained himself, first in small fragments, then scenes, births and deaths, old men, old women, children, words with them coming back. And when he was feeling better, he volunteered to go back to work.

He owed the Master five days. He accepted it as a duty and did not mind, not in the slightest, to work under the sun for five more days.

Ray shook his son's shivering shoulder, "It's time to go to work. Put your boots on."

They walked together to the barn.

The orange Carolina sun rose above the scattered pine trees. Light filled the barn and lit the meadow. The grass was wet with dew. Slaves began the work day in the cornfield. Others were standing in front of cotton gins. Others, like Neddy's mother, were servants in the house, Fancy Pants, the other slaves called them. They had warm food. They were spared the labor expected of the other slaves. They dressed in silk clothes, made just for them, as the Master would not have his slaves track mud and dirt around the house. He did not fully trust the slaves, however, but refused to hire a white man to do slave work. He believed all white men were created equal and the slaves, if they could be more, he thought, they'd put up a fight, like a white man would. This is what he believed.

"You shouldn't have to work," Neddy said. "It's disgraceful. You've still got a knot on your head."

"It's a nice one, ain't it?" Ray said, smiling wide. "One day son, when you're my age and have kids of your own, you might have a bruise as nice as this one. This one's a good one. Purple is my favorite color."

"But you're still hurt..."

"I'm fine, son," Ray said. "I'm not going to die. I'm going to be late. I'll see you tonight son."

"Are you going to come by when you're done?" Neddy asked. "The maze is almost finished. I want to take you through it."

"Oh, you'll have to," Ray said. "I'd get lost for sure without you, son."

Neddy smiled.

"I'll come by with a horse when we're done tilling," Ray said. "We gotta take a statue from the house out into the maze. So I'll see you then, not too long after the sun goes down."

"They'll light the lanterns," Neddy said. "Just follow them. Okay?"

"I'll see you then, son."

Ray led a horse out of the barn, into the meadow, and then down the hill to the tomato and squash plants. The leaves were changing colors, falling, breathing their last breath before old man winter's chill.

A group of slaves were waiting with a plow. It was near the end of summer just before the lukewarm autumn. The day was cooler than usual. The slaves were happy to breathe the cool air.

Neddy walked up the hill toward the mansion. Two horse drawn carriages waited out front. The Master's son, Thomas, called Neddy, gesturing with his finger.

"We want that maze pruned just right before this comin' Sunday, you hear me?" he said. "Y'all boys might have to break a sweat for once in your lives. How does that sound, boy?"

"Sounds very nice," Neddy said. "I love working, keeps me strong, and it's so pretty out."

"There's a pair 'a clippers in the back of that carriage," Thomas said. "Get 'em and get to work."

"Yes, sir," Neddy said.

Thomas gestured toward his gun.

"You see that?" he said. "It's brand new—just came from out west. You just look at that like insurance. If the work ain't done, all your strength won't save you from this thing. It's called a gun. Works real good with the Indians out west. They're just like you; ungrateful and uncivilized. But we'll teach you a thing or two about manners."

Neddy smiled.

Thomas, a young man of eighteen years, flinched. Neddy's bright smile made him uneasy.

"You think something's funny?" he asked. "How 'bout I stick this in your mouth?"

"I'm sorry," Neddy said. He turned around. Metal clashed against the side of Neddy's face. He stumbled to the ground, his arms splayed out in front of him, face first in the gravel. Thomas took hold of the back of Neddy's neck. He pushed Neddy's face into the gravel until dust seeped into his nose. Neddy coughed and gagged.

"It's not so funny is it?" Thomas asked. "Is it funny?"

"No, sir," Neddy said. "It's not funny. I'm sorry."

Thomas let him go.

Neddy stood up slowly, coughing, and dusted his pants off. The side of his cheek was bleeding and the rest was scratched up. He tasted the dust in his mouth.

"I've seen y'all together," Thomas said. "Y'all don't have no shame. Y'all just like horses; only dumber, least them horses got some sense. Y'all stand around naked, like animals... no shame, no shame at all! You make me want to puke. Ain't nothing more disgusting."

Does this make you feel like more of a man? Neddy thought.

When Thomas was young he went to one of the slave houses with his mother. He saw all the slaves naked, more equipped than himself, and felt a great deal of shame. It was that same shame behind the words he spoke to Neddy.

Thomas straightened his collar and walked away. Neddy's chest began to hurt and twinge. He couldn't breathe. His heart slammed against the inside of his chest. His body went numb, as though he had no body, and then all the feeling returned at once. It felt like he was inside a mason jar with a tight lid on it, like one of his pet lizard's, with no holes for him to breathe. He faltered as he walked, thinking, worrying about dying. His nerves lit up as panic shot from one node to another in his mind. He was certain he was going to die. He slumped against the wall by the porch.

You'll be fine, he told himself. *Just breathe. Concentrate on breathing. Just do your work old man, not an old man, you will be, and you will die. Not yet. Get up old man. Do your work.*

Neddy spent the rest of the evening trimming and pruning. The sun went down slow. Fireflies began to appear in the dark, hovering under the trees, and under the glowing lanterns on the porch. He wiped his brow and, seeing the lights come on, walked to the archway at the beginning of the maze. The grass corridors of leaves and grass ran symmetrical to the right and left. Another path went in. Neddy waited, his head throbbing electric pain the butt of the gun leaving a square shaped bruise.

Thomas returned to the main dining hall and stood in front of the mirror with a cowboy hat on, looking at himself as he twirled the gun around his fingers awkward, his real life imitation of a man.

Neddy waited, wandering through the mazes of his mind and memory, and waited, waited, waited.

At last a carriage bounced down the gravel road. Neddy, startled, ran into the maze. He walked to the left at the first turn, then right, and came into a circular clearing with paths in adjacent angles. Then he became afraid and left. He feared he would get stuck in the maze, condemned to run in circles, forever and ever by himself, in the dark, no one to help, no light to follow—just the endless infinity of grass corridors. He cut a hole through one of the smaller hedges, stepped over, and came out on the eastern side of the mansion, where the slave quarters were. He ran home. He knew his father would not lie; he never did. If he was unable to keep his word, something was wrong.

Neddy's father was a heap of screaming bones on the floor when Neddy arrived. Ray had tears in his eyes, and, Neddy knew, his father never cried out in pain. Neddy was startled to see his father, who intimidated him so, with tears in his eyes, confusion, shock, the look of a wounded dog. Neddy could remember two occasions when his father shed tears: when Galilee was born, and when Galilee died.

The first dead body Neddy ever did see...

Neddy's mother had a warm towel to his father's head. He had a long cut down his side.

"What happened?" Neddy asked.

"Your daddy fell," his mother said. "He was carrying that 'ol angel statue an' he tripped. He got dizzy again. That's all. He had it on his back when he fell. The statue fell on top of him and one of the wings broke off."

"I ruined it," Ray said, sad like, sighing "The wing cut my side. I let the Master down. I'm not some weak old man! I can still work... I just, I don't know... I'm making excuses. I don't make excuses. I was walking... I was... about to come and meet you... and I fell, got that feeling again, that vertigo, and my vision went blurry. "I didn't want to break the statue. I'm sorry I couldn't meet you."

"It was an accident," Neddy said. "He won't punish you for a mistake. That wouldn't be right at all."

"He shouldn't have been working at all!" Frannie said. "Neddy, son, fix your father a bowl of grits. Your father's strong. He'll pull through. He always does."

Neddy walked into the room with a bowl of grits. He handed his father the old grey bowl. Ray's expression was strained, sweat and dirt on his brow, disappointment colored in the rusty grey pallor of his face, not the pain--that he could deal with--but his inability to perform his duty.

"Dad," Neddy said, "I wish you had a chance for something better than this. You're too nice a man to be a slave..."

"I'm not a slave," Ray said. "I work to protect my family. My family has a place to sleep and food to eat. We have each other, and that is all we need. That's the most important thing in this world to me. Master is going to tan my hide for this one, you can bet on that."

He smiled. How he was able to do so befuddled Neddy. He was sitting on the edge of the cot, wincing in pain, blinking his eyes a lot as though the room was out of focus.

"Hand me that chunk 'a wood, son," he said, gesturing towards the angel made of wood. "And find my knife."

"You're not in any shape to work," Frannie said. "You get some rest. You can whittle in the morning, Ray. Get some sleep and relax."

Neddy thought that the Master would be furious at his father. Whenever the Master had to deal with a slave who had an accident, he never cared about the conditions. The Master did not know Ray had suffered bouts of fainting and delirium and vertigo. Ray never said anything about feeling bad. He never asked for preferential treatment. All Ray was to the Master was another means to an end, an end which would benefit not himself, but the Master. The next morning the Master walked through the door with a gun in his hand and anger in his eyes.

5. *The Love Songs Lost*

Neddy froze with fear. Everything slowed down, *something must be wrong,* he thought. *Master never comes out here. Why? Because then he might think of you as human.*
"Get up!" the Master shouted at Neddy's father.
Ray just laid there. Neddy noticed blood pouring from his father's nose. The panic took control of him again. The tightness in his chest got worse. The energy from his extremities went to the center of his chest and disappeared, leaving him out of body, numb, in full fledged hysteria, unable to move or act. Seeing his father's bleeding nose did something to Neddy's mind. The thought of suicide entered his mind. His thoughts were racing, a thousand words a second, an unrelenting torrent through his mind.
Suicide, why not? Neddy wondered. *What does it matter if I'm dead? I'm just another worthless slave who lives and works and dies unpaid, an animal without a face, not even thought of as a race. Just a means for Master's end, a stairway to nowhere once again. That's how it's been for my whole life, all my working, turmoil, strife... Why bother to begin to climb, step by step into the sky, when nothing's on the other side? No gates of Heaven open wide. Galilee doesn't play inside. She's cold and damp trapped underground, her once lovely songs forgotten.*
His father didn't stir, which was rare, and, infuriated, the Master kicked him in the ribs. His father winced. He opened his eyes but could not stand.
"Leave him alone!" Neddy shouted. "He's hurt! You're going to kill him!"
The Master slapped Neddy with the back of his hand. Neddy fell to the floor. Master kicked his father again. He coughed up blood, startled, and jumped to his feet, faltering, and collapsed again. His eyes sagged in sadness when he saw Neddy on the floor, with a black eye, crying.
"I'm sorry, sir," Ray said, struggling to keep his balance. "It was an accident. It won't happen again."
"Just get out of bed...stop crying like a little girl," the Master said. "And follow me."
Crying like a little girl...
Ray put his work clothes on.
Ray followed the Master to the courtyard where the whipping post was located. They tied his arms behind his back and bound his feet. All the slaves were allowed to watch. The Master

21

believed the demonstration would be educational.

Thomas stripped Ray's dirty work clothes off. The Master lashed him with the belt over and over digging into the skin with the belt's heavy silver buckle. Blood in thin crooked lines ran down Ray's back. He did not scream, but winced, eyes clinched shut, biting on the rope that bound his mouth, cringing and writhing like an insect as they beat him.

Neddy stood there in absolute hysteria, though calm on the outside. A terrible war went on inside his mind. A hundred or so other slaves showed up to watch. No one tried to help. No one could. Anyone who interfered was taken to the trail and shot, and then thrown in the river, weighted down with bricks, sinking down into the silent darkness with their mouths wide open screaming trying to breathe.

The nameless slaves amid the crowd stood in a terrible silence, watching, terrified, unable to act, unable to do anything but watch. Ray stumbled and fell to the ground, blind stumbling arms splayed out, his bloody body rolled around in the dirt, mouth open and no screams, the dust in quiet storms stirred when the frail old man collapsed.

Ray lay there unable to move, dust seeping into his mouth and nose. Neddy stood in quivering silent shock. Ray's frail chest struggled to expand and contract. Blood gathered in his eyes and he suffocated in the dust, hands tied behind his back.

Neddy's father choked to death under the last sun of a long summer.

Terrible thoughts entered Neddy's mind. *What would it be like if there was no Master, and all of us were free? Surely there must somewhere be a thousand other slaves like me who wish to be something more. I don't want to be a slave, to always work, not have a thing, like a bird that cannot fly, in a cage condemned to sing.*

Neddy once believed Master was merciful. To see his wounded father beaten without mercy instilled hatred in his heart. In his mind he imagined beating the Master, tying him to a post, and forcing him to beg before putting a burlap sack over his face and tying it shut with yarn, forcing him to suffocate in the dark, his screams unheard.

He snapped out of his trance when his mother shook him, screaming, hysterical, "He's dead!" she wailed. "They killed him! They killed him..."

"Oh dear God," Neddy said. "Oh dear God..."

And, he thought to himself, *Sometimes I don't see any God at all. We are alone in this world. God on Earth is that old man, our Master with his Master plans. Why not punish us himself instead of through somebody else?*

Neddy knew, for the first time in his life, real, blinding hatred. He watched them carry his father's limp, lifeless body to the barn.

Oh   God,   he   thought.   Oh   God.

6. *The One Winged Butterfly*

Neddy's father was buried two days later in a plywood coffin on the western end of the meadow. The day was overcast and grey and cold, windswept autumn leaves in the air. Neddy's uncle Nate and a few of his old friends managed to make a gravestone. Neddy chiseled his father's name into the stone with a hammer and a railroad spike. His mother gathered flowers for the grave.

Only a dozen slaves gathered for the funeral, which was quaint, and nobody knew what to say. Nobody said a word, save for Neddy's uncle. He stuttered, trying to mask his tears. He read his dead brother's favorite Bible verse.

"Verily, verily, I say unto you, except a grain of wheat fall to the ground and die, it abides alone; but if it dies, it brings forth much fruit.

"Ray was a good man," he continued, his breath a white cloud in the air. "He was always laughin' and playin' the fool, even when we was kids. We used to play hide and seek, in the old country, and one of us would go and hide. I remember one day I went to hide and Ray crossed his arms and leaned against a tree to count. He counted for a minute and then said, 'Ready or not, here I come!' I walked into the woods and climbed a tree.

"I saw him walk by me, under the tree, and I started laughing. I know he saw me. He had to. But he kept right on lookin' and lookin' and actin' like he couldn't find me, calling out, 'I'm gonna get you! You can't hide forever! The way we played in them days was if he didn't find me in thirty minutes I would have to run back to base before he tagged me. Ray liked looking just as much as he liked finding.

"So thirty minutes goes by and he still acted like he couldn't find me. So I jumped from the tree and ran home. When I got home Ray was sitting on the front porch watching a butterfly, crying. I said, 'I won! You didn't find me!' He just stood there, not saying anything, with tears in his eyes. He was sniffling like he had a cold.

"I looked down and there was a butterfly on the porch, with one wing, beating its wing against the ground, in circles, and Ray just stood there, really hurt, crying because he couldn't help the poor thing.

"He caught the butterfly in a jar and kept it, nursing it, hoping one day he'd see her fly again. He found out how to feed her and take care of her and the day he saw her fly away he had tears in his eyes. That's the kind of man he was, warm and loving, brave and smart. He was tender and kind. I love you, brother, and I'll miss you." He paused. "That's all I have to say."

Neddy's mother cried in silent gasps when the slaves started shoveling dirt onto the grave. Neddy's uncle had to hold her back. The shovel had a cracked and broken handle.

Back at home Neddy's mother was hysterical, her back heaving, breathless in the corner, arms folded, head in her lap. Neddy sat across the room, against the wall, in stunned, unbearable silence, watching his mother cry.

"Everything happens for a reason," Neddy's uncle said. "God has a plan for us. Ray is in a better place, Frannie."

"You know daddy," Neddy said, tears clogging his throat. "He will be alright. He's with God now..."

Sometimes I don't see God at all. Why lie to her? Trust me old man, if God is there he laughs at you. How could he allow such tragedies? Because if he's there he doesn't care or has something better to do, some better life to save. It's not fair. It's not fair at all. Daddy was a good man and he's dead. Master is a monster and he lives a life of ease, never in pain, while we suffer and live in a rundown shack, in the cold, like animals.

"We are all the children of God," Neddy's uncle said. "I know things don't make sense right now. My brother was a good man. He was a real good man, and I loved him. He was my big brother. He took care of me when our parents died. And wherever he is now, I see him in a rocking chair, glass of the sweetest tea, like momma made, looking over a cornfield in the shade.

"And all our old friends are there with him, working together for no one but themselves, tilling and plowing and picking in peace. If there is a Heaven for us, a Heaven for the slaves, we'd all live in one big house together, all of us, old and young alike. We'd have a big bowl of grits every morning and a glass of tea.

"We'd work under a cool autumn sun and come home to our loving children, long gone from the Earth, and put them on our laps and read to them. And they'd be happy, in the shade, forever smiling just 'cause we're together. We'll have picnics in the meadows and play hide and seek in the woods.

Neddy thought about the day his sister died. She thought she could hide in the well, holding on with her hands, so Neddy wouldn't see her. A woodpecker startled her and she fell. Neddy heard her high pitched screams inside his head. The pain in his head returned and his thoughts began to multiply and race like a broken feedback loop.

"I don't think I'll ever get to Heaven," Neddy said. His uncle

Nate was silent.

"You know," Nate said, "your father always kept a dictionary with him. It's in the kitchen. I'm sure he wouldn't mind if you looked through it."

Neddy smiled. His mother was asleep, face cupped in her hands. Her chest rose as she breathed. Nate stood up and went to the kitchen. He came back a moment later with a dusty, leather-bound book. Neddy took it and thumbed through the yellowed pages.

"Maybe one day you 'a speak real nice like your daddy," Nate said. "He was smart as a whip, wasn't he?"

Neddy nodded.

"Maybe I'll be as smart as him one day," he said. "I'm going to read this book."

"It's been a long day," Nate said. "You try to get some sleep."

"I don't want to sleep," Neddy said. "I have such bad dreams..."

"So do I, Neddy," his uncle said. "So do I."

It will pass, he thought, at last, *within another hour. All this pain takes place inside where grows a broken flower. Inside bone walls where hides my mind freeze tragic scenes when I rewind. The same scene is in my dreams, a moment long ago, when Galilee sang a song I know. A moment long, now long, long gone, as winds along the waste her song. Where her once vibrant voice was heard, again sung by a mockingbird. Then it's over, and is stole, down into the memory hole, where dead, a red rose withered blows. Its beauty the beholder knows, at the end of season goes, like my father, me, and all, and like these words just listless fall, just more lines scribbled on the wall.*

Neddy was silent, closed his eyes. "Goodnight, uncle," he said.

"Goodnight, Neddy."

Neddy tried to go to sleep, eyes tight closed, discomfort in his chest on one side, rolled to the other side, two many faces, sounds, *one two three four five six seven eight nine ten sleep.*

7. *The Reflection's Shame*

"Help me!" his reflection screamed. "I'm going to pull out my hair! I'm going to pull out my teeth! I'm going to scream until I'm mute."

He stood there frozen, unable to move, unable to speak. The reflection disappeared. In the place of his own face he saw the Master's puffy cheeks and bloodshot eyes. The Master's reflection smiled a slack jawed gape of a sarcastic grin at him. Neddy spit on the mirror, the goopy liquid dripping down the glass, and, in horror, turned to run.

In front of him the maze appeared, smaller than he remembered, by the master's porch. He saw black silhouettes in the shape of moths fluttering in idle circles under and around the lantern's pale cast yellow hue.

The window by the door was open, a breeze wafting the curtain back and forth. Neddy took the lantern and crawled into the window. The room was decorated with paintings and statues. The fireplace glowed on the other side of the room. He held the lantern in front of him as he walked. At the end of the hall he saw something fall and shatter on the floor.

Shining fragments, mirror's glass, reflected light that Neddy cast. Fireflies around him passed. He picked up his pace and ran to the place where the mirror fell. In each fragment on the floor he saw a family, his mother, his father, and his sister.

He saw them pulling a carriage in the rain. Each of them was tied up like horses, pulling the heavy carriages full of bricks. They were harnessed like workhorses. The Master and his son held the reigns, taking turns whipping them and laughing.

They piled more and more bricks on the cart and whipped them harder and harder, screaming worthless and laughing, lashing the naked back of Neddy's family.

Then he saw his mom walk by, like a zombie, vacant eyes, carrying a bowl of grits. Neddy followed her. Master waited in his rocking chair, in the living room, by the fire. The room was full of classy mirrors in heavy frames. The Master held a pair of scissors and a noose. Neddy became afraid and ran. He disappeared into the hallway.

He found himself in another room, dark, at the end of which a mirror loomed. He walked slow, and did not know, where the passageway would lead. At the end of the hall, with transparent paintings on the wall, he saw another mirror. He stopped as though afraid, closing his eyes, and stumbled forward in the dark, blind with outstretched arms.

He felt his fingers touch the glass. He opened his eyes. In front of him he saw a body without a face. The body was his. The face was black and blank, no ears, no eyes, no nose; the blank face set on a slumped over broken body, wires hanging out like a disconnected robot. Neddy blinked in disbelief. He opened his eyes again; the broken body had changed. His face appeared in the mirror again. The doppelganger, Neddy's replica, on the other side of the mirror looked down, refusing to make eye contact. He tapped the mirror on the shoulder. The reflection would not return his gaze. He shouted, "Look at me!" over and over. Neddy's reflection put his fingers in his ears, shaking his head back and forth, going, "La, la, la."

"Look at me!" he screamed. "Look at me!"

And Neddy slammed his fist against the glass and felt the cut, rousing him from sleep, straight up in bed, gasping and sweating.

8. *Life in the Bush of the Sun*

"Wake up, Neddy," Nate said, shaking his shoulder. "Just a dream, son, you'll be alright."

Neddy turned to face the wall, pulling the covers over his head, still trembling, still wet with sweat, still stressed and scared. Nate sat down and put his boots on, tied them, and went into the kitchen. He fixed two bowls of grits, one for him, one for Neddy. He filled two cups with water, one for him, one for Neddy. He walked into the living room, setting the glass and bowl beside Neddy's mattress on the floor. Neddy uneager to work wished for sleep and for a long time, *too tired, old man.*

Nate shook him, saying, "Come on, Neddy. Time to get up. Sun 'a be up soon."

Neddy sighed, rolled over, and sat up in bed, feet hanging off the mattress. He put on socks, long johns and dirty pants, a long sleeve shirt his mother knitted, and his wool gardener's gloves. He put on his belt, stood up, and knelt to tie his boots.

Neddy looked at the plate of grits with disgust. He stuffed his father's old dictionary in his pocket, drank his water, and sat back down, looking at Galilee's empty bed, looking where his father once slept, where he sat awake at night and hummed, reading Bible stories in the dark.

The tension in his chest grabbed him like invisible hands, squeezing him from both sides, making him cringe in pain, unable to breathe.

"Eat your grits," Nate said. "You'll be hungry later. I ain't gone let you go without eating, Neddy. Your father's gone and I gotta take care of you now."

Neddy sighed.

"I'm not hungry," he lied.

"I'm not asking," Nate said. "Eat your grits."

Neddy ate with slow, disconnected bites. His mother was already at work, her bed unmade and messy. The barrel of coal in the middle of the room had a dying fire in its belly. Neddy warmed his hands.

"What's wrong, Neddy?" Nate asked. "I can tell when something's wrong."

"Nothing, uncle Nate," Neddy said. *Father... choking in the dust... us just watching him die. We just watched daddy suffocate and now* "I keep thinking about the same day, a terrible..."

"What day was that?" Nate asked, concerned with waiting wistful eyes.

"I've only been off the plantation once," Neddy said. "It was the worst day of my life. Daddy was with me. Everywhere I looked were free and happy people, with nice clothes, clean hair. We had cotton stuck in ours. Their hair was slicked back, groomed with pomade, and the women tied their hair in pretty bows. They all smelled so pretty, like flowers. And we smelled like pigs and horses.

"I looked at all those free people, coming and going as they pleased, and felt ashamed of myself. They were better than me and free, to live their life as they saw fit, and I cried in anger, hating them for that. What makes them better than us? Their pretty clothes and slicked back hair? Their white skin? I didn't see any difference between us and them, on the inside, but on the outside they wore nice clothes and spoke all proper like, making me hate myself more and more. I wondered why that made them better than me. How was being white better than being black? It's just a color. I was too young to understand things, then, but I remember that day like it was yesterday.

"I was a little boy, just seven, maybe eight, and Master woke us in the early morning. He told us to get our coats, since it was in the coldest days of February, and told us to meet him in the driveway. A special job, he said, just for us.

"Daddy bundled me up warm as he could. We got to ride in the front seat. I was so proud. We had to ride in the back seat every time before that. The job must be very special, I thought, since we got to ride up front like people, not like dogs or tools, behind the wagon in the cart.

"It was a long ride. I never imagined the world could be so big. I never thought there'd be so many people in it. People were all over the place, everywhere, and their children walked behind them. They could choose when to eat, where to eat, where to sleep and when; they were free. It sickened me. I envied them. And that sickened me more.

"We arrived at a large house by Lake Murray, about two hours away from home, and we were told to collect firewood. Two of the host's own slaves had died the week before. We was on loan. We chopped the firewood and prepared the fireplace and then prepared their meals. Then Master sent us back to the carriage. Master finished his meal before he returned, leaving us in the cold carriage without heat, rubbing our hands together for warmth. 'Good steaks, boys,' he said. 'Harold was impressed. He might wanna borrow you boys a couple times a week.'

Borrow us boys...

"I was proud when I heard that, yet now it shames me. Back then it felt like we were good workers, valued, you know? Now it feels like we were tools, rakes called in to pile up leaves when their paths are cluttered. I don't want to feel like that anymore. I want to be something more important than a tool."

"I know how you feel," Nate said. "I've felt like that too. But your father knew the only way they could make us slaves was to make us do what we didn't want to do. As long as we do our duty because we wish to do so, we are not slaves. So just keep your mind on your work. It's time to go, Neddy. Get your things."

Neddy grabbed the hedge clippers and walked out the door, looking at the ground as he walked, avoiding eye contact. He did not want his uncle to see him crying. He sniffled and coughed, then faked another, hoping his uncle would think he was sick.

"You catchin' a cold, Neddy?" Nate asked. "Take my toboggan. Pull it over your ears. Winter's coming and if you don't be careful you'll catch pneumonia."

Neddy slid the wool toboggan over his ears. Neddy and Nate walked into the grey morning together, Neddy behind his uncle, staring at his feet.

A group of slaves carried a large fishing net across the gravel drive way, going to fish in the river, Neddy thought, *fish is tasty.*

He fished with his father when he was a child. As he got older, his father always went fishing alone, sometimes without his rod and reels and tackle box, which Neddy did not understand.

How can you fish with no bait?

Whenever the slaves went fishing they brought back bass and brim. Neddy liked fish. Sometimes Master let them have some of the food they caught.

"Where you working today, uncle?" Neddy asked.

"We gotta harvest today," Nate said. "We 'a probably shuck some corn when we done with that. You just keep yourself busy. You'll be alright."

"I don't have a choice," Neddy said.

"You always have a choice," Nate said. "That's what makes us human. But anyway, your friends are already at work. You better hurry."

"Alright," Neddy said. "I'll see you tonight, uncle."

"Have a good one, Neddy."

Neddy spent the morning planting shrubberies around the hedge. The other slaves trimmed the top of bushes, making sure they were even. Others cut the grass until it was even like a soft, dew soaked carpet. The older slaves raked the leaves and burnt them behind the house. A group of children from the Galilee church down the road, played ring around the rosy, pocket full of posy, ashes, ashes... *they all fall down.*

Master's wife sat on a lounge chair with a straw hat pulled over her head, reading a book in the shade while the children played. The Master was up stairs on the patio overlooking the maze and garden. He had a hand-rolled Cuban cigar in his mouth. He wore white pants, a white sports coat, a black vest, and a black fedora. His portly belly hung over a leather belt with his name, Alexander, imprinted in thick black ink on the leather.

Thomas paid close attention to a group of slaves shoeing his horse. The young horse kicked and whined and Thomas, angry, disappeared into the house only to return with a hunting rifle. He coughed and hacked to draw attention to himself and his gun. The slaves who saw were much more careful with their work once they saw the gun.

They all get nauseous when they see my daddy's gun, Thomas thought, disappearing into the house again. The slaves, relieved, worked on.

Neddy was never bothered by the sight of a gun. The device intrigued him, the odd killing mechanism fascinating.

Thomas came out again around lunch time to make sure the slaves were up to speed and sweating good, played with his gun, chamber spin, click, click, no bullets, *damn,* loaded the gun, shot idly at some birds and squirrels. And Neddy from where he worked saw the birds fall from the sky with tears gathering in his eyes and hated that he had to see them die, *like daddy and Galilee...*

Neddy threw the clippers to the ground and kicked one of the shrubberies.

He watched Thomas disappear into the house. He knelt to pretend to tie his shoes, seeing a limping squirrel. It had been shot in the stomach and struggled to walk. The poor animal lay under a shrubbery, his chest and back rising as he breathed, weak and sickly looking.

Neddy felt a profound sadness and empathy for the wounded squirrel, knowing how the poor creature felt. He picked him up, cupping him in his hands, petting him soft like on the head.

Neddy walked through the maze, taking random turns, not caring where he went. He was not afraid of getting lost.

He feared the squirrel, however, feared the wounded squirrel would die. He would bury him under the birdbath in the center of the maze, he thought, under a small stone sculpture with cherubs around the base, stone birds on the top, and a shallow pool of water.

Leaves floated on the surface. Neddy sat the squirrel down by the sculpture and washed his hands, dust and scratches covering his palm and fingers, bits of gravel embedded.

The squirrel had blood dried on his mouth and the bullet hole stained the underside of his belly. Neddy picked dry blood out of the hair under the squirrel's stomach.

He held him in his hands, seeing his own reflection in the dying animal's eyes. He felt better there, in the bush of the sun by himself with a wounded animal, like himself, finding consolation and warmth in each other's company.

The dying squirrel looked at Neddy, breathing slow, then slower, nesting in Neddy's palm, calming him, soothing the holes in Neddy's heart, until they both fell fast asleep. Neddy, in the dream, looked up to an overcast sky the grey of nails with clouds that frowned.

9. *The Dream that Bled*

Overhead a grey sky looked down on him with clouds that frowned. Neddy stared around in all directions anxious, panicked, his sweat the color of blood.

The machinery of twilight ran like clockwork above. He was lying by the bush, as he was before he fell asleep, and the squirrel was stiff and cold, unmoving dead in Neddy's shaking hands. The maze was overgrown, the reeds of grass so long and tall, the bushes and the hedges thick and dense. It looked as though it had not been attended for perhaps a thousand years. Brittle branches, leafless trees, swayed back and forth with twilight's breeze. The sound of wind went flying by. A whistling empty voice of Mother Earth surrounded him. He became afraid, looking up, seeing catacombs of clouds like rusted prison bars up above. He dropped the squirrel, afraid, a feeling he could not understand, perhaps overwhelmed by the emptiness of the grey fugue up above, blanketing the dying eve.

The sun held its breath, puffy cheeks, a tired shade of black, not golden as the sun of Carolina Neddy knew. It heaved like his breathing mother, when he by her went off to sleep. The wind in whispering tendrils drifted by as raveled fleeces in the sky. The wind assumed a human voice, the Master's Southern drawl, "Failure," said the wind, and, then, "No, no, not again."

Neddy looked down at the squirrel, lifeless on the ground, tongue hanging out with vacant, cancelled eyes, around which flew a thousand flies. And the sorrow filled his mind, as a broken levee drowned the screaming city in his head. The sorrow colored every picture in his mind he had, his mother and his father and his dead sister Galilee. Neddy, in tears, got on his knees and dug a shallow grave by leaves. He placed the squirrel into the hole and made a cross from two sticks tied together. He stuck it in the ground where the bleeding squirrel had died, by the bird-feeder and its cherubs made of stone. The wind went by again and this time screaming; high pitched it hung a moment in the air. It came from Master's house. Neddy cut a path through the hedges, walking toward Master's house. He heard screaming as he walked, back pressed against the wall under the window trying to hide. He heard his mother say something, something about food.

"Why don't you stay with me?" he said. "You got no old man to go home to tonight."

He heard his mother's subdued sobbing, the choking, the

gasping, trying to catch her breath. She said something Neddy could not understand. Then he heard the sound of tearing clothes, another scream, glass shattering on the floor. The sound of his mother kicking and screaming found its way to Neddy's ears. Something metal clanged against the floor.

Neddy looked in the window. The Master had his mother against the wall, holding her by the throat, with his pants down, between her legs. He held her hands against the wall, and Thomas, laughing in the corner, clapped for his performance. Neddy's mother struggled and screamed. Neddy yelled, "Leave her alone!" but no words came out. "I'll kill you!" he shouted soundlessly. "I'll kill you!"

He tried to run but could not. He tripped, falling face first to the ground, and jumped back up. He peered into the room over the windowsill. His mother lay slumped against the wall, naked, bleeding. Master was putting his clothes on. Thomas began undressing, walking over to where Neddy's sobbing Mother lay against the wall, "My turn," he said. Thomas took her hand and guided it to his crotch. "I think you dropped something, ma'am," he said.

Neddy woke up screaming.

10. *The Definition*

"You dropped something, Neddy," his uncle said. "You dropped your clippers. Come on home. It's almost midnight."

The dead squirrel lay beside him on the ground, stiff, tongue hanging out, the eyes a lifeless dead.

"I'll be home in a bit," Neddy said. "I got done with my work early so I sat down to get a rest. I wanna take a look at daddy's book out here where it's nice. I want to talk smart like y'all."

"You can read at home," Nate said. "It's late."

"But it feels good out," Neddy said. "I'll see you soon."

Nate shrugged. "Alright, Neddy," he said. "Don't stay out too late."

"I won't," he said. "I'll see you soon."

Nate turned around and disappeared into the maze. Neddy knelt beside the squirrel, as he did in his dream, and dug a shallow grave. He put the squirrel's stiff body in the hole and covered it with dirt, sad like, tears swelling in his eyes. He smoothed the dirt out and patted it.

Neddy leaned against the birdbath with his father's dictionary open. The lantern light behind him was barely bright enough for him to read. He turned to the bookmarked page, held in place by a reed of grass. He looked the top of the page, N, and began looking for his name. He couldn't find it. This depressed him, to think his name meant nothing, and instead he found the closet word to it:

Needy, adjective: 1. in need; impoverished. 2. Wanting or desiring affection, attention, or reassurance, especially to an excessive degree.

Neddy was not a very good reader, but he spelled out the words, memorizing them as he went. Then he came upon a word that stuck out like a sore thumb.

Nobody, pronoun: No person; not anyone; nobody told you to go. Noun: A person of no importance or influence.

He sought out another word he knew how to vaguely spell but could not find it. At random thumbing through the pages the word schizophrenia stuck out as he liked the tonal quality of the word.

Schizophrenia: noun. 1. Any group of psychotic disorders usually characterized by withdrawal from reality, illogical patterns of thinking, delusions, and hallucinations, and accompanied in varying degrees by other emotional, behavioral, or intellectual disturbance. Schizophrenia is associated with dopamine imbalances in the brain and defects of the frontal lobe and is caused by genetic, other biological, and psychological factors. 2. A situation or condition that results from the coexistence of disparate or antagonistic qualities, identities, or activities.

He thought of the last word he found in his father's dictionary: Redemption: noun. 1. The act of redeeming or having been redeemed. 2. Recovery of something pawned or mortgaged. 3. The payment of an obligation, as a government's payment of the value of its bonds. 4. Deliverance upon payment of ransom; rescue. 5. Christianity: salvation from sin through the sacrifice of Jesus Christ.

He found another word, idly flipping:
Nirvana: noun. 1. Often Nirvana a. Buddhism—the ineffable ultimate in which one has attained disinterested wisdom and compassion. b. Hinduism-emancipation from ignorance and the extinction of all attachment. 2. An ideal of condition of rest, harmony, stability, or joy.

Neddy thought about the concept for a moment, attempting to picture his Nirvana, if there would be such a moment in his long suffering life where he would know or attain rest or consolation, harmony and joy, or even come to terms with what he thought he was.

Neddy folded the book and put it in his back pocket. He climbed to his feet and jumped, hearing a loud nose, like glass shattering on the floor. He made his way through the maze, back to the entrance, hearing the Master shout as he walked. The anxiety overtook him again.

His fingers shook and trembled. He walked in quietly, so he wouldn't be heard out so late, he'd get a lashing for sure, he thought, if Master saw him so close to the house. The panic overwhelmed him. He stopped, looking into the maze again, daunting, hopeless corridor that never ended. Then something changed inside his mind. He decided he didn't care if he got lost. He walked into the maze, eyes shut, taking random twists and turns until he was certain he was lost.

His father always told him to pray when he was lost and he refused; Neddy wanted to figure it out for himself. Though he did not know why, and did not believe in God, he knelt to pray, clasping his hands together, finger over finger, saying, "God the father, creator of Heaven and Earth, show me the way that I might do your will."

A loud noise interrupted him, a squeaking horse drawn

carriage sound, the tussle of gravel and rocks, muffled conversation obscured by old man winter's breath, dry and cold, grey faces passed in the cold.

Neddy peered through the hedge and saw a group of slaves, one holding the reigns of the horse, one with a shovel over his shoulder, one carrying a lantern, its muffled glow illumed the dusty path; light beat off the broken angel statue. Mortar and dried cement held the once broken wing together. It glowed in the dark behind Neddy, captivating his gaze.

The angel's wing seemed to point to a path to the right. Neddy followed the wing until he came to another fork in the road. He heard a sound, like glass against a wall, to the left, and followed the adjacent corridor of grass. He walked as though by instinct until he came upon a lit window.

He could see the master inside, talking to someone, though Neddy could not hear. He seemed angry. His wife came into the room with a broom. His expression changed when he saw his wife sweeping. It turned to an expression of happiness.

"I hate they have to work in the cold," Master's wife said. "They could get sick."

"I know," Master said. "But if it's not them, it's our boys. And I want them to get a college education. It might be morally ambiguous, but it's the only way we can afford to live right now. And besides, we give them a place to live, and food."

"But do you have to whip them and punish them so?" Master's wife asked. "It's inhuman."

"I get carried away sometimes," he said. "Nobody's perfect, Paula. Especially not me. But your father could tell you all about that."

She laughed. So did he. His stomach jiggled. He said something else, lit one of his big cigars, then stood. He walked out of Neddy's sight, by a window, back into sight, and onto the veranda.

He sat in the rocking chair, about ten feet away from Neddy, the chair squeaking as he rocked. Neddy watched him as he sat and smoked.

His wife walked onto the veranda with a plate full of biscuits and a pitcher full of sweat tea. She went back into the house. The screen door creaked behind her.

Another cart came up the road. Neddy was startled. He ducked behind the hedge, looking out through intersecting limbs and bushels. Shovels and pickaxes clanged together in the back of the cart. The thought occurred to Neddy that the broken shovel with the duct tape on the handle, the spade that buried his father, could be in the cart.

They turned to walk toward the barn but stopped when Master called them. They left the cart not too far from where Neddy hid behind the hedge, looking out, obscured by the dark.

"Where was he buried?" Master asked the group of slaves. "What was his name?"

"Ray," one of the slaves said. "He was buried by the meadow."

"They ought to have buried him in the woods," Master said. "How's it going to look when children come to visit? I don't want them to find a gravestone while they look for Easter eggs. That ain't gone do, fellas. That ain't gone do at all. Y'all gotta bury him in the woods. We can't have his grave out in the open like that. He's dead and that's sad, but we don't want to make everybody that comes here sad. The children would find a gravestone looking for an egg and their ma would give me an earful, that's for sure."

While they talked Neddy crawled over the wall of the maze and walked to the back of the cart. They talked about digging up Ray's grave as Neddy looked for the broken shovel.

"Tomorrow after sun down," Master said, "I want y'all to dig him up and bury him in the woods. You hear me?"

"Yes, sir," one of the slaves, a young boy, almost Neddy's age, said. "We will, sir."

"Alright then," Master said. "Y'all put that junk in the barn and get to bed. The sun 'a be up early in and we gotta get the rest of the corn shucked."

"Yes sir," they said.

Their footsteps got closer to Neddy, as did the glowing lantern, bobbing toward him like a large firefly in the dark. Neddy took the shovel and ran into the maze. The slaves pulled the cart the rest of the way to the barn. The Master went back to enjoying his tea, relaxed, his rocking chair squeaking as he rocked.

Neddy exited the maze by squeezing his way through a wall of grass and crept along the edge of the mansion with his back to the wall. He ducked under the kitchen window, listening to Master's wife talk to his mother.

"These flowers would be lovely," Master's wife said. "Yellow jasmines are so pretty. I think they're my favorite flower. And I've been all over the world. There's nothing more beautiful than the jasmine, the yellow ones that grow in Carolina. As pretty as they are, no flower is as pretty as those on a grave, life in the presence of death, the beautiful in place of beauty gone."

Neddy passed under the kitchen window towards the back of the house. He picked up a rock and threw it against the back porch, breaking a window. He heard Master's wife say to his mother, "Did you hear that? Sounded like something broke."

Neddy crept along the edge of the house again, walking toward the veranda, ducking under the window, pausing to listen. They left the room, headed toward the back of the house.

Neddy walked to the edge of the veranda by the porch, the master's squeaking rocking chair right above his head. He leaned against the wall, shovel clasped in his shaking hands. He stood and looked through the kitchen window.

His mother and the Master's wife were around back, sweeping up the glass. Neddy crept along the base of the veranda, stopping to think. He'd hear me if I ran up the steps, Neddy thought. Neddy decided to pick up a handful of gravel and throw it across the porch, hitting the banister on the other side of the veranda, drawing his attention.

Neddy listened to him rise. He walked to the other side of the porch, back turned to Neddy. Master's wife and his mother were sweeping up the glass out back.

Neddy stood there for a moment, frozen, watching him, sweat on his forehead. Neddy knelt to say a prayer, hands together, saying, "Forgive me, father...God of all, if you are there; forgive me for what I have to do."

11. *The King is Dead*

Neddy tiptoed up the stairs while the Master's back was turned, shovel held tight in his hands. Master leaned over the banister, looking into the dark, his head swiveling back and forth. He did not hear Neddy as he approached. When he turned around, Neddy swung the shovel, with all his might, into the side of Master's face, in the temple, a sickening thud.

Master stumbled forward, spitting blood in Neddy's face, grabbed him by the shoulders, sinking to the ground, fingers clinging to Neddy's pants as he fell. Neddy shrugged him off and hit him in the face again. He stopped in his tracks, reaching for the door. Neddy hit him again, over the back of the head, and the Master fell to the ground, a puddle of blood gathering in his ears and eyes.

He lay in front of the doorway, the living room light illuminating the Master's body, the glowing red rivers of blood pouring from his ears and nose. Neddy turned him over on his back, sticking a boot to his neck, choking him with his feet.

The Master stopped struggling. Neddy slammed the shovel into his face, over and over, until there was nothing but a bloody puddle, where the Master's face once was, and Neddy saw, in his mind, his Master watching as his father died.

Neddy looked at the puddle, the puddle of blood and brains, and saw his reflection in it and, disgusted, slammed the shovel into the puddle again and again until his strength was spent.

Neddy turned and ran, first through the maze, weaving through the corridors of grass, hoping to throw off the scent of Master's hounds, which, he knew, would soon be after him. Then he crawled through the wall on the opposite end of the maze, leading away from Neddy's cabin, and then ran to the edge of the woods. He took off his shoes, covered in blood, and threw them in the forest. He ran back to his home barefoot, in absolute panic. Master's lifeblood dried on his face as he ran.

His mind was racing. Thoughts floated in from nowhere as the panic ran down his body in evil currents, electricity wrapping 'round the blood vessels like copper wire, his being on fire, like a cigarette screaming in a grey tray full of smoldering ash.

Where can I go? Hitch-hike. Hitch-hike to where, Nirvana? You'll never get there now. I'll wait on the shore for her, for who, for Galilee, with my thumb in the air, watching free birds, bye they fly, with the water's lullaby, like hers, kings and queens and pawns, walk on, blind with outstretched arms, a life long gone, a man, a child, vague shapes, a blur, stumble into Earth's wide urn, a place from which she can't return. That caravan back to the sea, the rats behind the piper sing in glee. Behind the song the rats walk on. Back to the sea soliloquy, sonnet for the dead. As faces in a mirror, first, the Master got what he deserved.

And at twilight, late tonight, locked away in plywood box, the procession of the lives, nonstop. One after another down the mountain, like Sisyphus, from the mound, casts a downward frown, me too, sits to sob, lament, another stone is sent. Sisyphus shrugs, says, 'Bye,' he goes, down into the memory hole, for why? Who knows, but goes like wind, and each time that old rock slides down again. Again, they shout, and he begins.

The empty sea, that nothing, the category gone, when we're filed away in the Earth like catacombs, the name of us, our deeds, the tomb, One Summer in the Sun, and in it our simple songs, of those like me in great despair, who long, for what they cannot reach, or the fear of the cold on their feet, not to act, nor cry, like Hamlet alone with his why and his sigh.

Perhaps one day I'll get to face, Karma and her Chalkboard, and Erase, all our sins she's penciled in, so all Nirvana Hitchhiker's like me can get in; I'd cheat them all, on our behalf, sneak the slaves into Heaven and lay back, laugh, as the wicked and the good and bad, are there, and love and live the same. I'd take all the slaves who pass my way, convicts to Nirvana, where there, together, perfect weather, we all can cry Hosanna.

He waited by the woods a while, delusional, hallucinating, seeing Sea gulls pluck the pearls. The tide came in, and, once again, he heard a laughing girl. Glass shattered in his mind, and, in reflection, all directions, birth and childhood, some woman too, disappeared into the blue hole of the Earth, the blue urn that bore them all. As soon would go another down, the Master's wife, by the cabin, picking flowers for the grave of Neddy's father.

Soon will go another down, into the memory hole, erased. Hitchhikers to Nirvana don't always find the place. Some wait with their thumbs out, all their life, hoping the wagon to Heaven comes by. If I could, I surely would, take every child and parent there, where they could sit, and laugh, and love, and live forever without a care. I would if I could.

Vanessa's butterflies, the butterfly seen by my father, with one broken wing who tried to fly, why bother? They try to fly, but can't, and go in a desperate circle, one lame wing against the ground. When I saw that butterfly, she sang without a sound. To me, she said, with dead lips, dead, 'Why do I have to die?' And, I said, 'Because you live. There is no why. Now you rest easy. Shut your eyes.'

Old Man, move on, and just look through, the prison bars that you call You, and stand outside, a happy stride, look at the prisoner's inside, in love and lust and hate. Chance's divisions separate, but in the end, they're whole, behold: life the divine ration.

In his mind he stood on the far off shore once more, his body frozen at the lip of the woods, the visions and the words clouding his senses, the world around him washed away, first from the corners, then the center of his vision, and he trailed off again, into that anxiety propelled fugue like state.

In front of him, far off, appeared a door; a satin sheet, red, and spread, along the corridor, and at the end, God's black limousine pulled in. Roses are thrown on the carpet, for him to walk, around the car Nobody's talk. He's returned, they say, they smile.

God is here again! He's here to save us from our sin! A long procession, eulogy, to the carriage on roses leads, an open door, the seat is empty, a thousand slaves shout in a frenzy. Another man, some other land, they take his place, instead. Alas, alas, they cry at mass, 'Our loving king is Dead, though Jesus never died, no Second Coming, never left.'

Children and the parents cried, as puddles in the sunlight dried, and now another long lost face, on Earth, has now been replaced, for some other man to sit. By the time the Master died another waited in the line, to take his place, put on his suit, his loyal subjects to recruit.

I'll wait on the shore for her, watching kings and pawns like me, walk on, into the Sea their life long gone. Into the sea, I visit, day and night, that I might see the dead. I see that girl, my sister, friend, and sometimes see my dad. He tells me he forgives me, I hang my head, and sigh. 'There's no need for you to cry. Be who you are, Nobody else, you are you, that's all, yourself, enough. If nothing else you this must trust.'

He snapped out of his trance. He felt for the dictionary in his back pocket, thumbed through the pages, until he found a suitable word:

Fugue: noun. 1. Music, an imitative polyphonic composition in which a theme or themes are stated successively in all of the voices of the contrapuntal structure. Psychiatry: a pathological amnesiac during which one is apparently conscious of one's actions but has no recollection of them after returning to a normal state. This condition, usually resulting from severe mental stress, may persist for as long as several months.

Then he looked for another word he did not understand, a word that had flooded his mind while in that other world, that blurry world where random images and words rain down on him.

Hosanna: interjection. Used to express praise or adoration unto God. Noun. 1. A cry of 'hosanna.' 2. A shout of fervent and worshipful praise.

He tucked the dictionary away.

"Hosanna!" he yelled and ran. His mind ran faster than his legs, the words in random clusters pouring from an unknown, unfamiliar voice.

Now you've done it. Done what? Think later. Run.

12. *Nothing But the Sun*

All the kings' horses, all the kings' men, couldn't put my mind together again. There's no such thing as Peter Pan, no such thing as Neverland, where children without worry play and sing. That is not the world, cruel maze, and judgment it's reward. I hope they have a phone in purgatory, so I can call my mother, High in Heaven, and tell her I got what I deserved.

If only I could somehow see the magic man for empathy. The door at the end of my golden road is closed. No neverland, no songs, just silence, God's one eternal song. And other men, now long, long gone, silence is their only song, whose high pitch is eternal. The tree, the world, that laughing girl, how beautiful is everything. The worms, the snakes, like me, the lice. Devil in the mind be gone. All is still, on the jukebox, Silence as recorded by God, and the man in boots, with his cowboy hat, never runs out of quarters. The devil is the busy boy, at the bottom of the steps, whose intent is control, the soul, and how it often wayward goes. A brief delay. Disillusion, before the curtain closes, and the drapes, what light! Of the night disposes, leaving nothing but the Sun.

He drifted into that dream world once again, out of body, out of place, out of time, a hallucinogenic episode. He was old, a white man, it was late at night. He had glasses on. All was quiet, with candles as his reading light. He stared all day into the sea, or in a dream, it sometime seemed, a book he held called, 'We.'

He heard three knocks on the door, just three soft knocks and nothing more.

The book he sat beside the table, on a lamp stand less than stable, and strode to the door across the wood floor. A candle huddled in his hand sat on a silver candle stand. He looked out to dare implore, and stood, gazing at the blue-tinged moon bathed wood.

Nothing and nobody there, just lonely trees and quiet, twisted elms with shrubs beside it, a shadow of its form behind it. Like shadow puppets on the wall, dancing lively, standing stall. Then he saw a young girl's dress drift deep into the wilderness, a smudge of blue under the pale faced sickly moon whose light the trees had barred, sending the light in scattered fragments through the trees that looked like bars.

A dress of blue, outlined in lace, by trees it blew, around her face. He followed her and then she turned her voice inside him burned. Behind him came a whisper, low-rolling and she said,

'Tell me, tell me, what's it like to be dead?'

Neddy was shaken, pulled from his anxiety fugue back to the world outside, the world without bars, and he saw, as clear as day, his sister cold and grey. Dead, and smiling, skin the color of ash. "Come with me," she said. "Neddy, I'll show you what it's like to be dead."

She turned and ran into the woods, through lonely nighttime trees and sand and, her childish laughing ringing out. 'What!' he said, and turned to shout: through all the rustling nighttime leaves into the wood he followed at full speed.

The same voice he heard just up ahead, a sleeping owl had turned, and said, like a jester from a palace read: through the darkness, he peered through, seeing a subtle shade of blue.

Strange it was that night to see, a lonely owl look down at he, saying, 'What's it like to be dead?' Who? Nobody. Who? The owl said, reclined his head, and laughed. On the ground not far away Neddy saw the curtail of a blue dress sway, then her brown eyes, as clear as day, held a mirror, from the ground, and she passed through without a sound. He went through too and then he knew, as he washed onto a pale white shore, and the words came, just as before, a small girl from the trees walked up to him and said, 'Do you know what it's like to be dead?'

There was a trap-door in the woods, they disappeared through, and now they stood; fireflies they saw, or thought they could, they glistened in the far off night like a star reflecting bright. Across the stream went flower seeds. They fell on the stream like silver beads, lonely was the water, settled still, laughing Galilee sat on the hill.

'What's it like to be dead?'

She, a reflection in the water said. She above the water whispered; dragonflies around them glittered.

'It is to lie alone and still, the world above your eyes might spill, to look above, like the lonely water does.

'What know you of truth, and lie?'

Again the same owl floated by, 'What could you know of life and death? Never does the water rest.

Tell me then of truth, don't lie. I oft-feel like a firefly, who random blinks, one moment then, away like wind goes with the sand.

The devil was made in our image, and we saw that it was good. This is me, the beast, a visage no realer than an angel carved from wood.

'Do you know the things you say?'

Because I've been there and I've seen. The trees began to sway. *This from the other world I bring.*

'Look into the water and you'll see too,' into the stream a stone he threw. The image changed, and revealed, plain, the Master's face looked at his own.

'Know you if by the hand of Heaven, or if you're held by the devil's hands? The voice inside, the voice that screams. That's what it is, not like the books of man, the laundry list of words that beautify the squalor. What mountains of creation could we ascend, if you upon the myths depend? If we on these myths rely, you'll drift around like dragonflies. Only there the silence lasts forever, regardless of life's stormy weather, regardless of the shovel or who it was made for. Only silence live forever more.'

Before him on the calm night sea, the silent tide, by Galilee, he could inside his future sea; drowning beside the birds that glide, in the silent tide where Galilee played. Neddy snapped back into his coherent mind again and stood at the edge of the woods, his hallucinogenic states coming and going at random, scaring and confusing him. His mind split into a thousand fragments with the grief weighing down on him, like God's boot pushing against his chest, suffocating, couldn't breathe, squeeze, Neddy writhing like a bug under a malevolent fingernail.

He heard the Master's wife screaming, snapping him out of his trance, his mother, too, was screaming, trying to console the widow. He turned around and returned to the scene of the crime with the bloody shovel in his hand.

13: *The Birth of Nobody*

His mother was holding Master's wife around her waist as she lunged forward, hand over her mouth, tears stealing down her cheek, shouting, "Why? Why?" at the dead man on the porch, whose lifeblood ran down the once rose white steps, now lined like arteries, intersecting down the stairs a biological red, red blood. It gathered in sickening gobs, coagulating, drying into sickening crusts of black.

"We'll have to call the police," she said. Neddy panicked. He ran onto the porch and hit the Master's wife over the head. She fell to the ground in quiet, her eyes fixed, unflinching, all the way to the ground. When her heavy form struck the ground her once alert eyes went shut, clockwork like, as though her off switch had been pressed. She fell into the blood of her dead husband.

"What the hell are you doing?" Neddy's mother yelled. "Oh, God. Neddy they gone kill you. Run, run and never come back. They'll kill us all for this!" She slapped him in the face. "How could you? How could you!" She slapped him again, throwing her small fists against his chest.

He went numb again, that distant, fugue like feeling enveloped his body, sending his mind far away from where his hopeless body stood in tears, his mother throwing her tiny fists against him in violent volleys. He felt as though his mother was a thousand miles away, beating against the empty shell of what once housed his self. He heard her cries, her shouts, as she fell to her knees, shaking the dead woman, trying to wake her. Neddy was in a state of catatonic shock, unable to move, pulled out of time, out of body, and taken to a far off place.

He stood before a judge, a man who looked just like his father.

"Guilty!" he yelled. "Guilty!"

A faceless jury of nobody's, like the ones in the mirror, all nodded their blank faces, mumbling in agreement. An old-time courtroom unfolded before Neddy's eyes, with the Master on the witness stand with his brains hanging out, "Was him," he shouts and points. The Judge, his father, slams the gavel and he's back in his body, the sound of the gavel being the sound of Thomas's gun.   All   he   could   do   was   run.

14. *The Judge of Me*

Reality swept over Neddy like a quilt of burning nerves. He ran into the Master's house. His mother remained on the porch, weeping, crying out I'm sorry upward trying to breathe life into the dead man's mouth she mourned.

Each portrait in the home that Neddy passed showed his Master in the past, not an evil being, but a man, a man who lived the only way he could.

There were portraits of him as a young man, with a black man to his side, smiling and shaking hands. It took Neddy a long time to recognize his father in the picture.

He dropped it, stunned, and turned around, coming face to face with a wall of portraits of the Master and his family, loving smiling, fishing, picking flowers under a yellow sun orange on the shore of Myrtle Beach.

There were portraits of Master and his son, a wee boy, holding his hands as he walked. Him riding a pony, always smiling, wearing his father's oversized hat, Galilee with Paula, Master's wife, in a field of yellow jasmines. He thought of stealing the picture and despaired, feeling like a thief, then ran out of the house, out the back door by the broken window, and disappeared into the darkness running full speed to his cabin, adrenaline setting his veins on fire, sucking and squeezing his chest together as though some alien or malevolent force was shaking him like a frightened kitten with no idea why it was being punished.

It was his uncle, frantic, breathing in deep gasps as he spoke.

"Neddy," he shouted, "are you hurt? What happened? You've got blood all over you."

"It's hard to say," Neddy says. "Something is wrong with my brain. I was walking in the maze and trying to get everything straightened up for Sunday that's what Thomas told us so I worked hard tonight and I tripped and fell and Master started cussing at me so I picked up a shovel and hit him and he tried to choke me so I hit him again they're going to kill me Uncle. They're going to kill me. He was gonna bury daddy in the woods and they are gonna dig up his body and put him in the woods by himself. I didn't mean to hurt him. I think he's okay."

"You have to leave and never come back," Nate said. "Thomas is going to kill all of us.

"No!" Neddy said. "Tell them I killed myself. I can fire a shot and you can say you saw me shoot myself. By the river you can say, shot himself dead and fell into the water. As long as they think I died, you and mama will be safe. Just tell them I was possessed by the devil... tell them what you have to. They have to think I died."

"Where did you get a gun?" Nate asked.

"Picked it up on the porch."

Just one shot and I'm done.

"You can sleep at the Galilee church up the road but you 'a have to leave just in case Thomas gets them hounds to look for ya."

"That's where I planned on going," Neddy said, not meaning to say *planned* instead trying to say *decided.*

"Alright, Neddy," Nate said. "I'll never see you again. I'm too old for that. You gotta stay gone forever if you make me tell 'em you killed yourself. How am I supposed to make them believe that?"

"Put up a gravestone for me by the river," Neddy said. "Thomas would expect you to do so where I died. He doesn't think you'd work... not on a grave for someone who wasn't dead, anyway. If he sees you working, he'll think I really died... He doesn't think you'd do it if you didn't have to."

"How do you know what he'll think?" Nate asked.

"Because I've listened to him talk, at great length, workin' under the window."

"Alright," Nate said. "Goodbye, Neddy."

"Don't use that wretched word," Neddy said. "I'm a nobody now, a nobody..."

"You're Neddy."

"Not anymore. Neddy was a slave who killed himself in Carolina long ago. Now I can be somebody else. I can be anything I want to be. I can do anything I want to do. I'm free. I can decide who I am on my own. Nobody's the judge of me now."

"Are you sure the Master's dead?" Nate asked, worried at the look in Neddy's eyes, the eyes of the delirious.

"I could see my face in the puddle of his brains," Neddy said. "Go tell 'em I killed myself."

"What do you want me to tell ya mama?" Nate asked. "You want me to tell her that?"

"Don't tell her the truth," Neddy said. "Tell her that her son killed himself because he was overcome by de—by grief. I'll be gone before you get to tell them.

"Just put up my grave and put those yellow flowers on it. I might come back someday to see it, if everybody could somehow forgive me."

If I could forgive myself...

Arriving home he found his dead sister waiting, still as grey, like cigarette ash in a tray, and she sat with her legs around the barrel of fire. She had a gaze of unwavering stillness and concentration. She looked into the wall of fire between her and her horrified and delusional brother.

Neddy stood there frozen, lost in his mental universe, locked away from the responses of the body. His sister said, "Where's daddy?"

"I don't know," Neddy said.

"Where's mama?" she asked.

"Uncle took her for a walk," Neddy lied. "She'll be home soon. Uncle took her for a walk on the trail. She'll be home. She'll be home."

"You're bleeding," Galilee's ghost said. "Did you cut yourself again? Why do you always cut yourself, Neddy? I've seen you."

Neddy looked at the blood on his clothes, the dried flakes on his face, the scab of blood encrusted on the shovel.

"You cut yourself, again?"

"No," Neddy said.

"But you're bleeding."

"Not my blood."

"What happened, Neddy? You have to face the truth sometime or later. What happened? I've seen you with the knife. Did you cut yourself again? Why do you cut yourself, Neddy?"

"Cut myself in the maze," he said. "Just got a little dizzy is all, fell asleep reading daddy's dictionary..."

"Neddy..." she tried, but he held his hand up to interrupt her. "One thing's for sure, sister," he said, "I will never see Heaven. I have to leave."

She saw the shovel in his hand, covered in almost black scabs of blood on his face. Neddy found it hard to lie to her, even though she was dead, and a hallucination. She cleaned his face in the kitchen, washing the rest of the blood off with a washrag. He rushed back into the living room. Galilee's grey ghost sat by the fire with the same far off gaze, looking into the blue hue of the barrel of flame.

"Look," she said. "You can see your life."

Neddy sat down and looked into the fire. He saw bloodhounds, barking, police officers tracking him across the state, his suicide or surrender, he hadn't decided; he saw an image of his mother tied to a whipping post, naked, with lash after lash levied into her back. He saw his father's ghost looking at him as he swung the shovel at the puddle of blood which once was the Master's face. He frowns and shakes his head and disappears. He sees a gravestone by overgrown grass. An angel sat by him on a wooden log somewhere in the woods, a green world of humid grasslands and woods for him to roam, to search for himself, for what he could make of his life, having been a slave and now a homeless man.

He saw Thomas as an old man in a different sort of suit, a different sort of place, kneeling by a nameless grave.

Neddy saw himself with a trashcan and a broom, sweeping for the Master's horrible son. He saw them hug each other, their forms cast by the curvature of flame. The image faded from the fire and Galilee too was gone.

He jumped to his feet and ran from the room, back to the maze, where the statue of the angel with the broken wing still stood. Neddy smashed it into pieces, jumping up and down and screaming and cursing unintelligible sounds of hatred and disgust no words were apt to articulate; it was as a blind man shouting at Da Vinci to describe the Mona Lisa and little boy Blue, as Neddy knew, was himself color blind. He called out for help but the sound echoed back to him in Galilee's voice, just like the hopelessness of that dreadful dream, now followed him into the land of the living, hand around his throat, the sound of dogs, the Master's hounds, *they smell my feet.*

He ran in circles almost blind before finding himself at the nature trail, not knowing how he got there, his mind still locked into a random loop of screaming sounds, the wall of fire littered with faces of when's and where's and then's and there's and through it saw a star.

Galilee's church just down the road...

Neddy ducked and dodged the branches and silent shrubs over brittle quilts of dead leaves. He tried to remember the way to the church, and, unable, just ran, fast with no idea out of breath and gasping. A devil figure appeared before him with dribbling teeth and mirrored eyes. Neddy saw himself inside the eyes and screamed.

The horrible monster grabbed Neddy by his throat and stuffed him into the slobbering mouth, bones crunching, child screaming, silence.

Neddy lapsed out of conscious. An indeterminate time passed and he woke in someone's familiar arms, black and strong, green and yellow sagging flowers going by him at an awkward angle, as though growing downward from the sky. Dizziness, a spinning sort of grey fugue blur, a memory hole, infinite stretch of confused faces walking in different directions, dirty clothes, shovels on their back. Images flitted by the theatre of the mind, sounds far off and muffled, mumbling faces smiling clapping, towering monuments, pyramids and dust storms in the desert.

The pyramids outlast the kings, you know. That Wall in china will outlast the slaves who made it and the kings for whom it was made. This will all end in tears, you know. It's the slaves, the endless line of nobody's with different names, who pay for the monuments with their lives and neither the maker or the Master get to see it in the end, when the curtain closes and the show is over.

What is my monument?

The maze.

15: *The Bars of his Cage*

Neddy opened his eyes, blinked, refocused—lanterns passing by his eyes, up a hill, a sigh, dizziness, panic pulsing wicked in his chest, burning numbness, tingling electric currents. His body felt detached from a mind unwired, sparks above the damaged circuit board where memories and images went in loops, in one side and out the other, Neddy repeating in dry monotone, "Wrong place, wrong time."

"I've been looking for you," Nate said. "I brought you a blanket. Your mama told me to find you."

Panic answered, "You told her the truth?"

"I couldn't tell her that her only living son killed himself. You know what that would do to her? She knows you're alive. That's why I had to bring you a blanket. I told everybody else you just went crazy and shot yourself."

"Did Thomas see them? Did he see them dead?"

"Your mother had to go upstairs and tell him... he lost his mind, Neddy. Master's housecleaner told your mama that he hanged himself in the barn, but we didn't see his body. They must 'a got it down. Said it was his fault, saying he had insulted you or said something to you, I don't know, this is the story that I was told. I don't know what to make of it, or if it's true at all."

"He wouldn't kill himself," Neddy said. "It's fabricated..."

Ever notice how people who are guilty of a crime are the first to suspect one? Did you ever think about that, old man?

"Thought you were going to the church?" Nate asked. "The church is the other way. You lucky I know you so well. You gotta go the other way to get to the church."

"I don't know if I can make it," Neddy said. "Everything is...all confused...mixed up... It was bad, uncle Nate. What I did was wrong. I'm no better than a dog. I still see my reflection in the blood... like I'm still standing there...and his wife...she..."

"You'll be fine, Neddy," Nate said. "Just stay warm. Mama made me bring the blanket so you better use it."

"I don't know if I can be alone," Neddy said. "I always feel lost when I'm alone, no matter where I'm at, but I've noticed something, uncle, about myself: I like being lost... I like being able to find my way. I'm more comfortable when I'm lost in the maze...but I've only left this place once. The world is more complicated than the maze behind the Master's house."

"Pray when things get bad, or too much for you to handle. Pray every day for the rest of your life."

"But I don't believe in God," Neddy said.

"Then pray twice," his uncle said.

"Praying won't make life any easier. If praying worked, I'd have a father and a little sister and I'd be happy now. It doesn't work. Where was God when my father suffocated in the dust? Where was God when Galilee screamed in the well? Where was God when the shovel shut the Master's mouth for good? It's all just people being people...and we had to hear them die! I hear it when I try to sleep... I can still hear the sound of my daddy dying. Where was God when daddy died?"

"Neddy..."

"There is no God! There is no guide, no paradise, just hell on Earth and then a grave, then silence, nothing. Just a little stone sticking out of the dirt with our name on it; that's all we have. That's the only way it ends. Every story is the same... someone lives and someone dies. Ever been to Lee Cemetery? Look at all those nameless graves and all those dead flowers and tell me if you see God. A single line between two dates—that summarizes all our life. I won't even get that."

"We'll dig a grave for you, when no one's noticing, and as long as I'm alive I'll visit it, every year, on your birthday and leave those yellow flowers for you."

"Then who will leave them when you're gone?"

Nate didn't answer.

"Nobody," Neddy said. "That's who..."

"Neddy...do you still have that gun?"

"Yes," Neddy said.

"Will you give it to me?"

"No," Neddy said. "I might need it."

Neddy turned to look toward the hill.

"Did you hear that?" Neddy asked.

"Hear what?"

"The dogs! The dogs!"

His uncle tried to hear but failed.

"I don't hear anything, Neddy. Just the sound of night..."

"No! Listen close... There! You hear it? Listen!"

Nothing, nobody there; a blanket of whispering wind goes by.

"They're after me," Neddy said. "They'll eat me alive."

They won't but your mind will. It's tasty too. The face is good. I've always liked the lips, so soft when you chew on them, the blood like sweet sweet fillings. Yum. Would you take a bite? The sweet yum yum taste of mama's mouth...

"Why would they be after you?" Nate asked. "They think you're dead and they saying Thomas killed himself. Nobody is after you, Neddy. Just go to the church, get some sleep, and try to get yourself together..."

"The dogs! The dogs!"

"I hear them too," Nate said. "They're on the trail."

"Bye uncle," Neddy said, turning. "I love you. Tell mama that I'm sorry."

Neddy ran into the darkness through the jagged limbs of dead trees, grey shapes, crickets and their songs and silence, tobacco plants and stale aroma.

Neddy fought the sleepiness, blanking out as he ran, stopping, running again, stopping, standing, looking in all directions, unaware of his surroundings and who he was. Then he'd gather himself and run again. He ran until his bleeding brain trailed off.

Mother against a tree, Galilee, father too, laugh and laugh and laugh, ha, ha, ha they laughed. Neddy stood in front of them naked, crying with his arms bound behind his back, unable to cover himself as they pointed and laughed.

Obscure sounds, smudging bending trees, Thomas with a mirror, Neddy saw his face; then, in shock, saw the Master's laughing ha-ha face in the dusty glass.

He blinked and the images changed, revealing instead inside his head a coliseum of the mind, giant pillars to the ceiling, a bunch of copy's of himself wandering blind around the chipped marble floor under the sagging ceiling. His mother lay by lantern light under a tree, naked, covered in blood, her face smudged out and blurry.

He closed his eyes and held them shut, tight until his mother's face appeared behind his eyelids.

"Goodnight, Neddy," she said.

She turned to walk away.

"Hey," Neddy said. "Where are you going?"

No answer.

"Mama?"

Nothing.

"Mama!"

She disappeared into the hungry black gullet of the night. Neddy closed his eyes.

She can smell the blood on you, old man. Did you see how strange she looked at you? She doesn't know who you are anymore. To her you're just another monster like the Master, another murderer. And you're crying? She's better off without you around anyway.

Neddy opened his eyes to find his mother sitting in front of him with a glass of tea, transparent, a bit blurry, trees behind her visible.

"Good morning, sunshine," she said. Her eyes like black marbles glittered in the dark.

"I thought you were lost inside the maze again," she said.

"Yes, I was lost," Neddy said.

"We found you in the maze," She said. "Sleepwalking again... You were delusional so we gave you something to calm down. You'll be okay."

He knew it wasn't his mother; his mother wouldn't have lied.

"I'm lost," Neddy said, indignant. "I don't know which way to go. One voice says yes and one says no."

"Sometimes I think you like being lost," she said. "Sometimes I think you don't want to find your way."

"They'll never let me into Heaven, mama."

"They might," she said. "That's up to you."

Neddy blinked again, the vision faded like breath upon a mirror.

She fixed her eyes on Neddy's. He turned his head, avoiding her face. She looked at the dried blood on her son's neck, chipping away in little scabs, made visible by the lantern light. She looked Neddy over, head to toe, and vomited.

Neddy put his fingers in his ears, collapsing. He opened his eyes and heard the barks again; he saw the real world once more. His mother's face was gone. He looked at his bloody hands, floating orbs of light about the woods bobbed close and closer still through the thicket of a rose bush and its thorns.

There had been one execution in Neddy's life time, other than the accidental death of his father and sister, when another slave, whose child was killed by antique looms, killed the Master's niece and nephew. The Master's disciples hacked off the head of that old slave with that old rusty blade.

Go ahead old man, he heard, *jump into the river drown ashamed you should be ashamed of what you did well murder isn't the best thing you could do you know I don't know where to go you'll go to hell no I'll go to the church like uncle said long road paved rocks loose gravel the dusty way to that abandoned church, three crosses clothed with scarlet robes, windows and doors overran by grass. A mile from here, just follow the river. Remember the baboon in the zoo?*

No.

That's just a story.

No, it's not. It is. But do you remember?

Remember what?

The old baboon's painting... They tried for weeks, remember that? They showed him how to paint and gave him a canvas. They worked with him for weeks until he produced his painting: grey smears and smudges, vertical strokes: the bars of his rusted cage.

And I'm the weakest baboon of them all, unable to paint, unable to work, unable to do anything but run...

...because you're a coward...

I'm not a coward...

...yes you are. If you weren't you'd kill yourself now.

I hate you. You should. We're a terrible person. You are, not me. I'm in your head, old man. Can't run from me. That tiny fragment of a decent man named Neddy is dead.

Oh, what shame unending.

16. *The Confession Box*

Neddy staggered drunken on the river's edge, a fork in the road, straight ahead under a subdued yellow moon that sighed.

Scrambled mind, fantasy overlapping reality, fleeting hallucinations, dead faces, father's, mother's, sister's, that sun, memories cooked up a fantasy and stress deep-fries the mind, a fugue, teeth clicking together, gagging noises, just grey, tree shapes amid the fog, unwired mind no memories vague symbols distorted face, *you did the right thing. Then why debate yourself, old man? Remember those bulging bloodshot eyes, that purple throat, puddle of brains...*

He deserved to die. The woman too? Why did she deserve to die? It was an act of mercy. Act of mercy? I don't think that's what Jesus meant. You should've listened to your father and been a good boy. Now you're a little windup toy, your broken brain, just grab the gun. Wouldn't want your uncle to be a liar would you? A liar like you. Like me? Who else would you be talking to? Talking at. Talking to. I live in your head and I'll chew on your brain like a slab of beef.

Neddy stood frozen in front of the time-worn and forgotten church in ruins, tired his body spent and sighing burnt out mind, his aching feet dragged along the dusty trail the tired sigh sang the dirt.

Malevolent menacing trees lined the road. In the distant sky into the stars a black cross made of iron bars hid a tired moon behind it quiet.

Neddy stood at the front door, double doors covered in moss, gold handles.

No place for a murderer, you know. There's no one there to listen to a nobody, his tawdry confessions blah, blah, blah and sobbing sad sad stories, confusing tragedies how comic. This is a place of beauty, no place for a wretch like me. There's nowhere for a wretch like you. You'll pay for all for nothing.

The double doors were boarded up, held by crooked rusted nails, stained glass mural by the door a mural of Jesus shone, the Christ held forth a book, somber eyes and knowing smile. Another mural, Gabriel, carved out of stone and darkness covered with dust and grit and moss.

Neddy in a sing song drawl, "No place for a wretch like me."

Neddy crawled through the back window in an empty room, a row of pews and scattered yellow bibles, a confession box. Neddy walked into the confession box, *feels like a grave to me,* with God on the other side, he sat, feet curving inward resigned posture, shameful.

"Forgive me *father*...for I have sinned."

A familiar voice said, "It's the same old story, isn't it? Kill a man and say you're sorry sin erased. You want to find salvation now? You've thrown that all away. Why would a louse like you deserve freedom or salvation? You're a nobody, a tool, a slave, a faceless one without worth to the world, a soft machine that has no function, an engineering flaw, might as well hang yourself, old man. This will all end in tears."

"I'm sorry," he said, no sound. "I'm sorry!" he yelled.

"You've dishonored your family and yourself," the voice said inside his head.

"I'm sorry," again.

The apology echoed back at him, repeated in his head.

Kill yourself.

Kill yourself be free. Let the carcass die and get your peace.

Neddy enraged stormed out the door to the other side of the box, opened it, nobody there, just still and dust and quiet, his shadow on the wall scattered by the stain-glassed windows hues of blue and red and gold.

God himself in that old man...

Neddy's collapsed, brain shuts down, unconscious, ear full of clotted blood, arms spread an angel shape the wings the lines of dust.

And Neddy wandered on.

17. *Neddy's Monument*

By the River Tyger in the dream, he stood and waited, gun to his head, full, six bullets in the chamber, chamber spin click done, waiting for the demon dogs, the Master's snarling mutts, weaving through foul spectral trees.

Neddy hears them howl and sees their teeth, a shouting mob with lanterns, rifles, shotguns and a rope. Neddy waited by the fake grave for a while, where innocence filled the grave, hearing the devil dog's call, just fireflies imagined lanterns drifting careless lazy in the grey, the orange sky.

"Drop the gun!" he heard—just fireflies—no words, no contorted angry faces mouth agape and shouting, the sound of guns, chamber spin click spin click, click. Click click click click click click...

His bloodshot eyes focused on the exaggerated maze of twisted trees in front of him as stinking sweat stole down his cheek, tasting it, still waiting, no lanterns coming, no shouting men with rifles, just the dark, nobody in sight, just crooked trees into the sky like crooning shadow figures, the twisted bone like branches, the wind in hush-hush whispers by, cooing soft the shadow's voice.

Neddy put the gun to his head, pulled the trigger, slumped over like an actor's lifeless husk, a sickening empty thud on soft ground, rose above his body and he saw a theatre empty, nobody in the hall: a poor performance for the trees and fireflies, for the imagined men—with guns and rifles and broken shovels—who never appeared by the river bank, where he performed his trashy show for no one, *old man lost his mind. It's in the Trash—can they look for me now?*

Words and sounds swam like fish in the broken fishbowl brain:
   Who is they?
   Everybody.
  It's everyone but you.
  My mind is breaking down.
They're trying to take my mind. The devil's chewing on_____
      my—mind...
                  Your mind? Who's 'they'?
      All madmen have a they!
     Who can be yours today?
   The people I hurt.
    The lives I ended.
    La, la, la, la, la...

That's not who you should be
afraid of, Neddy. Them you can outrun. You can't outrun what
will chase you.
The maze?
　The maze
　　and the shadow
　　　too, your
　　　　monuments,
　　　　　what you'll
　　　　　　become, another
　　　　　　shadow on the Hill
　　　　　where once a
　　　　　thousand dead slaves
　　　　tilled in morning
　　　and the evening
　light...What now?
　Who am I?
　What can I do
with my life?
Not much. You're homeless
　and alone in the world,
　　just you old man,
　　　your old self dead,
　　　　floating down
　　　the make believe river Tyger...
　Death, ah,
　and then you rest.
Death—one shot away. One shot, bang,
　　it's done,
　　　no more need
　　　　　for you to run.

Neddy leaned against the pulpit, hard wood on his back, a sigh, canceled eyes, chest pain, miserable blood burning like electric eels in evil torrents.

No need for me to cry, he said, *the weight on the back, the pain in the chest, the devil choking the mind in distress, that's all it is I'm sure.*

So now I am the devil? I'm just in your head.

I hate you and your cause, the stress, devil anxiety. Leave me alone and let me rest.

Why do you hate yourself, Neddy? Why don't you get the gun and listen to its sing song lullaby and let it lull you off to sleep just like mama's arms?

How ridiculous and hopeless games against the self, what melancholy pays, sometimes it seems to me that an hour lasts a thousand days. Melancholy sounds and forms turn into beauty if they're right. What joy! I can be anything I want to be.

And what's that, old man?

I don't know. I'm not a slave anymore...

Yes you are, just a different type is all.

I can be a king, like the Master Alexander. I can be happy, sad, angry, miserable, whatever it is I wish...

As long as you have to wish... you're never going to be free, a puppet that dances by desire is a puppet controlled by me.

The real world stabbed away at him, the anxiety like acid eating his chest from the inside out in violent bites as he stood there, wondering if he'd just fall over like a prop, an empty mannequin hours spent, bug eyes like a dead fish on the shore.

Tired he closed his drooping eyes and on his eyelids there to find, pass by the glass ball of his third eye, a black man Master, puffy cheeks, smacking away at toast and treats.

And *he looks a lot like...*

Yes? A lot like who?

Nobody, nevermind...

Nobody indeed...

The vision faded like a cloud of smoke as quick as it appeared. Neddy shook off the dizzy feeling and stumbled around the main hall of worship, the wasting syndrome symptoms glowing, anxiety, doom, and dread, the panic in his blood electric screams. He made his way uneasily to the rain-stained pew, read a Bible verse or two, the dog-eared books, the yellow pages, hanging from compartments behind the seats.

He thumbed through the pages, finding a song his mother once had sung, when Galilee was born all those years ago. Neddy thought back to that day under the shade in the woods, reading the hymn his mother sang.

Amazing grace, how sweet the
sound,
That saved a wretch like me.

Images rewound in his mind. Christmas time, four years ago, Neddy and Galilee played in the snow, bundled from head to toe with thick winter jackets, zippers down the front.

I once was lost but now am
found,
Was blind, now, I see.

Neddy saw himself walk through the snow alone. He stood by a snowman in a dim and grey type snow covered noon. His warm breath hovered in front of his face like Master's cigarettes.

And grace, my fears relieved.

Neddy's father walked through the door, no jacket shivering with a smile, a bowl of grits, a cup of tea. Neddy and his family ate a while, and then for a while they sang. They said their prayers, went to bed, Neddy without a thought in his mind, just the songs of before.

Ray sat with his bowl of cold grits, Galilee whittling in her bed, cheerful little smile brighter than the stars.

The memory began to fade, leaving Neddy in the dark church alone. He heard them eating and laughing, the slaves in the other cabins bawling hymns into the morning, clapping their hands. In Neddy's mind, the memory changed, and the smiling faces turned to clapping skeletons, their gums smacking as they clapped, the brittle bones like sticks against each other.

The song played on:
We've been here ten thousand
years,
Bright as the shining sun.
We've no less days to sing
God's praise, than when we've
first begun.

The memory began to bleed and change. His mother grew terrible teeth and chased a naked Neddy through the maze, Thomas behind him laughing with a whip, a bird was crooning:
Amazing grace, how sweet the
sound,
That saved a wretch like me.
I once was lost but now am
found,
Was blind, but now I see.

The visions on his eyelids dissolved like a bubble, the drab dark of the broke down church crept in again, washing away his fantasies and fugues. He lay there in the dark with whispering all around him, tossing and turning, trying to sleep, pain on every side.

He walked to the dusty pulpit where a yellowed Bible sat, opened with a burgundy tassel holding place, and Neddy knelt.

He could not believe in God, not with what sorrow he saw in the world, but he prayed every night anyway, in quiet in his mind, never out loud, not like his proud father would. Neddy was ashamed of his vain needs and whimsy and the prayers that grew from them.

God, I'm sorry. I'm wrong, I know. I shouldn't have done what I done and I would never do it again. I'm not asking for forgiveness, because I don't deserve it, I'm asking for…

Neddy paused. He looked around the pure black church, just little pools of light in places. Neddy went back to his prayer:

…for your empathy. I will suffer the rest of my days, gladly, if Master finds a place in Heaven, or if my father gets to drink iced tea up there with you, or if you see my sister Galilee tell her I don't think I'll make it this time, but I love her. Don't tell her what I've done. Just that I love her.

If there is mercy in your heart for the louse, absolve me; let my life be an anathema to undo the crimes I've committed, to undo the anguish and leave beauty and goodness in the world, wherever I take it. That will be my life. I hope there is forgiveness, like in that song, for one as me, a louse, worse than a wretch, a bug that dreams of one day being a man again.

In the dark beside him, Neddy heard and saw a choir of old time ghosts, crooning Amazing Grace, dressed in their Sunday best, pearls and hats and linen gloves and clapping, surreal tenor soothing until Neddy went to sleep, mind shutdown, blood still drying in his ears.

That night Neddy had the dream again, the dream of Nobody, the louse. That fearful dream again appeared, the cruel fingers from the sky, that dusty sun, those strange giants that turned massive eyes on them, the lice, tragedy after tragedy until only one poor louse remained.

And   Nobody   was   his   name.

18: *Inside the Bone Wall*

He often dreamed he was a louse, back at his quarters, in the slave house, trapped on a free man's head. He always had the dream and to him it was as real as waking life.

It was as though he once lived a past life as a louse trapped in a maze of hair, the hair the giant bars into the sky, poor lice in search of a queen he never saw. The lice lived blissful lives for a time and Neddy didn't suffer the endless maze of hair.

Then the fingers came for him when he tried to sleep, as though in a dream, he ran in and out of brown corridors from the fingers, fingers with crusty blood under the nail, killing Neddy's family one by one, songs for forgiveness, screaming at the bone wall of the mind.

Then the light went out and the tense and terrible fingers left and Neddy lay against another louse, unable to sleep, but content and warm. The light came on again and he crawled like a slave under the sun, that dim apartment light, a monotone music box playing tranquil songs for dying bugs becoming conscious.

When he was that Nobody louse, when the light swam overhead, he fled as though a moth burnt by the light, always running, never knowing to where he ran.

The lice made up stories about the head, the origin, the God whose fingers killed them, whose will it was to suffer the delusion of a life lived as a louse.

They cried Hosanna, flinging themselves to the ground. They were happy and lived in peace, holding hands and singing songs for God. To live was enough for them and all the lice were free. The lice rejoiced under their plastic sun, singing hymns about its beauty holding hands smiling at the world above them, poor understood but marveled. The fingers came down again onto the scalp, killing them by the thousands, a genocide a second, wiping them away as they sang, while those still alive would sing and sing for the murderous hands, the hands and fingers that killed them, then flicked them into a trash can by the sink, a little treatment to get rid of the pests. Millions died under dirty fingernails, what had they done to incur their Master's wrath, flat against the forehead, flicked off, category gone.

The free man, Master, prepares for lice a great disaster, though they appreciated still their world, and kissed the scalp and cried in glee as the poison drowned their sounds nobody heard.

But the evolved lice, those who survived, become sentient and conscious beyond their ancestors and built miniature ships and telescopes and began to explore the face on which they lived, the freeman turning into Neddy. They planned a great expedition into his ear in search of consciousness within their world.

Nobody the louse was an explorer in his mind, inside a microscopic ship, in his ear and through the ear drum. The lice in Neddy's mind cut away the tiny membrane that led through the eardrum and into the physical brain. Mounds of throbbing pink globs and purple sections and pink reddish type pulsing veins like snakes showed up in the dim light of the open mouth, to their side coming oxygen as Neddy breathed in his sleep. Pink, breathing, pulsing, threatening mountains throbbed in the distance, strange structures brushing against the ship of panicked lice.

Their plan was to reach the soul, the conscious mind, what it was that separated Neddy from all the other lice and men on Earth, and the explorers arrived in the center of the brain, looking at parts and organs arranged in large structures inside a self contained wall of bone.

No consciousness appeared but sounds, in unknown murmurs, filled the cavern, words like why and how and who am I rattled the exploration ship. The lice did not comprehend the words as they went by the ship, *nobody, nobody, zero, murderer, failure, maniac, maniac, garbage, a louse, worse than a snake or maggot an animal without a face not even thought of as a race.*

They came upon a seaside scene, something out of Neddy's dream, a land sublime, a sublime Sea, and beside it sat his Galilee. The sun was going down and his mother hummed, ever present, filling the exploration ship as it plunged further into the mind.

The same song his sister hummed, on the gravestone in sleepless dreams as they neared Neddy's subconscious mind, hearing random words adrift, a stream of thought.

A girl with jasmines. Blood shovel. Never make it now. No more need to run. No more wisdom. Terrible louse maniac fiend garbage not worth the breath you have but you take it thief.

Vague shapes and massive beings passed before the screen, women, men, neither, walked by slow and spoke in slow stuttering low pitched voices unintelligible backwards nonsense, rewound and replayed, saying, "Wrong place, wrong time."

Little girl, blue dress, murmuring *no more need to go home now,* a child, back turned, at a dock, fishing line in the water waiting, turning around, never checking the line for fish, no bites anyway. His father's grey ghost showed up and talked but Neddy couldn't hear him only his lips contorting into silent patterns misunderstood, "I can hear you too."

The side of his face was lashed, though he laughed, still not letting on he was hurt; a scratch, he said, no big deal.

A child. Someone crying. The other side of the door of the brain. Neddy refused to let them in. They battle the defenses for hours before they break down the wall to Broca's area, the core of Neddy's being, where the demons of his past waited on them.

Center of the mind, absolute dark, in Broca's area, Neddy became trapped, as a man in bed, and a louse in an active dream. The words from his father's dictionary fluttered by his eyelids as the catatonic state over took him again, a grand mal seizure.

Failure try loser why win accident ruined abortion redemption forgive me song hymn forgive me God, my crime, I somehow went mad, lost my mind, and that man who I killed that day, not so long ago, has been on my eyelids since, smiling with his son, with his daughter, with Ray, the father. A noble man who sometimes lost his temper but a kind man to his kids, who I killed, taking Thomas's father from him forgive me I was wrong calm down louse bastard now the father die stain obsolete dictionary self panic backwards never full, not even half empty, when the glass itself is broken, nothing in it to be held, no bottom with which to hold.

The lice arrive at the center of the mind, poor light, boarded up doors and two by fours with rusted nails to all the pathways but one, the door called Hope was closed, not locked, and the lice passed through the door.

19. *The Death of Oedipus*

A king in a gold suit sat on a throne placed just in front of a door, above it reading: NO EXIT. Guardsmen sat by the king, swords at the ready, as the ship of the lice slowed down, arriving in the center of the universe of the mind, whose impulses and responses ran under thought.

Neddy's father stumbled into view and the lice saw him choke on dust. His father disappeared. And where he sat, that Oedipus Rex, pulled out his sword.

The lice attacked and smarter, in greater numbers, won; and Oedipus Rex, who in the throne of Neddy's misery sat, had been slain, and the eternity conduit of Neddy's mind, the golden doorway, opened.

And there he stood, at the edge of the opened doorway, looking, as a louse, into the vastness of the soul. The conduit, which linked all consciousness, had once been shut off, blocked in the mind of a melancholy man. Melancholy blocked the doorway but it became unlocked. Neddy cried Hosanna and rejoiced. He was connected by tiny chords to other universal rivers merging into one infinite ocean. Love from all sides escaped into Neddy's mind and out his mouth and the once said man cried, 'My God!'

Neddy stood for several hours a tiny being looking into the soul, thunderstruck by the beautiful doorway opened. He rejoiced. He felt the heartbeat of all creation, and despaired at the heartbeat murmur he had severed from the song and thought about hanging himself like Uncle, no more pain for Uncle Tim.

He stood there conscious, as a louse inside his mind, just above a sleeping body on the floor of the old church, and in front of him he saw a flash of light, a flash of truth; a revelation. He saw the conduit of eternity in all beings. He saw how actions against another was an action against himself; he felt connected to them, to the world entire, and for the first time in a long, long while—connected to *himself.* For the smallest of moments, Neddy tasted freedom and liberation.

How sad was Neddy before, whose mind and doorway to the soul was locked, who saw light through cracks in boarded windows of the mind. Tears streamed down his face as the soul swept through the doorway and out his mouth. Neddy opened his mouth and a high pitched whisper oh slipped out, his eyes rolled to heavens, and he said, "The beauty...the beauty..."

An old man sat on a stone wall. "The Oracle lives at Delphi now."

A woman sat in a chair the shape of a triangle, spinning in a circle, grey skin, bags under her eyes a thousand lines, silent looking at tiny variables.

Neddy tried to speak but the Oracle put her finger to her lips and shook her head, finger to her lips; she bid him leave.

Neddy wandered through the desert and found a small puddle of water by an empty house of rotting rosewood. Cot on the floor, pages all over the floor, Neddy holding a burnt spoon, eyes rolled to Heaven, "I believe," he said.

Neddy wandered on, up a hill in the desert, vague shape, a girl with an ebony leg and ivory dress. She opened her mouth and Neddy heard, distorted, "Wake, you fool!"

Neddy woke and expected hounds with bloodshot eyes all watery and spotted. Neddy was still on the floor under the old and rotting crucifix being consumed by the ivy of the Earth. He thought about running again, couldn't decide which way to go, closed his eyes and spun; he opened his eyes to run. "What can I do now?"

Wander on old man, he heard. *Just wonder on.*

He stopped, restless, and could not see. *What the hell can I do now? Pray? No. Give it a shot. Why not? If it doesn't work, it doesn't work and you're done, but if it does, you'll be free. Apologize why I'd rather die I'm not going to say that to someone who let my father die. Revenge is what it was no justice where is justice you did to him what he did to you and you know how you feel about it. Say another prayer and see if it works.*

I'm sorry for the things I've done. I would change it if I could. I am no better than the man I hurt, and his fair wife so full of love now gone it's me who did wrong my father I miss him if he's with you tell him I love him.

And still you're lost. The prayer didn't work, old man. What will help when a prayer won't? Just run around in circles and it'll make as much sense. Oh this one likes being lost but doesn't admit things to himself. I hear he's crazy? I think I might be crazy. Think about thinking if you might be crazy is crazy enough...I'm afraid you're losing your shit, old man. Praise God. Praise yourself. Forgive me, sir, a crowd draws near...you just going to stand there and look like some sort of queer?

A group of wandering slaves on a dusty gravel road walking North, or so Neddy thought, not having any perspective of direction, appeared like scarecrows in the fog half visible grey shapes lifeless walking no expressions.

"Where are you going?" Neddy asked the tallest of the group.

"The guy up there knows," the anonymous man said.

"Would he tell me if I asked him?"

"I don't know where he's at."

Neddy wandered through the crowd and confronted another man, another tall grey expressionless man with drooping lips and sagging eyes.

"Where are you going?" Neddy asked.

"We're not going anywhere," said the old man. "We're supposed to walk this road until the carriage comes by."

"Where does the carriage go?"

"Up North," the man said. "To freedom."

"May I walk with you?" Neddy asked.

"If you'd like," the man said.

Neddy fell in line another shadow shape wandering in the grey of twilight night arriving.

Neddy had made a masque of lead before he left the church, to hide a face, he'd say, a wounded face by flame. He walked amongst the other silent slaves in the dark, passing on a blue-tinged highway under a yellow sun, wrapped in blue clusters as it descended on the horizon, the slender tendrils of gold going blue as night fell like a blanket on the road, the moon the only light above.

Neddy could not fathom the sound of his name in his mind, so he decided not to bother with having one, and never sign his name. *Stupid killers get caught. Who will you be? Nobody, anybody, I can make that up as I go along. The slave is dead by the river where he once lived but Nobody is free. Someday you'll go back. No I won't. Yes you will. They always return to the scene of the crime…This will only end in tears. Of course you can be anybody now, you're still Nobody, in truth, and a series of affectations take your fancy and you hide under the sickening veil of lives a slave no one should see, only at night when the mirror exposed the sadness when the mask comes off. I'd rather die. You will. Just wait. You will. They all do. They all will. The figures in the grey all disappear.*

20. *The Lives of Nobody's*

The sun went down and the group of tired slaves divided into two groups, each on a side of the road, trying to sleep. Neddy had trouble catching his breath and breathing when he walked to the left side of the road with his head down eyes on his ashy grey feet the dusty road where ants crawled over his feet lost too in the grey of the dying day. Neddy couldn't remember when he last slept and mingled amidst the tired anonymous slaves who never spoke just trod autonomous like soft machines.

"What's your name, son?" an old faced man said.

"Nobody," Neddy said.

"Nobody?" the old man asked. "Your daddy named you Nobody?"

"He hated my mother for having a son," Neddy said. "He wanted a daughter, not a son. Makes me want to choke myself, really."

Silence.

"Where you from, down in Carolina?"

"Yes, sir."

"I knew an old man in Carolina, blind man, thought everything his dog barked at was a duck. I took care of him until he died."

"They all seem to do that," Neddy said. "Everybody seems to die. Have you noticed that?"

"Nobody ever really dies."

"That's why he gave me that name."

Silence.

"So where are you going now, old man?" Neddy asked. *Old man...*

"North," the old man said.

Neddy looked at the wrinkles in the man's hands and the crevices of age under his eyes. Neddy thought he must be seventy, or even older. The thought of the old man having to work made him sad and did not know what to say.

He fidgeted, uncomfortable shaking hands, thinking the old man sensed his moral dilemma of having nothing to say. Finally he said, "How long have you been walking?"

"Seems like a thousand years," the old man said. "Two thousand years before we passed you. I hope we don't have to walk too much longer."

"How long do you have to walk?" Neddy asked.

"Until the carriage or any carriage picks us up."

"What if the carriage never comes?" Neddy asked. "What will

we do? What if they catch us?"

"Relax, young fella," another slave, appearing out of the darkness said. "If the carriage doesn't come, we'll walk all the way. Relax, and go to sleep for a while. You'll feel better."

"I don't sleep," Neddy said.

"Bad dreams, eh?" the man asked. "Where are you from?"

"Rose Hill, down in Carolina."

"What was ya daddy's name?" he asked. "I might have known him. I worked there once. One of the old man's other slaves had got hurt on a wheelbarrow or something, so we worked for a few days until the old man was good enough to work again.

"Then we have to leave, sent us back down state, near Charleston, and there we hear that we could meet some people to take us up North. Won't have to be slaves no more. I don't know what I'll do with all the time. I'll be bored. Nothing will ever happen and then, as crazy as it sounds, someday I might miss working in the mornings in the field, maybe when I'm an old man who can't piss for himself I'll think 'maybe I'd like to plow a field today.'"

"You think it'll ever end?" Neddy asked. "The slavery—will it ever end?"

"I never thought about that," the other slave said.

"Neither have I," Neddy said. "I can't let myself think like that. It'll never end. It never ends. Even when we go to some other place to live, even free, we'll still be slaves, to some white man, or even if he's not white, but he'll make us offers, pay us off you see, and make us his worker bees, same thing as a slave with only the right to choose what kind of slave you are and to what. That's not the kind of freedom I'm looking for."

"You got to have hope," the slave said. "You can't let these white folk take your hope, man. Can't let nobody take ya hope, that kind 'a thinking is bad for a kid your age. You don't look eighteen in ya bones, but I can't get a good look at you behind that mask."

Neddy wondered for a moment if the man might mean to look behind his face, not the mask that sat on it; he had forgotten he had it on, more comfortable, less anxiety without it, a perfect feeling of liberation in being whatever and whoever he decided to say he was.

For Neddy it was easier to be anonymous, to wear the sweating, stinking mask over the face that he once had: the rusted contraption worked well enough: it concealed the skin color, that ever-present stigma of his heritage.

The makeshift mask itself was painted white, black lashes, above narrow slits of grey for eyes, curved outward.

The mouth was an emotionless leer, loose, no sign of happiness or otherwise—Neddy strived to imitate the mask with the face underneath.

He struggled as he spoke with altered speech, masking the inflection of his words, monotonously reporting each word as though it was the end of the sentence, robot like and final.

"I was burned," Neddy said. "I was fixing eggs for my little sister and the grease splashed on my face. We didn't have money for a doctor, and it scarred my face. I'm terribly self conscious about it and I'm more comfortable with the mask on. I wouldn't want people to be taken off their meal by my deformity or shock some child with a face the look of charred beef. I still feel the pain."

"A terrible thing," the old man with his old face said, "happen to me once, to my son. We were workin' in the mines not far from here out west though but not too far out where we had to carry axes and chip away at rocks. Rock slide happened and it hit my son on the side of the face, makin' him slow, slow to answer. He didn't talk no more, just stared out into the woods, blank look on his face, like he wasn't seeing a thing. It was like he could see but couldn't look. He went crazy as they come, piled himself in a room full of books, and he seems like he's peaceful enough, considerin' his troubles. He seems happy enough."

"A lucky man," Neddy said. "Not many people find it. My daddy's book..."

"What kinda book?" a woman asked. "I can't much read, myself."

"A dictionary," Neddy said.

"What's that?" the old woman asked. "I wish there was a word for somethin' that kept track of all the words so we'd know 'em all."

"That's a dictionary," Neddy said.

"What's that?" the old woman asked.

Neddy laughed under his breath, feeling a little shame at having mocked the woman's lack of understanding.

"This book has the meaning to all the words in it," Neddy said. "I learned the meaning of life from this book. I also learned about a place called Nirvana. It's this real happy place, where everything is just right, and no matter what, we all go there when we die. There's no rules but to live, to learn, and die, and you go to Nirvana. I don't think you'll need dictionaries there."

"What's that?" the old woman said. "Something like Heaven?"

"Something like that," Neddy said.

"What's your name?" the old woman asked.

"Nobody," Neddy said.

Uneasy look, "Is that your real name? You're pullin' my leg."

"No," Neddy said. "My brother's name was Somebody."

"I'll get a fire going," someone far off said. "We'll get some rest for now while we can. We don't know when they'll arrive for us, but all we can do is wait."

"Goodnight, Nobody."

21. *Déjà Vu*

Neddy walked with the slaves for weeks, through bayous, down old gravel roads, in and out of riverbeds, across the water while it rained. They made their way further north. He shared the same outward hope the other slaves expressed, the carriage up North, a good job, nice house, opportunity everywhere, just got to be there when it happens, you see. It'll be there, they said; it'll be there.

Neddy did not particularly want to ever arrive anywhere, instead he would rather wander with the slaves, as he had been for near three months, three months since the Master's eyes bulged out like a fish when the metal shut his mouth, his wife's mouth too for good, and that ate away at Neddy, those images, the stark, staring eyes, the absent, vacant, dead eyed stare.

His dreams were vague and irregular, too abstract for him to ever piece together or interpret, but they were of a confused sort, about the same thing each time, longing, desperation, need, but different in context; in each dream a dog was lost, and Neddy was the dog, and he was lost in the dark, in the rain, unable to find his Master's house, unable to find shelter.

And when he arrived, as the shaggy dog, now wet with mud and stained, the Master doesn't arrive, just a shut, locked door, no food, no water, no warmth the longing mutt had sought, a locked door, no Master, nobody, just cement steps to a locked black door.

So the mutt wandered on, to a new and brighter place, where everybody cared and fed him and treated him real nice, thankful, Neddy as that shaggy dog shook their hands, tail wagging, rolled over, begged for treats and love, begged to feel the kind rubdowns that Master long ago gave—the rough kind, caring, tough, harsh love that bled away the hours in the mind where the clock had stopped and the only thing left an image of a love long lost, lost like a shaggy sort of dog in the dark, hungry, scared, and cold, where there's no porch to lay on, no umbrella under the sun, just a continuing search for what once was, now gone; searching for the embers of a flame once warm, now cold, ebbed away unto the heart until it, like stone, was cold, as the stone becoming heavier and heavier the more it takes shape, the more its accented angles invoked the misery of what was gone again, tearing Neddy away piece by piece, until he saw what he thought to be a ghost.

A young girl was walking by the trail, picking jasmines, a hallucination, he thought, how like Galilee—she looked at him and he saw, because of her bottom teeth, Galilee had lost hers, fell face first onto a pile of bricks, and she was a bit older than Galilee, but she had looked to be a ghost, Neddy mind returning to the body.

He had not seen her, in all his roaming; she must be new, a new slave who has escaped to find that freedom, he thought, another hitchhiker like himself with a thumb out on the road. He walked over to her to introduce himself.

"Hello," he said.

His altered voice was faultless now, no longer sounding anything like the frightened slave from South Carolina, beyond recognition. He wondered if his mother would know his voice.

"Hello," the young girl said. She went about picking jasmines, putting them in the waistband of her dress.

"What's your name?"

"Nobody," Neddy said. "Nobody, really."

"Well," she said, "Nobody, it's nice to meet you. Do you have a last name?"

Neddy laughed, *a last name...*

"Where are you from?" he asked.

"Just a ways down south, Beaufort," she said. "I'm going to be with my father's family up North. What do you do? How long have you been walking?"

"I'm a writer, you see," Neddy said. "I want to write stories about these slaves."

"Why would you want to write stories about slaves?" she asked.

"Because somebody has to," Neddy said.

"But that'd be a sad story... My mother was a slave."

"I'm sorry to hear that," Neddy said. "Your father?"

"My father was a Hindu man, a Punjabi poet," she said, a bit of joy creeping into her eyes, suppressed. "He met my mother at the slave quarters and the Master there, since he was friends with my father, the Master there let him speak with anybody he wanted 'cause he was respected like. That's how he met my mama..."

"What is your name?" Neddy asked.

"Nirvana," she said.

"Buddhist word, right?" Neddy asked, knowing if he didn't know the answer, he wouldn't have asked the question.

"My father was a Buddhist man. I guess that's where he got

the idea to name me that... but I'm a long ways from Heaven... but he always said that's what I was for him. You can put that in your book."

"I will," Neddy said. "I used to make up songs for my sister when I was young... I never wrote poems...but I make up rhyming sentences in my head when I have trouble going to sleep."

"Do you remember any of them?" Nirvana asked. "Read me one. I loved it when my father read his poems to me."

Neddy did not know how to maneuver his way out of reading a poem for her. He didn't, until the very end, consider telling her the truth.

"I could write them down for you," he said. "I'd be embarrassed..."

"How are you writing your book on slaves if you ain't got paper?" she asked.

"I write it in my mind first," Neddy said. "By the time I get the pen, the story is done, finished inside my head. And the story I'm writing, you'll come in at chapter twenty, yeah, that's about right, and I'll describe how young and pretty you look, and how you walk with disinterest along the road, as though in a world of your own, picking those yellow jasmines, just like my sister did, even reminding me of her to see you, as though you were her ghost returned. Then I'll tell about my sister, how brief the time I knew her, and then I'd go into the rest of the information about you that I manage to get. It depends how far into the story you want to go."

"What if I wanted to go to the end?" Nirvana asked.

"Your name is Nirvana," Neddy said. "That's what the story is about... Hitchhiking to Nirvana."

"There you go again," she said. "You sound like my daddy. I bet your poems aren't as bad as you think. My father didn't like his either, so self conscious, but they were always beautiful to me.

"He was a well respected writer really I'm not lying but I don't think—I don't think he was good enough for himself. Everybody in the world knew he was a good man, but I don't think he knew, and if he did, I doubt he believed it."

"What happened to your father?"

"I don't know," Nirvana said. "But I think he must' a died by now. He was old when I was born. They took me and mama to Charleston and we didn't get to see him again."

"I have nothing to say to that," he said.

She handed him a jasmine, a *flower from the field*... The déjà vu of the moment swept over him and his mind trailed off, remembering a day, his birthday maybe, when he got to leave work early and Galilee, waiting for him, handed him the jasmine, smiled, just as the young girl in front of him was doing.

Behind his mask he blushed and again, that nagging feeling, the feeling to tell the truth, to let her in—to show her what was behind the mask, Neddy and the scars on the old man's legs and daddy's knife and what caused those cuts what made them bleed and scar and turn white then grey before turning into another tear later when he looks down a river of crisscrossing misery for every single sin he could count.

By his reckoning, he was running out of leg room.

You could whip your back, if you like that kind of thing. Could cut out your own heart. Offer it to God. He still won't answer your prayers. Answer them yourself.

I can't.

Just try. You can show her. You saw it—that understanding, the empathy and her likeness to Galilee what a bleeding déjà vu...

"Follow me," he said. "I want to show you something."

"Follow you where?" she asked.

"Just into the woods for a second," he said. "It will only take a moment. You have to see. I... I nee—I want you to see."

22. *Unmasked by the Stream*

They ducked and dodged low hanging branches, fanning them from their face, into a small clearing, brushes and shrubs around their ankles.

"Is it that important?" Nirvana asked, out of breath. "Wait! Just slow down. It's hard for me to keep up. We're going to lose the others."

"I want to show you something," he said. "Everything with those people, my face... It's all a lie. It's some different persona I've made up in my head, the personality, the family, the occupation, the name—always the name, I either make one up or just say Nobody and walk off. I never talk about my place of birth unless it's a lie and I've never been there. The stories are always different. The lies begin with my family; sometimes I'm an only child, sometimes I have a brother and a sister, sometimes my father died before I was born; sometimes he died when I was too young to know him. Sometimes I knew my mother. Sometimes I didn't. Sometimes I slept with her every night. Sometimes we picked flowers in the morning. Sometimes she brought flowers home for me. It's always something different, something make-believe, never me."

"Why don't you just tell people the truth?" Nirvana asked. "I'm sure people might like the real you."

"If they knew who I was and knew my name, they'd cut off my head and bury me in a grave without a name...at least without a last name..."

Oh, what I've done, gone too far now, waiting on you old man. Say something nice. Same something sweet. She'll laugh. Calm down say anything that smile will appear tenderness again, what tenderness conveyed, what tenderness apparent, what love lost, how long ago, where somewhere her dad did go, leaving her in the totality of her loneliness, her mother gone, herself, on her own picking flowers by a lost dirt road somewhere down south.

Who is she to tell, and know?

The mask forever could replace what was once called a face, how scarred now, not burnt, yet pained, wrinkled by the stain of time in narrow streak steal downward, one of those old men, move on, same old doubtful withdrawn song, unsure of anything, of life, how it might go, what melancholy tidbits he could arrange to surmount a thousand hours of grief and doubt, the doubt that not even time can wash out.

"I've lost," Neddy said. "I don't know how long ago it was when

I looked into that blood and saw my own face look back at me and I hit it again and again and again until where a human face once was lay a black tinged pool of blood. I killed a man and killed his wife. It felt as though I killed them twice. I keep seeing my reflection in that puddle of blood and when I see it that's what I want to hit, that image of what stands above the crime, what I hide with this silly mask. I call myself Nobody and after that, if they even ask again, I just make something up, whatever takes my fancy at the time. My charade is the event of the season for every person I meet, and they all get such a grand story of my life, but such a contrived, improvised lie. They never even know my name. That's what I wanted to tell you; I wanted to tell you my name and show you my face."

"Okay," she said.

"My name is Neddy..."

"I know that word," she said.

"Which word? Neddy? It's not in the dictionary..."

"It's a Buddhist word," she said. "I think it is anyway... He would meditate after supper and would say "Neti atma," over and over until he ... he always trailed off. He looked so happy."

"What does that mean?" Neddy asked. "Neti atma? I've read this dictionary a hundred times and never came across my name."

"Well..." she said, reluctant, "I'm not sure what it means."

Neddy's eyes dimmed a bit.

"Do you think I'm stupid?" she asked. "I just don't remember what it means. I think it means this is not me...and I don't know what that means...so I don't know the meaning of the ... the meaning. I'm not stupid... I just don't understand all that Buddhist stuff."

"I don't think you're stupid," Neddy said. "I don't think that at all... I just... I never know what I'm supposed to say, what's expected to be said, if I'm supposed to say anything, if I'm supposed to let somebody just ask questions if they need to know or just act like I'm deaf and can't hear them or blind and can't see them. I could make those stories up if I wanted to and they'd work, because the story would be just as real as the truth, because in truth, what once was there seems murdered, as though I took who I was and murdered it with a shovel, and every day since I hit that face in the puddle I have these dreams, these nightmares where I walk into a house of mirrors and every image the same—the image of myself without a face just a brown smudge, or an X or some other obscure image just obscuring the face... and I can't escape my reflections... they run at me and laugh and do terrible things and I just run in all directions trying to get away but I can't.

"I always tap talking people on the shoulder and they turn their faceless face to mine and I feel terror and I run and try to tap these talking murmuring not saying anything I can understand type people and I say please can you help me can you show me where I am, somebody please, I know what I look like, if I could only find the door..."

"The door?" she asked. "Which door?"

"The door that leads... the door that leads outside the maze."

"Are there other doors?" she asked.

"Yes," he said. "There are thousands... and I try to open them all. Some of the doors are locked... some of them lead to a wall... some of them lead to another door...door after door after door after door...and that's my favorite door. I always look for it."

"Why can't you tell everybody the truth? The truth about you, I mean."

"Because the true story is a tragedy... in my case, anyway. It's a tragedy. It will only end in tears."

"Those are the tragedies that mean the most, at least in my life," she said. "Those were my favorite stories when daddy read to me."

"Why do they mean more?"

"Because it feels more real," she said. "You can always tell if it's going to be a good one... you can tell it's a good one when you care about the main character when they die."

"And that makes it more real?" Neddy asked. "How does it make it more real?"

"Because you care about the character..."

"I don't think anybody would care about the character in my story."

"Your story?" she asked. "You have a story?"

"We all have stories," Neddy said. "We just don't have enough people to tell them all."

"What's the name of yours?" she asked.

"Nobody," Neddy said.

"Tell me about the story," she said.

"I can't," he said. "The only book I've ever read was the dictionary. I wouldn't be a good writer I don't think."

"You never know until you try," she said. "You know... how can you read the dictionary?"

"Because it's beautiful," Neddy said. "I've read it so many

times... it's the only poem I've ever read and it's about everything. That's just how I see it... I have so many favorite words, and words I hate. What's your favorite word?"

"I'll have to think about that," Nirvana said. "What's yours?"

"I have several," Neddy said. "Farewell door sunset autumn warmth hello see you love I lay for sunshine lullabies Galilee's cradle and wonder why. But I hate ... I hate the word goodbye. It's a lie. There's nothing good about a bye."

"Can I see your face?" she asked. "You should take off that silly mask."

That silly mask... What's silly lies behind. Your face is what is silly old man. Watch her run when you show her that ugly face of yours. You look like a baboon...

Nirvana took off the mask.

The mask came off.

Neddy's eyebrows raised. He turned to look away, kneeling to grab the mask. She kicked it out of reach.

The cold air around the mask turned his grey lips a saddened leer cold lines cracking in his chapped lips.

Naked now...this is when they laugh and point. Just like in the dream Thomas with the mirror and your hands behind your back... That... That's what? That's just disgusting. She's looking at you old man. She sees the naked slave. Run. Just run. Run. Run. Run!

"We need to get back," he said. "We'll lose the group... We'll be lost."

"We're alright," she said. "They'll be on the same road. Let's sit down. I'd rather talk to you than follow those old fools. Tell me about your story, Neddy. I want to hear about *Nobody*."

"I wouldn't know how to tell it," Neddy said. "It'd be easier to tell you as though I'm not telling you... like I'm the narrator of the story instead of the person in it... That I could probably do."

"That's good enough," she said.

"Okay," he said. "Neddy was a slave who lived in Carolina long ago. His father had to plow the fields his mother had to sew. For his sister Galilee he wrote a little eulogy..."

"The eulogy," she said. "Do you remember it?"

"I only remember the end," Neddy said.

"Then how did it end?"

"It's a stupid poem... it's not good, really..."

"Tell me!"

"Okay," he said. "...And now another flower in the field will lay it's head back onto the garden where once it lay in bed."

What a pathetic little piece of poetry that is. Seriously... you don't understand how terrible it really is. Look at her. She can't even speak it's so stupid. Run! Run! No. Give her time and she will speak.

"It's beautiful," she said. "If I ever read *Nobody,* that would be my favorite line."

"I'll keep that in mind," he said. "There are parts you wouldn't like."

"Like what?" she said. "I can accept people for who they are."

"Well, in *Nobody,* Neddy kills an old woman while his mother holds her. He goes into a state of shock, a numbness, as though he became locked away in part of our—in part of his brain. I became autonomous, like a soft machine made out of metal, a prisoner tucked away in the suffering corner of the brain while a young, dumb slave slung a shovel at a nice old lady's face and they hit the ground, such a sickening empty thud, I think about it all the time... Vacant eyes, can't sleep, nervous wreck, the same words over and over. 'Move on, old man. Run, old man. You ramble, you dabble, you don't know who you are, and he—I don't. I knew who I was until I killed that woman. Until then I was a person... after that I was a murderer... and I'd rather be a louse than a killer...I... I talk too much. I'm sorry."

Nirvana was silent.

"You know..." she said. "I just remembered my favorite word. It just came to me."

"What is it?"

"Redemption."

"That's what concerns me now," Neddy said. "There will be no redemption for me."

"But..."

"There will be revenge... I'll get revenge, revenge on myself, and I'll put myself under some sinister looking glass and look at all the blemishes and stains and then wipe them away with some new fantasy, some new person I was, some new mask I've plucked, and in the end, there's Nobody, the man with no idea what to do, no idea where to go, no idea what to be or how, just a man walking blind in the dark in random directions with tired hands trying to feel through the night... It's a horrible feeling, just a feeling of not seeing what is, rather what private hell I've fashioned for myself. All I see is that I have to atone... I can't just cut myself... and I have... I have several times.

"I've bled for every sin I've committed and I don't have enough blood for that *one*...well, it was two people. Don't you see? I have to…I have to sacrifice myself—that's what I see: the end of the road, me by myself, bottle or two of whiskey empty by some bed alone with a shotgun barrel in my mouth and boom, like that—out like a lantern and then sleep, endless, restful, eternal sleep, from which no pain by this life acquired can reach, not past that barrier, the people of this world cannot reach into the next.

"We cannot hold the ones who leave, not my sister, not your father, we can't reach that world. And when we do we won't even know it. They'll dump us in a hole cover it up with some dirt put a flower on it and then it's pretty, like your tragedies, and then somebody else comes along, and he wants the grave to be moved, the anger, it grows and grows until that little maggot crawled into my ear. I think I might be insane.

"That's the only definition to explain it, tuck it away real nice and tight, just insane, and I'm sorry that I took so much of your time, so much of my sad song to hurl at your ears, unfair of me I know…"

"Come on," Nirvana said, taking him by the arm. "I'll show you the way back."

Neddy grabbed his mask.

Neddy followed her until they were back in the line with the other slaves, some stragglers far behind, the old and invalid.

"Nice to meet you, Neddy," Nirvana said.

23. *The Brain that Bleeds*

They merged back into the crowd, Neddy's mask secured, his hand still held tight by Nirvana's as they walked. It was overcast, a day of grey, and raining just a bit, the type of rain that feels like air playing with the skin, just mist really. It felt good on Neddy's arm. He felt as though the rain clouds were sent for him, their refreshing little beads washing the crusted blood off Neddy's fingernails.

He felt empathy with the rain, their long and soundless journeys, not knowing where they'd end up, ending up on Neddy's arm, rolling to the side, dripping drop by drop onto ground. He watched the drops of rain bead off the boarded planks of the porch he with the other slaves huddled under. He watched Nirvana from across the road, her downcast glance a curiosity, watching ants crawl over stones stolen bread on their frail backs, running under the porch to get out of the rain.

They set on their hands and looked around in nervous twitches waiting, worry stained their face just like the rain, down the creases of their spectral faces color of ash.

Neddy stared at one for a moment, wondering what his tragedy was, then thought of Master's cigarettes, how like them the slaves sit on the tray, stubbed out, thrown away in the evening ash their breath before their mouths white clouds dissipated as breath fades on a mirror, disappearing, where the smoke goes when it's gone. Neddy tried to imagine where the smoke went.

Same place your father went. Same place his father went. Same place his father went. They're all gone. That's where you'll go you know.

I have that choice.

No you don't. You broke the rules. What can you do with your life, really? Run?

I could write.

It wouldn't be very good writing, as you've only read one book and that's...

...the most important book there is.

Just because you can read doesn't mean you can write.

I can try.

You will FAIL.

Neddy stood and walked into a raggedy off-white country store.

"Do you have anything I can write with?" he asked.

He looked down his slender nose at Neddy's black arm on the counter. Neddy withdrew his arm, knee jerk reaction nervous.

"You're alright up here," the man said. "White or black, money's the same color."

He flashed a toothless smile.

Neddy returned to the front of the store with a packet of paper and a couple of charcoal pencils. The slaves were walking again. He decided to try to write and for a moment tried, until he decided to close his eyes: a field of graves, towering in every direction, yawning open, black tongues wagging, father's grave, no last name, Galilee again, scribbled plain with no last name, the shame.

Graves rose in the distance, jagged against the grey sky; they appeared and clouded graves with names on them, blocking out the mad men and women and the nameless others under Master's gun, and Neddy read as shadow shapes with shovels filled the graves:

Hope desire empathy anathema love stillborn dying failing atone butterfly Master mama dying clothesline panic love respect pride filth jaded naked shame alone suicide slave.

A shadow shape beside the *gravestone hope* turned Neddy's way, hacked a smoker's cough, and laughed, flicked the cigar in the grave and walked off. He hummed some sort of country song, a twang like hymn as he walked, his boots echoing like horrible hammer blows in Neddy's mind as there again he stood, disconnected from the world, disconnected from the solemn faced worker bees who waited up ahead, carriage coming calling out in random moments of false hope, not this time, tomorrow it'll come, they say, tomorrow it'll come.

Nirvana found her way into his mind. She was sitting at the edge of the one of the graves, her little feet dangling down, down into the darkness disappearing. He looked at the grave stone *hope* and saw her little legs like twigs dangling in the horrible hole amidst the sea of stones and words removed, and he thought;

Why now, for me, the wretch, a wren or starling, heaven sent, should flutter by the drab bars of my baboon cage, her, if she was who she appeared to be, the ghost of love's adored at today's doorway brought by fancy or by fate, stumbling as she was along the way, those yellow flowers, how like her.

How like me to see, happy at that time and now, no future with redemption a variable, with consolation a fairytale, a poor word plucked, perhaps a slip no way for that, but yet that glimmer fills the cage, a bird, as fair as one once was, has fluttered by the shore, a shore that ever lives in mind, the nuances and universe a totality, a totality of living images

Where once a young girl played, a finch, a bird, now flounders by the shore. The wounded animal, how often that repeats, wounded, catatonic, miserable suicide a hopeless sunset goodbye sad where lovely walks today. Nirvana just across the road, eyes down at the ants the slaves themselves before the Queen, to feed, the long haul up the mound. The Queen now fed nods off to sleep, perhaps not where hope, that grave, her feet fall in, swallowed by the days obscured by others, lanterns in the desert glimmer, a rare bird in a grey cage to brighten the whole world has flown and here it flies again. It flies into those painted bars to where retreats the déjà vu, self portrait as a circle screaming Silence!

If only that soothing voice of God could come, when she slept by me, no graves or lice type dreams, just that warm sea again. She's there with a dress, like a little lady smiling wide happy just to be alive, if only happy now, if such happiness was possible, is it for the wretched not deserved?

The wretched pitiful potmarks along the ashy road, blood that lines that road, a bit of rain like blood on the steps, beautiful with different eyes, an understanding noun to feel as though one understands the jokes on you old man, how can it be me if it's you?

'Cause I am you.

How do you know?

Because I have your name. I know what you're up to.

Up to? What do you mean? I'm just trying to be happy.

You don't deserve to be happy you wretched piece of shit. You don't deserve a fragment of the happiness she could hold for you.

Even the wretched deserve to find consolation and redemption.

Not when they're murderers. Murderers don't find redemption. And you deserve it? Fiend. You liar. You pitiful slave you pitiful little fiend! You give fancy to your melancholy and try to string together little tidbits of inspiring words. It will come to nothing. If you were a dictionary, redemption wouldn't be in it. Salvation wouldn't be in it. But Nirvana is. A woman dressed like contentment, really; Nirvana is not the girl, it is what she represents, consolation, salvation, and you are not capable of finding it.

I thought I could atone for my sins.

How could you do that? Apologize?

I could do something. I could do something of great tenderness and love with my life.

Like what? The troubles of slaves with faces no one sees? They see faces, not the wrinkles, not the ridges or the pours or the crust on their lips. They don't see life as it is before the eyes, yet, under a giant looking glass, a passing curiosity, giving fancy unto pity, if anything, and turning it into some sort of confession box game stop it stop it just stop it I just want to be happy just STOP IT STOP IT STOP IT STOP IT. I DIDN'T DO ANYTHING TO YOU. IF YOU DON'T STOP I'LL BLOW YOUR—MY FUCKING BRAINS OUT.

Watch your mouth!

Listen to your mother, old man.

I'd rather see him blow his brains out.

Calm down old man. It's just your brain, doing it to yourself, you know. You'll make it, man. Concentrate on breathing. Let the panic subside. You'll be alright. Only a moment has passed. They do not notice when you trail away.

What if they do they'll think I'm some sort of invalid.

You are.

I'm not.

You see things, Neddy. You drift in and out of your body Neddy. You talk to dead people, Neddy. You are out of your mind insane to the point that it really staggers your conscience.

You're not my conscience. What am I then?

A voice in the head.

A voice?

What kind of voice?

The accusing voice! The voice of Satan!

You're calling yourself Satan, Neddy. You just killed an old fat man, not God himself. You're just a pitiful little murderer and I understand. I understand the stress you were under. The attacks were rough.

Rough?

I understand that you were under some stress. Your father's death was tragic. It just drove you mad. You don't need a big reason for murder. People do it every day. Sometimes when someone is murdered people cheer and applaud and go Got what he deserved that guy. Some people get rewards for their murders.

Then what do murderers get?

They get what they deserve?

And what is that?

NOTHING. ERROR ERROR THERE IS NO ONE TO HELP YOU NOW OLD MAN, GOT INTO IT WITH THE BRAIN AGAIN, AGAIN AGAIN AGAIN THE SIN PLAYS YOU LIKE A VIOLIN NOW SHUT

UP AND WALK. MOVE YOUR BONES.

The girl is here again.

What girl?

Your Nirvana in a little girl's dress, you pervert! I know about your dreams. Ooh look she's naked! Ha!

Don't talk about that, why think about that I don't want to see her naked. Shut up.

Just some sort of delusion of yours. You have a lot. Right now you're lying unconscious in a field full of people.

That little girl that you've got such a thing for is shaking your body, screaming for you to wake up, screaming for you to answer her.

There's blood coming out of your ears. You keep mumbling things, but they don't understand you.

You just mumble on, a bunch of random dictionary words, vague, insane; they might give you something to calm you down. That'll be nice. Then you and I can get along.

You don't need redemption. You don't need salvation. That's for the goody-goody. The murderers have so much more fun. They wear it as a badge of courage. There are people in the world who would not abhor the fact that you killed a slave-owner. That's a different perspective.

I don't want to go into that perspective.

You can't justify murder with anything.

You can. You do. You're doing it now.

What am I doing?

You're mumbling in some sort of trance while everybody around you is thinking that you've just lost your marbles. They're giving you an injection of morphine now. Here it comes. You're on a bed. The little girl is by it.

She's distraught; she really cares. And you had to make her care about you only now to see her cry? What a miserable little maggot. The calm comes in. That's the morphine singing to you. What warmth, like your mother's thighs, how you clung to her like some baboon.

I'm not a baboon.

But you say it. You think it. You say, 'I'm the weakest baboon of them all.' What is that even supposed to mean? Do you care?

It's just a generic statement of despair. You could do so much better. Look through the word book. That's where you'll find the definition to life. That's all you need.

Sleep little baby, said his mother's voice, and just think back, when we went to the stream; your daddy caught a brim and your sister found a red rock looked like a heart, remember that? Looked just like a heart that stone, remember that Neddy?

I do. How is everything back home?

They think you're dead.

They think you killed yourself.

Could I break in for a moment? Yeah, you were talking about a baboon and what happened? Your mom came in. What shame. Is that how you see your mother; are you some sort of monster? I bet you are. And a pervert too, the warmth of her thighs?

Neddy lost consciousness, darkness enveloping him like a warm rug, then cold, and long lapsed silent eons, empty space, baby cries in the dark, row after row of faceless people rooted in the ground rolling over and over and over, hitting their head and bouncing back up, then down again and over, the tumbling of the mind stressed to the breaking point, the breaking point where thoughts themselves press physically against the skull until either blood comes out the ears or screams come out the mouth or a gun goes to the head. Bang the little lullaby and then, blinking at first, focusing, the blob like shapes appearing around the bed, Neddy opened his eyes, room spilling in, seeing a young girl he had never seen before standing by his bed. She had flowers for him. It was his little friend, Nirvana, though his mind out of some sort of amnesia had forgotten her, and, somehow, taken the rest of Neddy away as well.

He felt dry flakes in his ear, though he knew not from what, sleep glue in his eye, flicked it away, dug it out, sat up.

"Something is wrong," he said. "I have no idea who I am, where I am, where I'm going, or where I've been. Do I know you? Who am I? What's my name?"

"Your name is Neddy," Nirvana said.

"What's my last name?" Neddy asked.

"You don't have one," Nirvana said. "I think that's what you told me. You don't remember anything? You don't remember talking to me by the stream? You took off that terrible mask you wear, though they surely took it off when they put you to sleep. You scared the hell out of everybody. You started shaking and rolling around on the ground and mumbling, like you were screaming at yourself, like you were arguing with yourself. Some old guy brought you here. It's a hospital. They said you should be fine in a couple of days, and we can be on our way."

"On our way where?" he asked.

"Up north," Nirvana said.

"Why are we going there?"

"To get away from where we were."

"Where were we that was so bad?"

"We were slaves and lived in little rooms and up north they'll let us live and not treat us so bad like they do down here sometimes but there are nice people around here. Yes, I've seen them. You'll be fine."

"I want to go home," Neddy said. "I want to see my mother and my father. I have no idea where home is, no idea what my mother looks like, or if my father is alive at all. We have to leave."

"But you're sick! Stay in bed until you recover and your memory comes back. You can't just go off wandering in the dark. You might bump your head."

Neddy stood up.

"I have to go," he said.

24. *Merry Out of Focus, Bye*

Neddy walked into the unknown. The area around him alien, unfamiliar, as though it never were, as though conjured, spread before his eyes as unknown shapes, every direction déjà vu, confusion.

He didn't hear the people at the hospital when they told him he could leave. He didn't hear Nirvana when she stood beside him holding his hand shouting, "Neddy! Neddy? Neddy! Say something. Say something! Say anything!"

He did not hear her shouts and she left, crushed, with the other group of slaves, their wagon finally pulling through the fog above the roads. Neddy's mind was blank of memory and association, though littered with the words plucked from his father's book.

Neddy wandered blind-like, nothing familiar, nowhere, Neddy's nowhere known, what face—sadness wrapped in blue dress lace, giggling laughing, going by, laughing sounds a merry-go-round, one face after another dradle spun, all by him a blur, a smudge, again again Nobody spin, by hands unknown they grip and hold and won't go.

Lilacs flowers merry-golds golden moments happy lands oh how they fade and change, rolling over as a cube like dice, changed in and out and in and out, Nobody in Nobody out, Nobody, who are you?

Awake.

Who are you?

I don't know.

Well you know how to string words together. Very nice. Welcome back to the conversation. Everybody thought you died.

They were supposed to think I died.

No, you moron, this is another matter. This is something else, the collapse you know, the sad, sad face all going what's it going to be for him then, eh? They drag you onto a bed and stick a needle in your arm and you mumbled less and less until you lost it.

Pure black.

Yeah, now where you going?

I don't know.

You never have.

Nirvana.

That's the girl.

No, it was a place, where everybody got to sleep and rest.

Yeah, but murderers don't go there. You made a choice, old man. You had the shovel in your hand. Don't worry. Nobody gets there. Not even the goody-goody types you wish you would could be. You can't do that. Murder murder murder murder rattles when you yell it don't it? Don't act like you don't remember. Some pathetic little scuffle and boohoo goes Neddy's pride so down the old man had to go. Remember that, those fish eyes, all bulgy like just like mama?

I don't remember that.

Liar. Shovel, face, South Carolina. You killed a man.

I did not.

You're walking crazy, old man, slow down, take it easy. You trying not to be late for nothing? You in a hurry to get no where?

I'll get there. I'll find it.

Not if I can hide it.

I?

Aye.

No.

Where will you go?

Anywhere I want.

You have nothing. You're nobody. You'll have no home. You should have stayed on the farm, old man. It wasn't so bad was is it?

What wasn't?

You don't see their faces? Their beautiful round eyes, so glowing brown and perfect, the color of autumn's carpet, just walk; no need to worry, take pause. The other voice is not of us. You can exist outside that old bone wall and live and smile and be what you saw all those free people be. If that is what you want, Neddy's. That's your name.

Was his name. He don't got a name no more. Just ask him. He tells everybody that his name is Nobody. Just let him believe it, no need for you to flash hope by his eyes to dangle it like paradise on a hook for some worm like him to follow blind.

You were a good boy once. Everybody makes mistakes and it never is too late to turn around and walk the way to find what it is you wish, to smile, again those teeth to gleam, how infrequent they appear. Don't you ever get to smile?

He doesn't deserve to smile.

He does.

He doesn't.

I do.

25. *Around the Eyes Away*

Neddy wandered aimless dribbling through the woods alone, no danger to anyone but himself—something he understood less than the sun and other shapes around his eyes, words and thoughts no longer synced together.

He looked at trees and called them happy's, then looked at trails and called them sad's, then looked at clouds and called them glad; the autonomous recollection of words, from all those hours under twisted elms all those years ago, to him a thousand years at least, though to the world as it walked without him but a few years.

He took the dictionary from his pocket, not even remembering how or if it was possible that it was there at all or if he was off somewhere again inside his head where the landscape unfolded as he walked about, strange shapes like frowning faces cropping up.

He knew but four faces well, his father, his mother, little Galilee and Nirvana, though he attached no name to them, Galilee to that church, a vague construct blurred by white inside his mind, and Nirvana to that concept in daddy's dictionary back when he was still connected to the world, his tether to the normal torn by grief, enveloped and stamped in further by self hatred and overwhelming, misunderstood shame.

He felt it, that hideous shame with teeth no remorse or rest or recompense, just a gnawing away the day by day and poor Neddy's mind began to fray.

He felt a new bit of clarity bestowed on the world outside, the voice between him and the other, what he did not name, the startling voice he only thought he heard before. He smiled for a moment, for the first time in so long, sitting there, in the bush of the sun again, reading through his father's words for the first time like he did so many times before.

He thumbed the yellow corner of a folded page, a page stained red, a thumbprint, maybe his, and again by the blood thumbprint he found that terrible word and at once the forgotten appeared again:

Nobody: pronoun. 1. No person; no one: Nobody answered, so I left. 2. A person of no importance, influence, or power.

Importance: noun. 1. The quality or state of being important; consequence; significance. 2. Important position or standing; personal or social consequence. 3. Consequential air or manner: an air of bustling importance. 4. Obsolete. an important matter.

Obsolete: adjective. 1. No longer in general use; fallen into disuse: an obsolete expression. 2. Of a discarded or outmoded type; out of date: an obsolete battle ship. 3. Of linguistic form, no longer in use, especially out of use for at least a century. Verb: to make obsolete by replacing with something new or better; antiquate; Automation has obsolete many factory workers.

He heard a sound in the woods behind them, sticks breaking, rustling leaves rolling one over another of their small blown sighs, muffled laughter fireflies.

His heart thumped a bit like irregular hammers against the sweat stained wrinkled skin pulled tight around him. He heard laughter in the woods behind him, stood up, the dictionary dropping splayed open on the page of X.

He peered into the darkness like outstretched fingers around the trees. The stare of eyes crawled over his body, head to toe, back up again. Neddy felt naked again, that shame around his throat, shaking him like a dog that pissed on the carpet, the poor dog miserably unaware what it was that brought such violence and abuse.

A shadow figure strode into the clearing, Neddy's size and height, an exact replica, but black, no form, no outline, a shape carved by the sickly moon who's light in limpid pools spilled into the blue hue of the darkness visible through narrow slits between the intermingled branches of the frail trees dead.

Neddy's likeness stood before him as a mirror, still, mocking movements, no smile, no frown, no laugh, some devil shadow puppet. Neddy stuck out his left arm. The shadow imitated. Neddy stuck out his right arm. The shadow repeated the gesture. Neddy turned as though to walk away and, like him, the shadow turned on his pivot in the adjacent direction. Neddy folded his hands in prayer. The shadow opened his mouth, a great big gape of a black hole the size of a sun, the suction, the gnawing away type feeling. The leaves and grass around the horrible hole begin to slide inside, distortion behind the horrible shape like ripples in the fabric of the eye shaped windows to the world. Then Neddy heard the shadow laugh and turned and ran and ran as fast, as fast as he could, in absolute terror, the gaping mouth of the shape pursuing him through the forest.

It's in your head. Can't run from that. You can try, though, it's more fun to watch such a hopeless victim run screaming through the woods like this, so pretty out, ain't it?

And the torrent in Neddy's mind rained from an unfathomable infinity of panic and desolation, the squinted closeness of his tearing eyes, a bulb on the cusp to spill, and steal softly to the wet wet grass that Neddy trod.

Oh, Nobody, obsolete, no linguistic form, no use, a century gone in a catacomb, so out of date, so dry; why poor creatures strung by hands of fate give pause to sigh, why on their minds and all the time, their ever present suspect of the crime, detectives of the why, why their alibi; their form, partition of importance for an old man lost his mind type guy just get a gun lake master's walk to the River and yell bye, bang another lullaby that lulling by in swift time waves and winks to linger, soft like ivy spread around the eyes away.

26. *Never Again, Again*

Neddy ran for several hours through the woods, in and out of thickets, in and out of consciousness, the terrible rotten rape of the shadow still in pursuit.

It had been hours since the appearance of the shadow in the woods and every time Neddy looked back, or to the side, or anywhere but forward, he saw the same terrible laughing figure running, the distortion in perspective like a cone shaped tunnel suction cup that swallowed and devoured all the trees and leaves.

A light appeared in the distance, dim, a glowing square, something like a lighthouse in the rain. He felt a rare and not oft felt emotion: hope, seeing the girl by the grave, her legs dangling in the hole. She turned her face to him: the smudge, a blank white oval, half-cocked shrug, turns around back toward the grave still empty, but now more full than before, dirt just below her feet. The man with the cowboy hat and the cigarette walked up, cigarette glowing, light spilled around the crevices of his lips curled to a leer.

"We'll be filling this one soon," he said. He took a shovel, a broken shovel, familiar to Neddy but vague, that kiss of déjà vu again. Pain flooded through the chest again that panic nasty, crippling, dirt going into the grave one sigh and dump and sigh after another.

The young girl looked at Neddy. A faint face began to glow, came into focus, and he heard the word *Galilee*. The man in the cowboy hat looked up, dropping the shovel by the now half full grave. The image of the face came more into focus, bit by bit, until it was alas so clear.

Little girl, Galilee, singing little songs for me, flowers too that dress so blue those rhymes and lullabies sublime washed away by time how goes, over and over memory hole, piling piling piling high all the way up to the sky the bodies on the shelf go by, bye say they for moments glimmer and then aft summer, adjacent, rest back into sleep, while alive to dream, Rose Hill, blood shovels dream never again, never again again.

"Wake up."

"Who's there?" Neddy said, opening his eyes, looking at the glowing face of an old woman by the bed he lay in, not remembering how he got there, not knowing if the shadow waited just outside to swallow...

"Jesse found you in the woods," she said. "She brought you in out of the rain. It's cold out there."

She put a warm washcloth to Neddy's face. Feeling the water on his face provoked a cringe. *The mask,* he thought, *how could I have left it, where'd it go? Where have I been and will I know?*

Some day you will.

Not this one, never. He can't handle that kind of weather. He panics all the time. He blanks out too much. Can't march that dusty road to Heaven if you go passin' out like that. He's a nervous wreck. I bet he'll shoot himself, either with a needle or a gun or both.

"How long have I been here?" he asked. "I hope I haven't burdened you. I'll just be on my way..."

"No, no," she said. "You're fine. You look pretty exhausted, though, so I've given you something to help you sleep. Jesse used to take it when he lost his finger. It'll help."

Neddy glanced to the wooden stand by the table, a glass of water a brown bottle labeled MORPHINE SULFATE.

That name rang a friendly note, reminding him of warmth, images of sleeping beside a woman, the warmth of her thighs keeping his little toes warm. A vague feeling of desire for the bottle nagged at him and, at first, he shrugged it off; then came the chest pains and the worry and the anxiety chewing on his side, then the bottle planted itself inside his brain and would not disappear.

"I don't think it helped," Neddy said. "My chest still hurts real bad... I think I might have had a heart attack."

More ... more ... more ...

Fiend.

"Well," she sighed, "I'll give you another teaspoon full. I don't want you to take too much... How much pain are you in? What happened?"

"I..." Neddy hesitated. "I was helping my father brick a chimney and a brick fell and hit me...right on the side of my face... I fell. I fell onto a wheelbarrow...chest has been hurting ever since and where I lived they don't have anything for pain... I've been in a lot of pain for a long time now, ma'am."

Another teaspoon please... Please, God, make her give me another please.

"Okay," she said. "I'm sorry you had to go through that. I'll give you another teaspoon in an hour..."

"Is it that strong?" Neddy asked. "I still hurt..."

"That stuff can hurt you if you take too much," she said.

"Jesse…had some problems with it when he lost his pinky. After a couple of weeks he didn't want anything but that bottle… That seemed to be all he cared about."

"But it takes the pain away," Neddy said. "That's what's important, ain't it?"

It surprised him to feel shame in saying *ain't* in the company of the smiling woman by the bed. He could not place the source of this shame on anything other than a vague impulse, like the accumulated memories he had before his first collapse, symbols, words, sounds adrift around his mind.

"When his finger stopped hurting…" she hesitated. "When his hand was okay… he wasn't hurting because of the pain anymore. He was hurting because he needed that stuff."

Neddy was silent. He averted his eyes when she pressed, "So, what's your name?"

"Ray," he said.

"It's very nice to meet you, Ray," she said.

"What's your name?"

"Helen," the woman said.

"Thank you for helping me, Helen," Neddy said. "I'm sorry if I've troubled you. I'll be on my way…"

"Oh no, it's fine… Just lay down and try to get some rest if you still feel bad. I don't mind helping…"

Neddy looked around the room, his eyes averted, pictures of young children on the yellow walls.

"I don't mind helping people," Helen said. "I just don't want to see another… I've seen that stuff turn decent… honest folk … into…" she looked up at Neddy's face. "Well, I don't…"

"Into what?" Neddy asked. "Slaves?"

If she answered, Neddy would not have heard. He was *out* again, mid sentence, unplugged, a disembodied mind adrift above the bed, looking at the lifeless flesh below.

He hovered for a moment, hesitant to leave the empty body on its own, sighed, rose into the air and got stuck on the ceiling; panic, struggle, menacing vibrations, then, with great effort, he managed to escape the magnet of the ceiling.

Neddy's mind went out the window, up to the sky, into a grey fugue of blurred shapes walking.

A young girl sat on a bench. A vacant body, empty eyes, sat beside her on the bench inanimate. Neddy's disembodied being went in through the mouth of the slave. The body became animate and alive, Neddy gaining control of the fingers and the toes, the eyes alight.

"Who are you?" the young girl asked. Her words were unfamiliar and unintelligible, as though she spoke a foreign language.

"Who are you?" he repeated.

"That's what I asked," she said. "What is your name?"

"Name?"

"Where are you going?"

"Going?"

"Yeah," she said. "I'm waiting on the carriage to come by."

"Where are you going?" Neddy repeated.

"I've been a good girl," she said. "I'm going to Heaven."

"Good?"

"Yes," she said. "All good little girls go to Heaven."

Her words began to make more sense, turning into meanings, though Neddy had no frame of reference in regards to experience.

"I don't know who I am if I'm anybody at all. I don't know where I am. I don't know where I can go."

"Have you been good or bad?"

"Does it matter?"

"Yes," she said. "Have you been a good boy?"

"I don't know," Neddy said. "I remember words, vague images, not what they represent, just words. What are you?"

"What do you mean?"

"What are you?"

"I'm Galilee," she said.

"What is that?" he asked.

"A girl," she said.

He felt a little shyness for a moment, naked skin, a well, splashing water, running, screaming, zigzags through overgrown hedges, a wall, no where to go, nobody to see.

"What's that?" he asked.

"Well, I'm a girl and you're a boy. I have long hair and you have short hair. You get hair on your face and I don't."

"Ok," he said. "How long have you been waiting now?"

"I died not too long ago," she said. "How did you die?"

"Died?" he asked. "What's that?"

"No longer alive."

"Alive?"

"A state of being."

"Being?"

"Everything around you and inside you. Your body died. It carries you. When your body dies you got to leave. Then you wait here for a while and a man on a carriage comes and takes you where you're going."

"How do you know?"

"Based on what you did in life."

"What if you don't know?"

"Then somebody will come by and help you earn the money."

"The money?"

"The money to get to where you're going. You gotta pay the driver when he comes by. If you are in debt, you are taken down, down, down, if you earned your cash, you go up, if you leave with nothing, you go to no where."

"Where is no where?"

"You just walk around, no redemption, not condemnation, nothing. No punishment, no reward."

"But somebody can help me right?"

"Yes. A guide comes by. If you can earn the cash you get to go."

"Go where?"

"Go up, where everybody goes when not in debt, if they are in debt, they go back to life, yet with a guide; you'll get a chance to earn your pay."

"Or I go to no where?"

"That's right."

A raggedy carriage pulled up, two horses suspended by reigns; a blind man sat at the helm.

"Nice to meet you," she said. "What is your name?"

"I don't know," he said.

She climbed into the carriage.

"Tell me if we meet again," she said.

The carriage drove away.

He turned to face the dusty path toward which the horses in a hasty gait clamored on noiseless ground. A sign glowed in the distance, and it read:

NIRVANA

And Neddy walked the other way.

27. *Past Knocks on the Door*

Neddy woke to the sound of knocks, just three then no more, he turned, his aching body rolling over soft cotton, *Maybe uncle picked*, his mind with reluctance accepting light of day. He looked about the room, alone, nobody there. He felt an impulse to check the night-stand, brown bottle happy pain goes by, but that heart shaped bottle long was gone.

It took a considerable amount of effort to stand up. Neddy took in his surroundings, plain white walls, chipped white ceiling, little oil burning lamps, a bed, streaked wood floor. He took particular notice of the shadow cast by the sun at the bottom of the bed where the white sheets ended meeting dark.

Anxiety, that familiar chest pain twinge type uncomfortable numbness slaved away, setting his nerves alight again, alone, feeling like that lost dog in the rain again.

Knock, knock, knock.

Sounds, shuffling feet on wooden floors with slow pace, reached Neddy's ears; they perked, his head turning to the tall blue door, that golden handle gleaming, coughing, spitting, a sigh, a sigh, one after another by him by.

Old man, he thought. He remembered the face of the smiling woman by the bed, her full chest, warm bosom, that table-spoon, syrup of God's relief, what warmth so momentary, fragments of a summer in the sun plucked from a field of winter cradled by that bottle, that word again inside his mind.

MORPHINE SULFATE.

He looked in the cabinet under the stand beside the bed, nothing, cabinets poorly nailed to the wall, towels, napkins, a small white bowl, no warmth. He debated looking under the bed and let his fear decide; he walked away, toward the door, turned the golden handle, into a new room, alien, again another landscape of structures with vague impressions.

Lost like for a moment Neddy wandered through the home.

Knock, knock, knock, he shuddered to hear, thinking, God, the shadow's here.

He left the room in haste. The adjoining room was the living room, dominated by subdued browns, earthy colors; paintings of people lined the walls.

Neddy looked in a cabinet at the far end of the room, empty; he found his way into a painful bright white kitchen full of cabinets, a catacomb of drawers with possible consolation just inside, just in that brown bottle, what warmth, he thought, what consolation would a rusted body mend, a fix, and Neddy plodded around the home, looking in every cabinet and drawer he chanced across, still finding nothing.

Knock, knock, knock, startled panic, run old man, that face again gives chase if not for it what in its place a mask perhaps or layers too, old man, old man, what are you going to do?

Knock, knock, knock, came hammer blows, Neddy's sweating chest heaved clinging clothes, gaping mouth, fuzzy lines, random raining words that sometimes rhyme went in and out and all around and then within his body bound Neddy gasped for breath, again do something, fight or flight, live or die, run, run, run, along the dusty planks through picture covered corridors that breathed and swelled as though they too could swallow whole—Neddy's being, Neddy's soul, sucked into the memory hole, recycled made a couch for some other Nobody to sit in, and there it was, that sound, taunting again:

Knock, knock, knock, *come out Nobody. You can't run from me forever.*

Sinister laughs, menace, soft feet crawling cross that dusty floor a tiptoe type charade; the shadow with its mouth agape turned and looked at Neddy's face—not too far from him, down the hall, and Neddy at once saw again: the murder, the shovel, the well, and the blood, the trail in the woods, his sister, and mud; Nirvana picking flowers smiling unmasked by a stream under which moon neon gleamed and an out of tune type redemption song sing. Ray, his face, like all before, returned to Neddy and he hurt more.

He felt his face and missed the mask and kept on running from his past, into a bathroom, ran silver latch, alone in the room, alone in the world, Neddy saw by blankets twirl—a woman on her heel, deep purple dress and hair pulled back, and sweat, knelt a basket her to get. She turned to look his way.

Neddy ducked not to be seen. Ducking down he looked around and Neddy saw a bottle brown. His sad frown turned to glee. He twisted the top off the bottle and took a good sip, swallowed, debated, drank some more; he stumbled in the hands of God toward the door, a languid smile synthetic on his face like that old mask once replaced an ashamed slave whose shame could be wiped out with that name.

Morphine sulfate, Galilee, Nirvana synthetic warmth for me, what mirror dare give chase, that smudged out face, that open mouth, pulling me back to the South, back to the past now long long passed and leaves bleeding covered grass the maze a wall a slip a fall down down into the well frown frown don't feel too good, not that you can or should, and if you should, are sure you would? No; turn the other way, that glowing neon sign Nirvana adjacent to direction of the shadow's resurrection, and adjacent to me—truth, what now old man, what do I do but sigh? Live life artificial lie? Steal rob kill and drink that brown so far down down 'til it drinks me and leaves me vacant, like the slave on the bench, by the girl once used a wrench, now a wrench to fix a broken mind where random words rain down inside.

Panic replaced by calm, high strung nightmare with tranquility, and Neddy's thoughts trailed off, replacing the sadness of his own hell with that synthetic Heaven bought. He saw angels flutter by his eyes, the warmth of his mother's bed, all artificial circuits in his head rewired.

He forgot where he was, as he often did before, but did not retreat into his mind, beholding before him life, sublime: the beauty of the toilet and the bath, the beauty of the silver locks that blotted out the past. A cough in the other room a crooning trumpet blown by angels, old man walking rum tum tums and Neddy began to hum:

And now another flower in the field has laid it's head, back onto the garden where once it lay in bed.

Knock, knock, knock, real knocks this time. Neddy did not know the difference.

"Nobody home!" Neddy said with a smile, then he thought of the word for a while. Could it be, he wondered, that horrible shadow once again?

"I gotta take a piss," the voice said, unlike the expected hollow suction sound. Coughing, hacking, ding, spittoon. "Open the door."

Neddy stumbled to his feet, his mind a bit at ease at last, no longer expecting past.

The door opened. An old man, stubble on his chin, fifty years of time erosion on his face, looked down at Neddy with surprise.

"Can't you hear?" the man asked. "Go on, get. I gotta piss."

He shoved his way inside. Neddy stood to the side, still in his languid daze, adrift and timeless on his feet, that morphine singing oh so sweet.

Neddy heard frantic sounds in the other room, no lifting of the toilet seat, bad manners maybe Neddy thought, *he knows. Now a thief and a killer. Congratulations. Not only are you a louse but a thief and a murderer, and a lost dog oh how sad your pathetic soliloquies are. Why don't you work with that? So fascinated with words, aren't you?*

Words like what? Neddy thought.

Like morphine murder shovel blood Nirvana and Galilee pain, the screaming water bubbles drowned and silent muffled help me please. Master dying sister drowning madness itself explains. Thomas and his man-sized gun his boy sized thumb just on the trigger, kill you, you nigger, hang you like a dog.

And the world doesn't even care that down in Carolina when the sun went down on a little girl who drowned whose sad frown made a man with a thin face mask, a frown like prior. That's what you deserve.

Think you deserve salvation? What nerve? Who are you? What is your purpose? You've got a life. You're here. Now tell me; who are you? Just improvise, a laugh, a smile, nod and shake your head a while, and turn up your nose at things inferior to you, like Master did, you know.

Let Neddy grow, Nobody no, as to no where, where you go, another slave like merry go, and someday goes—again again, your mind, your friend who comes to say hello. Nod and smile or cast a frown. Turn your face a bit around and walk away from me. But stay a while and share a smile and create your fantasy.

You can be happy, can be sad or after long misery you've had you'll fire that gun before so good it's metal touch. Think about it. Don't like my voice? You've always got the other choice. Pull the trigger, use a needle, vain, morphine sulfate kills the pain. A slave no more though slave to it, and you deserve no part of it, such warmth not made for you.

Those are for people good and right, who wake in morn and sleep at night, and at work they play; some of them with this get pay, compose their lullabies—their pathetic murmurs last mere moments and, though in Heaven, not in your head, drawn sonnets have the letters bled and memory stole it, golden moment, now again is dead.

Not myself again, Neddy thought, and in reproach, a thousand pangs of despair wrote, scribbled drawl the words.

The door opened.

"You steal from us?" the man asked. "Who do you think had to pay for that? I did! I know some boys who'd love to get their hands on a little nigger thief like you. How does that sound?"

28. *A Nobody's Prayer.*

Neddy's hands were tied behind his back by the old man, Jesse, who brought him out of the rain the night before, who now would lay an hour away with a fake smile on his lips and la, la, la.

A black bag was placed on Neddy's face. At first it scared him, then he felt better, comforted by the layer over his face. Black in all directions, then Neddy wondered if the shadow was there, in the dark, invisible. He started to perspire, fast the carriage along in the grey husk of the day, drooping sad rain clouds frown overhead.

Two men sat in front of Neddy. A man sat on the outside of the carriage at the helm, the horses by his hands controlled. They drove hastily along the way and Neddy wondered as grew the day where they would take him why. In the dark he saw the sky, Heaven maybe, angels sigh, a shadow then the night-time brings. Panic, knock, panic, knock knock knock, the echoes back and forth inside his head, where comfort used to rest chaos slept instead.

"I didn't mean to kill him," Neddy said. "I wanted my own pain to go away and thought if I killed him that would happen and it didn't. It made it worse. Please let me go."

"Killed him?" silly laugh. "You just been takin' what ain't yours. I don't care if a nigger don't wanna be a slave but when he thinks he can take what belongs to a white man, we got a problem. You gotta earn things in this country, boy. You gotta work to pay for your own sauce, boy. You was fine until you took uncle Jesse's medicine. Jesse's grumpy when he ain't got his medicine. So, you're a thief and you're going to hang."

"What did I steal?" Neddy said. "I found the bottle spilled. I didn't know what was in it. You know us blacks can't read."

"He said he could smell it on your lips," man said. "We have a place for crooked niggers like you."

Terror, pulsing heart, Neddy tried but failed to start, saying, "I thought..." then stopped, "but I..." forgot. "I was thirsty. I thought it was water."

"You smile like that when you drink water?"

Neddy thought.

"My father did," he spoke, in truth, a terrible thing, he thought, to do.

"See?" man asked the other man. "He admits it. He says his father ain't know, but that don't mean that he don't know. He's too dumb to know he's admittin' to the crime. That's what I love about niggers."

They arrived at the end of an old dirt road, dusty, gravel loose, a turnaround at the end. A couple of men, same type of clothes, were sitting on a log, a tree and a river behind them. They took off the burlap sack. And Neddy saw the rope.

The man jumped from the carriage, opened the door, other men throwing Neddy to the ground. He landed on the sharp rocks and broken glass. They stripped him of his clothes and tied the rope around his neck, just a normal knot, no noose, and Neddy struggled and screamed and yelled, "I'm sorry! I'm sorry! I didn't know it meant so much! I'll go to work! I'll pay for it!"

They strung Neddy up by the neck until his dirty feet hovered just inches above the ground, rising, tip-toe rising into the air, strangulation, stark staring eyes, gasping, panic. Neddy's heart was racing.

The branch broke. Neddy fell to the ground. All of the old men gathered around. They pulled him by his arms, back of his neck, his waist, dragged him down a hill with speed. They neared a still brook, moonlit stream. Neddy was just screaming, unable to manage real words at all, his mind at a fever pitch too rapid to discern, images flooding the brain.

Two of the men pushed him to the ground. One kicked him in the face. Blood, fresh and shining red real bright, spilled at the water's edge. Neddy gagged and coughed and hacked. They stuffed his face in the water.

Neddy opened his eyes, dark blue tinge, seeing rocks and the bubbles from his muffled screams. The pressure on his neck was unrelenting. Neddy, for the first time in his life, felt that there was absolutely no hope of survival. There was no hope now. And though he didn't believe in God, Neddy prayed.

Father if you're there, father if you care, turn your kind ear to me. I've been a man without a plan for far too long, you see. I did bad things and had bad dreams I longed to see the light. If you could find it in your heart to let me live tonight— I'll try as hard as I can try and maybe as the time goes by I might alas atone, but please don't close the book on me, there's too much to read on. There's love in me, that's real, that's true, and if you're there you see it too. I might be a worthless slave a nameless face no last name grave but there is good in me. Give it time and line by line I'm sure that it might grow, but if I die, and go to hell, the reasons I will know. Forgive me if you can and please, forgive as well my family, Galilee, Nirvana too, who I'm sure will rest with you, I only long to see, and I know, with much sorrow, I am a Nobody, but my prayer is sincere and I hope that you draw near, I'm lost in life and now I'll die, no way for me to say goodbye.

Neddy opened his eyes. A young girl, with the look of an angel, appeared before his eyes. She held her finger to her lips. Her face was blue, outlined in gold. Neddy stopped screaming and kicking and flailing his arms. The men who held him by the neck let go. Neddy, alive, floated down the stream, the angel gone away.

But the next morning Neddy saw, and was so very thankful, the sun to rise, again another day.

I'll get to Heaven.

Maybe.

29. *The Flea's Nightmare*

Neddy floated down the stream as though in a languid dream again his mind astray. He was walking on in grey, from that Nirvana turned away, toward a desolate city in the dust.

Coughing people walked by forever ill and Neddy in the vacant slave stood still and saw an image on the hill, the Master he was running to, across a ground of dirt decay to in the end find his lost way. There he saw an open door, the Master there, and haggard, poor, he walked with an amber cane and uneasy walked into the rain.

Neddy walked by mirror, saw a dog, as though he was inside again, like that fantasy begins a dog alone out in the cold crying still and growing old. The Master by him, in the mirror, behind the wet dog drawing nearer, walked slow and picked him up.

"Who's a good boy?" Master said.

Neddy tried to speak but barked instead.

"Why don't you go get in bed? We'll go for a walk in the morning. Want something to eat? You hungry? Who's my little man? You're my little man. I ain't seen you in so long, where you been? On the prowl? You dirty dog. Let's get you dry."

The Master looked down at the floor and the left side of his brain fell out, hit the floor, rolled across the room up Neddy's leg, then up his thighs, then crawled in through his nose.

He looked down at a wet dog sad, but somehow someway also glad; the dog was dirty, soaked in rain, and Neddy the Master felt his pain. He rubbed the dog on the belly, tickling his belly till his leg started shaking and the shaggy beagle crooned, baroo, baroo, roo, roo, roo. Neddy the Master said baroo too.

The dog was itching, Neddy in the Master saw, scratching at some fleas no doubt, around the house he lounged, to pout, scratching until he bled. Neddy got a powder from the shed to give the dog a bath.

A piece of brain falls out the nose, lands on the dog a microdot a space of blood on a wayward flea, trapped on the body of a shaggy dog who tried to paw them all away. Why can't we live why can't we stay they say.

The dog doesn't hear, nor does the Master, but Neddy the flea saw giant hands destroy the valleys all the lands and kill his friends with shampooed hands. The terror as they ran so real he felt, while he inside the poor flea knelt—to duck and dodge the paws. They clawed the ground a thunder sound as Neddy ran and ran.

Until he was caught by the Master's giant hands and squeezed until his eyes went black.

30. *To Nowhere Done*

Black as night in envelope, around Neddy's mind just like a rope, tight and dry around his throat he fell; air passed by, a muffled hum, no flesh to him attached, just the night, the idle mind--his conscious downward spiral.

Bit by bit eyes came to see, hands and feet, elbows and knees, but still constant, everywhere the dark, red flashes, giant columns slamming one after another on the ground.

People were huddled together in tight knit groups, all panicked, scared, running from that metal column in the air. A flash of light, the dark alight, thousands of tired faces suffering, running, arms flailing their unintelligible murmurs, screams.

Neddy looked down at his hands: white hands, skinny, bones protruding, young man, intense worry, type-writer on his back.

The massive column slammed into the ground beside Neddy. He ran through the horrified faces in the crowd and into an old time trinket store, white and stained by rain.

The tired ceiling ached and strained as the fire from above down came, building shaking person like, giving off a sense of fright.

Trash blew by in clustered piles, and people walked amidst those aisles, to different doorways numbered one through seven. Panorama, seven doors, to each a person clamored toward, slumped over, drooping frown, their tired glance cast at the ground.

Neddy's father appeared behind a counter with a deck of cards. His shadow, exaggerated, towered into the sky behind him.

"A game?" he asked.

Nothing, Neddy said.

His father dealt the cards.

One faced down and once faced up. A ten of hearts, a jack of spades, on the table the ghost lay.

"Hit or stay?" the ghost of his father asked.

Neddy looked at his father's facing card, an ace of spades, and one turned over.

A ten, Neddy thought, *blackjack, twenty-one. All I can do is tie.*

"Hit me," Neddy said.

His father lay the card, a queen, "bust," he says.

Ray turned over his other card, an eight of hearts, nineteen.

"Would you like to play again?"

They played again, same result, same hit and stay, Neddy unable to stop the feedback loop, that hollow laughter of his father turned a devil doll, "Ha, ha, ha!" metallic voice, ventriloquist mouth, little wires dangling holding the flapping jaws, "Ha, ha, ha."

Neddy ran out of the shop, into the street, a beatific vision shone, Nirvana, blue dress, flowers held.

"Want to take a walk?" she asked.

"A walk to where?"

"You'll see."

He followed her along a trail, tall buildings decay drift further to the ground. A group of black kids jumped up and down, grabbing at a dangled apple from a tree, clown laughing holding the string children in despair forever longing always jumping never catching that apple, their feet taking root in the ground and they sunk down and down until Neddy could not see them, no more jumping, no more longing, trapped in the murk, alone, asleep.

Neddy felt better, sadness having taken him at their sight, being replaced by a pained smile at their descent into the ground, to rest. They sprouted again. The clown dangled the apple, them, happy again, hopeful, eyes cast to the sky, as, by and by, they sank into the ground again.

"Why are they punished so?" Neddy asked. "It's not fair. Everyone deserves consolation."

"Their punishment reflects their lives," Nirvana said. "So every day the apple orchard grows, and every day the apples prosper; every day the punished people get to hope and lose it, always trying to get one more bite, always one more bite. And see, there are people, up ahead, who walk in circles, long gone dead, the circle of the maze to them a nameless passage by. They run blind in random directions, running from the shadows of their past, then they begin to chase the shadow of the past; if only they would pause to see the beauty, the beauty of it all, the maze for them will disappear; when the children no longer desire the apple, the clown will become bored, no longer amused to make them suffer, and the apples will rain down. It might take them a thousand years, a million, but they'll die every day, get rooted in the ground, covered up, no more sounds, tree sprouts again their life begins and the bobbing apple up and down dangled evilly by a clown whose painted smile, what forgery, smiles, what leer, to watch them jump and climb and struggle."

"Then where is God?" Neddy asked.

"You will see," Nirvana said.

Neddy looked at the blind men lost on the trail, arms

outstretched their long way in the dark that did not end. He thought of his days living by the hill named Rose, where once a thousand jasmines showed, beautiful of that garden, that bed, abstract concepts tumbling around Neddy's head, broken fishbowl, broken flower, in hell again another hour.

What torment do those children get, a thousand directions, all with nothing, all to nowhere, all with that same blank stare, cold cheeks blush an autumn rose, what hole is there inside my mind that lets such thoughts leek out, blood on the pill, those brains that bleed, the brains that yearn, to be somebody, anybody, instead of Neddy, instead of Nobody, of worth to the world of worth to the beds of flowers by the hills that grow and blow and to me show a world of beauty shining bright though often times that shadow might, from the past emerge at now, eating all the light until all seen is what once was real yet now a gleam, in a mirror, closer, nearer, the ghost of past knocks on the door, cannot answer any more, just run, just run and run try to have some fun and then again to nowhere—done.

"Come," Nirvana said. "There's more to see."

31. *The Sign*

Neddy woke up by the stream, thinking back, thinking about his father. His father had once been a man of great misery and unrest, chest pains, always hurting, aching mind in a wounded body. His father later suffered a stroke, through his explanation of the feelings, the pain of the matter, the more it sounds like something quite different than a stroke.

Galilee had died and Ray was out in the woods. Neddy's mother told Neddy to let his father think, let him take some time, he'll be alright, you know? Your daddy is a strong man, you know? He'll pull through."

"If he wants to," Neddy said.

"He's going out in a boat today, get some fishin' done, might get some carp, you like carp don't you? If he don't get no carp we'll still have somethin' to eat, Daddy always catches something."

His mother sewed with dry tears on her face, a crochet pattern of brown and black and soft the color of blushing cheeks through plastic grids for Galilee, a vague outline of a little girl gone, her father in the woods with a revolver that he'd stolen. He had three poker chips; he'd found them at the river bank one day, not knowing what they were, and thought they must have belonged to somebody, so he kept them. He kept them on him at all times, in case he ever ran into the man who lost his last chips, game over, out of the game, blackjack, twenty-one.

Neddy's father rowed the boat into the middle of the Tyger river, down to his last chips, with no fishing pole, no tackle box, just a revolver and those three chips. He sat one on the plank of wood. He dumped the bullets out of the revolver, all but one, crying, no idea if he wanted to live, deciding to leave it up to chance, the whims of that great magnet.

Tears hit the plank, in each Ray saw reflections of Neddy, his still young, young man, miss him, I might, I won't, you'll be dead, won't miss nothing. No work no pain just sleep and sleep you won't remember if they lived regardless of when you die.

And his father sat alone, twilight in the center of the river, and spun the chamber, rattled, hammer back, click.

Where do we go and why does it have to be, that a slave like me whose melody forever is unheard, can sit here in the wilderness where no white bird has flown, no holy spirit by the river, not there, so long ago, no consolation for the worker bees, the drones, whose long long song is never to be sung, nobody there to read.

Nobody read the story none it goes and never rose like the jasmine withered blows bye blankets bye my wife my son, my sun, blotted out by Daddy's gun.

Click.

Crazy in pain nobody no last name a face replaced and imitated recreated someone else can do someone else can plow those fields someone else can love Neddy, oh Lord, let him love himself, let him learn, show him angels if you have the time, send them to save him, for if this gun the job gets done I'll no longer see, my son or my wife or the grave of Galilee.

Click.

If I've done wrong, my life for his; I will accept his sins, his crimes, so he can go to Heaven in my place. Let him look into the looking glass and smile once in a while, if not all the time, and if he must walk through hell to get to grace, don't make him walk for nothing, Lord. We're your worker bees who sometimes don't understand, your words, your message, your divine plan; could we at sometime see our divine plan and destiny?

Click, spin.

Can we change the story to save the lives of those we love, do you edit, could you erase a line and give my daughter back, just one edition to the plan, for a slave, no last name on her grave and none on mine. Neddy's sins are mine. If you want me to live, God, give me a sign.

He spun the revolving chamber again and put the barrel to his temple, closed his eyes, counted down from 10, 9, 8, 7, 6, 5, 4, 3, 2, 1...

Click.

He spun the chamber again.

Click.

Click.

Click.

Neddy walked along the river's edge, tackle box and fishing lure, his daddy's gear he left at home, Neddy there to bring it to him, *you forgot this, Daddy...*

"Daddy?" Neddy called out, seeing vague a black shape sitting in a boat a moon behind, that perfect riverside moon silhouette. His father in his grief and through his tears was unable to hear.

Click. One tear after another hit the plank, young son clamoring down the shore with his ragged fishing lure, wanting to help.

"Daddy, you forgot something," Neddy said.

And Ray received the sign.

He dropped the chips, his last, into the water, watched them
go   bye,   a   sign,   Neddy   stood   at   the   shore.
  Startled at the sight of his son, so young, his father, in his
daze, asked, "Who's there?"
  "Oh, Nobody," Neddy said. "Just your son, that's all."
  "And that's enough," his father said. "Who you are, Neddy,
that's enough."
  If only he could be enough for himself, his father thought.

32. *Somewhere to Go*

Neddy sat by the stream for hours, replaying scenes of his life, trying to make sense of what took place inside his head.

You must be mad. Of course you're mad. A mad junkie, we've seen your type before. What will you do for more?

Neddy stood up, turned in a circle, trying to decide which way to go. He decided to close his eyes, spin around and around and around, then go in the direction he faced when he stopped.

Spin, click, you'll be just like your father. He had the gun. You saw it. Remember? Repress, repress, repress. Why can't you just accept the maggot that you are and kill yourself? You could make quicker your passage to nowhere. That's where it is, remember that stairway? What matters how many steps you climb when there's nothing on the other side? Kill yourself. It's easy. You don't have to make sense of it. Just pull the trigger and I'll leave you alone. Pull it. Pull it. You'll feel that morphine warmth again, or will you steal some more of that just keep walking smile they know you're a killer and a thief and a nigger that's their word not mine well you might as well use it if you let it hurt you it doesn't hurt me of course it does it's an insult not to me but it is you little moron kill yourself it's easy get a gun put it to your head shut up I'm not going to do that of course you are just not now why keep on wondering if you're never going to get an answer the answer to what the equation in your head your body belongs to me not you and I'll lock you away in behind bars and force you to watch me act out all your poor thoughts choices play with people and destroy them and make you feel it until there's a boot on the throat of the body I've stolen from you. Kill yourself. Kill. Suicide. Suicide, the willful ending of one's existence what do you know about that nothing didn't say a word keep walking keep smiling nod and smile and nod and smile look old woman follow her home she might have some more misery medicine like that other old lady.

Neddy followed the woman.

There you go, and when she turns her back, slip in her house, look in the cabinets, what warmth, remember? Just like your mama's thighs you know she'll have some she has to the last old lady did just think she might have more and might not notice that you've stolen from her.

"Excuse me ma'am," Neddy said, "could you help me out?"

"Sure," she said. "What do you need?"

"I live not too far from here and my mama is real sick, lost her leg, and she told me to ask somebody if they had something called morphine sulfate because she's out of medicine and in a good deal of pain, crying really, I hate to bother you just hate seeing my mom like that..."

"I'll check my medicine cabinet," she said. "I'd be more than happy to help. Could you wait here for a second?"

"Yes ma'am," Neddy said.

He waited for a moment on the porch. Panorama, old buildings, country store, people walking slow, shuffling in the dust, wind blowing trash in circles.

The woman returned with a small brown bottle.

Just like last time, Neddy thought, relaxation, a brief escape from that anxiety, with such feet push down on my chest because you deserve it no I don't yes you do look at you you're robbing an old woman I'm not robbing her I'm asking but you're lying might as well be she's happy to help to help a liar and a murderer and a thief the sins just keep piling up, Neddy. And you're even guilty of the worse sin there is what's that? Hope. Hope isn't a sin. It is. If God is just, the world is as it should be, and your suffering is his will. I don't suffer. You could be like me. Who are you? Nobody, your shadow. You're in my head. I'll chase you through the woods and crawl inside your head when you're not looking. I'll plug my ears. I'll crawl in your nose and get in the brain and yell kill yourself kill yourself KILL YOURSELF KILL YOURSELF KILL YOURSELF STOP YELLING WHY LEAVE ME ALONE she sees you sweating she knows you're lying look at you robbing that old smiling lady. You ought to be ashamed of yourself. Now you're a liar. How do you think your father feels about you? Lying for drugs, killing a man and a woman, stealing from people trying to help you? He's disgusted. He should be. One trigger click will shut me up. Think about it. Click, click, click, gone. No more me or you or nobody, just rest, the silence that you want.

"Thank you, ma'am," Neddy said, receiving the bottle.

He put on his happy smile, nodded, walked down the steps uneasy, nervous trembling and sporadic pains like electricity running up and down his body, same old evil currents in his veins. He started running when the old woman closed the door behind her. He made it to the edge of town, by a sign, one saying Virginia, one saying Tennessee, two dusty paths of dirt. He looked left toward Tennessee. He looked right toward Virginia. Two dusty roads, windswept, trash and sticks and stems. He walked forward choosing neither, found a strange device in a ditch—a gun, *looks familiar, doesn't it?*

Neddy gripped the handle, turning it over in his hand, cold metal on sweaty hands. He thumbed back the hammer, hand along the cylinder, and pulled the trigger—click.

Hmm...

He saw an old man out of the corner of his eye, wiry grey hair, walking cane, stumbling as he walked.

"Excuse me sir," he said, "could you help me out? I don't know how to work this."

"What's wrong with it?" the man asked.

"I don't know," Neddy said. "It was my fathers and my father died recently and he left it to me in his will. It won't work."

The man opened the chamber.

"No bullets," he said. "That's why she won't fire. You can get some bullets down the road a ways for this one. Just tell 'em .357 bullets and they'll get you what you need."

"Which way is that?"

The old man gestured down the dusty road toward Tennessee.

"Thank you, sir," Neddy said. He walked towards Tennessee with the naked revolver tucked into the waist of his pants, covered by his shirt.

"Neddy!" came a familiar voice, just a ways down the road. Neddy turned around. A distant figure running towards him calling.

"Neddy!"

Keep walking, old man. You're seeing things. That was so long ago. She's much older than that... It's somewhere else. That's not your fantasy.

Nirvana walked up to him. She blinked and rubbed her eyes in disbelief, rose red blushing cheeks.

"Neddy?" she said.

"Maybe," he said. "What's left."

"Where are you going?" she asked.

"Nowhere," he said. "I don't have a where to go."

"Why don't you come with me?" she said. "A real nice family took me in. They don't live too far from here. You could follow me."

To the end of the world, Neddy thought.

"Sure," he said.

In silence they walked on, her hand finding its way to his, startling him with her touch.

"It's okay," she said. "Just relax."

Neddy tried but couldn't.

He thought of the morphine in his pocket.

"I'm sure I'll be fine once I take my medicine."

"Your medicine?" she asked.

"I've been blacking out a lot, think I might have narcolepsy... I think that is the word. I have to take this icky medicine every few hours."

'Icky'? Did you just say 'icky'? You look like a moron, you know. Icky is a word for children. Time to grow up old man.

"Grow up, how?" Neddy said.

"What?" Nirvana asked. "What are you talking about?"

"I don't know," Neddy said. "The medicine makes me... a little... confused..."

"Does it help any?"

"It helps a lot."

"Good," Nirvana said. "The house is just up the road."

33. *Neddy's Poem*

"Where have you been, Neddy?" Nirvana asked. "I've been worried about you."

"I really can't say the names of the places I've been because I have no idea. I was in the woods, some house, some old woman, some old man, chased me out, called me a nigger, people tried to hang me, called me a nigger..."

"Just tell me what happened," she said.

"I was staying at somebody's house," Neddy said. "I passed out in the woods, out of my medication, mind trailed off, it's hard to explain—I leave my body sometimes and go to different places. I don't know how to explain it. I'm going mad, Gal... I'm going crazy, 'Vana."

"I'm sorry," he said, "I know your name, you just remind me of my sister."

"Where is she?" Nirvana asked.

"In the ground somewhere near Tyger river. Her grave doesn't even have a last name."

"Life is so hard," she said, "and there's so much suffering. I know you're suffering now. I've suffered too, Neddy. We all have to suffer sometimes..."

"But people shouldn't have to," Neddy said. "They shouldn't have to. Nobody should have to suffer."

You're right about that, but don't worry, when the bottle's gone you'll have those hands around your chest again. I'll shake you like a dog and make her watch your misery until it crushes her. Your problems are your own. Don't put that layer of garbage on her. Just make up somebody to be. You don't have to be the paranoid slave all the time. You can be any sort of person you'd like. How about something she likes? Her father was a poet, bet she loves her father, why not play into that? Make her love you so I can make you crush her. Either that or suicide. Your only choice. Stop attaching affections to dying animals. It will only end in tears, you know, suicide kill drink the bottle you'll be fine Neddy are you there I'm not sure who the hell am I she's looking at you talk say something she has to be happy she deserves to be happy if I can't be happy with her, I'll offer what I can.

"I wrote a poem for you," he said. "I had to find my dictionary first, but I did write you a poem."

Her face lit up.

"Really?"

"Yes," he said. "I thought you died. I think terrible things sometimes. Things are always worst case scenario with me, paranoid a bit I guess, anxiety hurts but I, I, I need my medicine hold on a second it'll help I'll be fine then read you my poem okay? Sorry, I'm nervous I don't get to talk to people often anymore except myself and I don't like that guy too much."

"I'd like to hear the poem," she said. "If you'd like. If you're too nervous to read it, I'll understand. You look nervous. Take your medicine, Neddy, and I'll come back when you're feeling better and we can talk. I have to go back to work."

"Okay," Neddy said, crushed. "I'll talk to you then I guess how long do you think it'll be? Because if you could bring me some paper I could write the poem out I don't have any paper lost it in the woods but I remember the poem I made up for you I just don't have it written down have any paper or a pen?"

"I'll get one," she said. "I'll be right back."

She brought him a stack of paper and a fountain pen.

"I'll see you later," she said.

And Neddy was alone.

Alone again, he thought, the brown bottle in his fingers. He twisted the top off, swallowed the entire bottle full, ah, a sigh. He waited on the warmth, there feeling frail, the pallor of a bleeding nail, that cold, those arms release. Electric down the system warm vibrations mmm so nice isn't it nice to be alive?

Neddy saw a vision of an angel on a hill in front of him, pale legs like scarred dessert, wind in gales around the mound. She has a bottle in her hands and it's shaped like a heart. The bottle that to Neddy held him so kindly in their arms. He runs up the hill, dust against his face, falling, slipping, sliding. He gets to the top of the hill, reaches for the bottle, and Nirvana swallowed it. Then she disappeared.

A poem, he thought, *Angel on the hill to me an image to disappear just like the rest, could that say it, she'll go down the hole as well, you know, she'll get swallowed like your mother and your father. I'm telling you. It'll be much easier to kill yourself. Get some bullets. Spin that chamber. Play the game that daddy played. If you deserve to live, the magnet will not let you lose.*

He took the pen and quill and wrote:

For   Nirvana,   non   de   plume, who sorrow stole away too soon, and in my mind, time after time, and every where I go, your lovely face, so full of grace, before my eyes unfurl. Across the plains, pigeon coops and rain, a glass umbrella in your hand, under the sun with no sun, none, slow walking in the sand. And that face so full of grace freezes before the eyes when I rewind, angel frozen in your place on the screen where plays my dreams that nothing can erase. Nirvana, my sonnet, who, lives inside my mind, once lost to me, inside a timeless ballroom where, we once danced without a care. If along the lonesome shore you wash before my feet once more and smile to see me there, miss make believe, my fantasy, I hope I'll see you there.

Happiness once walked my way only to be stole away by time and locked and line by line me my love this world remind.

Neddy drifted off to sleep.

"Wake up," Nirvana said, hell behind her, giant column, screaming people. "It's time to walk she says."

Neddy stood. Hell again, he thought, the clown, the apples, laughing ha, ha, ha Neddy looked ahead. A young boy, perhaps Neddy's age, walked in a circle with a rope around his neck, face cast down, watching ants pull rocks, vacant look, mindless walking in a circle.

"They should sit down," Neddy said.

"If they did, the rope would come on." Nirvana said. "It will sooner or later; it's all up to them. Just follow me and see, the elevator's coming up, we're going down, further down, to the city of Dis where Satan sits. He wants to speak with you, Neddy. I can't go down with you, but I'll wait. He may talk to you for five thousand years, but I'll wait."

The elevator clicked open. Neddy stepped in, selected Dis, and was plunged into the utter dark of the bowels of hell a mile a second free fall his body weightless as he fell. A red glimmer grew larger and larger on the horizon, a black outline, a shadow shape, sitting behind a desk. Two cards dealt. The elevator opened.

Neddy stepped into Satan's office.

34. *The Shadow's Face*

"I'll eat you alive," Satan said. "Every day, I'll eat you alive. I'll eat your tallywacker, ain't that what you call it, southern boy? What's your name?"

A plate was placed in front of Satan. Somebody's head, his mothers face, lips peeled and eaten. Satan cut off her bottom lip and pushed the fork toward Neddy's face. Neddy opened his mouth. Satan laughed and put the fork down, clapped his hands: another plate, Neddy's father. His eyes were hollow, long devoured, worms crawling in and out of his nose. Satan gestured toward the plate. Neddy bit his bottom lip, watching in horror as his father's face was eaten bit by bit. Satan clapped again. The waiter brought out a bleeding brain.

"Your brain," Satan said. "Dessert!" He cut off a large chunk, stuck it in his mouth, chewed it up, paused, dabbed a napkin at the blood on his chin, pushed the plate away.

Satan placed a pipe to Neddy's left, a gun to Neddy's right, put down the napkin.

"Simply stuffed," Satan said. "I've saved the best part for you. Won't you have a bite? I can't. I'm stuffed."

Neddy picked up a fork and stuck it into the brain—feeling the metal prongs inside his head—closed his eyes, opened his mouth, chewed and swallowed.

Satan laughed.

"It's good, ain't it?" he asked.

Scene replaced, skipped forward, people walking backwards screaming, "Ah!"

Neddy walks into the door again, déjà vu. Satan is eating his mother's face again. He cuts off her bottom lip.

"Won't you have a bite?" he asked.

Neddy tastes the lips—sick and warm, liquid texture like melted butter.

Neddy takes another bite. Satan claps his hands.

Screaming people in and out two archways, NO EXIT in red above them.

The waiter returns with Neddy's face. He peels it off with an old timer knife, familiar whittled angels wood chips on the floor, pulls open Neddy's skull and puts his bleeding brain on the plate.

Satan puts down the fork, picks up the brain like a bleeding strawberry and takes a giant bite, sickly sucking sound. Satan licks his lips, picks up the fork, offers Neddy a piece.

Neddy looked at the breathing piece of fragmented brain and puked. Satan dipped the brain in the vomit and slurped it down with a sickening hedonist slurp and licked his lips and moaned, *Ah...*

"So, who are you?" Satan asked. "Nobody, that's right. Suits me. We're all Nobody's here in hell. Would you like some opium? It's Turkish. You've never been there, but it's good and nice just like those brown bottles are. Come on. Have a puff."

Neddy looked at the pipe, looked at the gun, that revolver, ivory handle, rose in the center... *rose red just like her cheeks, still waiting at the top where the slaves jump up go down...*

...The apples never hit the ground.

Neddy picked up a candle, placed it to the pipe, letting the opium heat up. He inhaled. Satan's face became distorted and changed, more shadow, an obscure, familiar face, a laugh, again familiar, though alien, no face to attach it to.

"You believe in Heaven?" Satan asked. "Nirvana, samhadi, the never ending valley? You're a fool. It's just suffering. It's an experiment, and God, though all powerful, plays cruel jokes on people for his own amusement. What a tragic farce. I disagree and I'm thrown out of Heaven. Choice contradicts predetermination. The old man upstairs don't like it when his controlling strings are cut. He believes that one must walk through hell to get to Heaven. That wasn't my idea of how to run a universe. We had creative differences, you could say, so I left."

"You are the one who tortures people," Neddy said unsure. "You trick people..."

"So," Satan laughed, "you *really* think I would punish people because they break my *enemy's* rules? That's just stupid. I reward them. They don't have to apologize for anything and they have here what they could have in Heaven. Everyone here exists as they wish to, a delusion for eternity, they walk in circles some random memories playing on their eyes. They create their own fantasies and live in them, a dreamlike stupor. You don't have to feel guilty about being a thief or a murderer or a liar. It's human nature. Humans aren't the most noble of creatures, you know. They crucified the son of man for saying, 'Love each other.' Is that a breed worth saving?"

Satan took the pipe, held it to a candle, took a long pull, smoke rolling from his nostrils in tiny tendrils, the thick opium, the fire in the pipe, revealing familiar eyes.

Neddy felt his face, looked to the glass of Satan's table, seeing Neddy, the slave, in his slave clothes, dirt on his knees.

"Have a pull," Satan said. "You won't need the mask then. You can't hide what you are around me. I know. I see it. I watch it. I enjoy it. I'm not so miserable, not like they say; humanity tortures itself so desperately I have little to do these days. I like to meet all the people who suffer the type of... existential dilemmas you face. You know what existential means? Your problem does not *arise* from existence. Your problem *is* existence. So, you're looking for redemption. There is no such thing. There is no Heaven and Hell hereafter; Hell is in New York, not underground, not like those stupid stories, and Heaven is *that bottle*; it's in the pipe, not the afterlife.

"Just have a hit. Another hit. It'll take the pain away. There you go. Feel better? No need to feel guilty; nobody saw you. You're in the clear, friend. No need for panic."

"It shouldn't be this way," Neddy said. "Everyone should go to Heaven, no matter what, no matter their crimes, no matter their names, no matter their life, just a little bit of Heaven for everybody."

"There's no such thing as Heaven, Neddy," Satan said. "That's a comforting fantasy for the deluded, of course, but it's just not there. When's the last time God spoke to man? Two thousand years ago?"

"God speaks to man every day," Neddy said. "They just don't always know that."

"Schizophrenia," Satan said. "It's understandable. You've gone mad. That's a natural response to the stupidity of existence. It's pointless. It's a temporary delay between eternal states of nothing. You come with nothing and go to nowhere."

"Then I'll go to nowhere," Neddy said. "It's what I deserve."

"What one deserves is irrelevant. What they get is not up to them. You come from nowhere, and that's where you go. Or you can live here with us and do whatever you'd like. Just pick the gun and come to see us. You won't need your medicine or your attachments anymore. No more pain. I want you to think about it. The bottle is temporary relief, you know, the bullet is permanent. Want some rest? Want some silence? Just get some bullets. But you'll have to get going now. It's almost supper time."

"Tell me a story," Neddy said.

"You don't want to hear my stories," Satan said. "They'll make you want to pull your teeth out."

"Try me," Neddy said. "You don't intimidate me. You're not going to make me cry. Tell me a story before I wake."

"But I'm going to be late," Satan said, now in Neddy's voice, candle light threw a glow on his face, Satan's face, an old time Neddy, wrinkled, bones protruding from stretched skin. And Neddy was intimidated. It was as though he peered into a dusty mirror, a category of the mind not faced, and Satan said, "I'll tell you a story," pause. "I'll tell you my favorite story of all. I might not make you cry, but I'll hurt you. The world is a world of suffering, and I will lay it before you, naked, without censorship, the creature man, under a microscope, his nakedness and scars exposed."

"Then tell," Neddy said.

"I will," Satan said. "Welcome to hell."

35. *Suffer the Children*

"You might need the pipe for this one," Satan said. "This is something I saw some time ago, last time I walked the Earth. It has been a while since I've had the nerve. I'm Satan, and human beings disgust *me...*"

"Just tell the story," Neddy said.

"There once was a morphine man, a happy chap for sure, like you, the miserable, self-tortured addict type, sitting on a balcony, overlooking a beach, sun going down, down, and further down, then dark: unhappiness, what unhappy generation whose bourbon bottles have ran dry, so when his bottle ran dry he put a pistol to his eye—pulled the trigger—then survived, teeth shattered like a wicker basket blood on the wall behind him. The maid found him, screaming, yelling, 'He's killed himself!' but he lived, went to the hospital, few months go by, the little girl, his daughter, was placed in the care of his aunt and uncle, morphine addicts bang around like broke machines, needles hanging from their arm an on switch that makes them twitch and shoot of sparks. That was the verdict. While the father recovered, this beautiful young girl, like your sister, was placed in the care of her aunt and uncle. Morphine addicts, your kind of people, smoking from a light bulb black with lighter stains, their spoons bent back burnt, discussing the world and God. They scratched their scrambled brains. An error in the code, perhaps, a word misspelled by God. He won't re-write it. Even when he knows it's not right. It's all the same.

"This radiant baby girl, just three years old, had to live with these monsters as long as her father was in the hospital. Court order, like I said, gunshot wound blew off his nose and shattered his teeth. He was in no condition to take care of a child.

"Before I finish this story," Satan added. "It's best you think what you're about to hear is fiction, some story of misery that tickles me to delight, but it's not fiction, and it doesn't tickle; it hurts more than you can imagine. So think it's fake, a fiction, some allegory, something; anything, it will help your well being to think this is fake, but it is real.

"These two machines, her aunt and uncle, were unfit to care for her. When she cried for food they just grabbed her by the hair and slammed her face against the wall or punched her or kicked her and once even kicked her in her sleep for crying during some sordid dream. They knocked her out to silence her cries and shouts, no hesitation, no concern for the beautiful child they are destroying. She deserved redemption in the closet. It was noise to them, and noise was bad, interrupting their songs and their junk shooting. Noise was bad, so they cut the cable that allowed the cries. She dared not cry from fear, for if she cried, again they'd lock her in the back room of the house with no way out, no exit, Neddy. Then they return to their semicircle of broken human beings, whom no band-aid could fix, murmured in the poor illumined light.

"They walked in circles, every day, needles in their arms, stuttering like broken toys, stumbling over their own feet. Nothing excited them like torturing that innocent little girl. That's what got them off, you see; the torture of the innocent, the suffering of the sinless. They hated her father and torturing the girl appeased that hatred.

"She was but a toddler, a wee little girl, like a butterfly with one wing as they watched her tragic circle with a laugh. Have you ever plucked the wings from a butterfly?"

"I would never," Neddy said. "Never."

"Never again, you mean," Satan said.

"I didn't know what I was doing," Neddy said. "I didn't know how wrong it was."

"It's alright," Satan said. "I understand. But what I don't understand is the suffering of this little girl. When the little girl got lice, what do you think they did? Did they care for her as they should have like decent sophisticated people should? Of course they didn't. They pushed her tiny face into the aluminum sink until they felt the pressure of her soft face against that cold, cold surface. They ran scalding hot water over her head. What dreamed those lice, Neddy? Did they think the hand behind the rain cared for them? Did they think the hand that caused the rains was there God? They did, and they thanked him, flinging themselves to the scalp, 'Hosanna! Thou art merciful, o God!'

"This poor girl suffered third degree burns on her scalp and on the side of her face. Her beautiful blonde hair fell out, bald, lice alive clung to blond strands of burnt hair in the sink.

"The last louse cried, as he circled the drain, 'Thou art merciful, oh Lord of hosts! Thou art merciful, but not to us.' They cried out to the morphine junkies, who abused such a beautiful girl, 'Hosanna! Thou art so merciful!'"

"What happened to the little girl?"

36. *The Robot's are Malfunctioning*

"She was bald and all the lice were gone," Satan said. "The broke machines kept her in the back room, walking about like machines, trains in blind circles, needles in their arms. These blank people staggered about the house, click-clack, click-clack, grinding their teeth, buzzing, and grinding their teeth, shooting off sparks electric blue. They were outraged. The lice survived, but this time, they were on their heads, though the little girl, her name Hanalei, was clean, no lice for her.

"Their heads went under the water too. The holocaust of the lice. But hey, mysterious ways, right?

"After they cleared themselves of lice, they stuck the young girl's soft face against the aluminum sink again, scalding hot water on a bald head, free of lice. Her hair was gone, once so beautiful. She had on a dirty dress that once looked so pretty before her mother died and her father shot himself.

"Because they gave them lice, they had to teach her a lesson. Her uncle placed her face between the door and the bedroom wall. He held her by the stumps of golden strands trying again to grow and slammed the door on her face over and over laughing until she collapsed into a pool of piss and blood.

"Their hearts beat faster and faster until the adrenaline boils their veins. They dragged the girl across the room, unconscious, and lock her in the closet. It was a sport of sorts to them, no concern at all. They didn't even consider the possibility that she might be human, a human being, a beautiful, innocent girl, when they slammed her face against the wall they locked her in the closet, in the dark, and threw beer bottles at the door whenever she managed to murmur in her trembling fear.

"On they walked about the dimness, dim lit misery, their living hell until she woke, the child again, slamming her face against the closet wall, crying, screaming, 'Mommy! Daddy! God!' And no one comes. Her cries hurt them more than anything. So they lock her in the closet, tie her up, put tape over her mouth, and fitted a noose around her neck, suspending the rope from the pole their clothes hanged on. Then they stood Hanalei on a crate and locked in the closet once again.

"If she moved and fell of course she'd hang herself and die. She stood there for three days in muffled silence sobbing beating at her thin chest in silent agony, beating her chest and screaming. Who was there to save her? Nobody.

"Some say God defends the right. Well, who the hell defends

the wrong? Who was there to save that suffering girl in the closet in the dark when she dry heaved unable to cry out loud. Where was God when the box shook and the noose turned those silent sobs into a silent scream a little dance then silence."

"Die she die?" Neddy asked.

"Not then, no," Satan said.

37. *Her Name was Hanalei.*

"Not from being hanged," Satan said. "God works in mysterious ways, or at least that's what I'm told. It seems to me that he's sometimes short on miracles. The bar the noose was suspended from wasn't sturdy enough to hold her when she fell. It collapsed and she fell to the ground, the iron bar on top of her little back.

"She had been there for three days, standing up, peeing on herself, going to the bathroom standing up suspended by a noose. Her urine covered the box and the carpet around it in sick little yellow puddles. She fell face first into the puddle and suffocated. God defends the right, I'm told, but how was this little girl so wrong? She was a child. Her name was Hanalei. She liked fireflies and coloring and listening to her suffering father read Bible stories.

"This beautiful young girl, not old enough to be a beast like you, a little angel—she suffocated alone in the closet, face down in urine, blowing bubbles desperately trying to breathe. How could anything but a monster or a beast do this to such an angel?

"Those broken machines have long since died but never paid for their crimes, but once I call them in my office, I'll make sure they do. They'll relive her misery every day for the rest of eternity. They'll drown in puddles of urine, be hanged, die, come back to hell, be terrified, panic in the crowd, only to come back into my office, learn what horrible hell I have reserved for them, and be led out into the courtyard, where their punishment will be waiting.

"Hanalei's father left the hospital rehabilitated, off drugs, ready to be a good daddy, a good daddy like yours. What did he find? Not his daughter, just a grave on which some roses lay.

"I was in the closet when he uncorked a bottle of champagne, out of the hospital, ready to celebrate. He sat on his un-made bed, and looked at a picture of his little girl. I saw him in the narrow cracks. I heard him pick up the phone, dial the numbers one by one, click, spin, and he spoke for less than a minute.

"He slammed the headset on the receiver and screamed. He screamed at the walls. I heard a thud against a table, metal spilling, spin, click, sound of gunshot. I saw his limp body fall to the floor. He had succeeded, the gun between his eyes, and he was off to nowhere, no redemption, no salvation, nothing. He got nothing; he got what he deserved.

"I stood there, emotionless, under the ceiling fan for a moment, looking down at him, and I felt immense, profound pity and empathy, something I'd never felt until that moment. Sometimes when I walk the earth, I visit Hanalei's grave. And I have planted flowers there.

"But, you'll have to wake up now. It's almost supper time."

"But we haven't even looked at our cards," Neddy said, gesturing to the two cards dealt to each, Satan showing a prince of hearts, Neddy showing a six of diamonds.

"We'll meet again," Satan said. "I'm starving."

The faceless waiter brought out another screaming face and sat it on Satan's bloodstained plate. Satan picked up his knife and fork, cutting off the ears, crunch, swallow, ah.

"I've always liked the ears," Satan said.

Neddy woke up, hell disappearing, Nirvana by the bedside reading, a piece of paper in her hands.

38. *Lost and Found.*

"This is a good poem, Neddy," she said. "I really like it."

"I haven't written for a long time," Neddy said. "I was taken in by some old lady and some old man. The man was racist and called up some of his friends and they tried to hang me. I know I don't have to explain, but I'm trying to come to terms with all of this, it's all mixed up, somebody has to know me as I am, not as I dream up, not as my fantasies, as me, but then I hide and obscure and misdirect concentration, trying to hide some facet I can't face.

"My shadow's chasing me. Literally. I see it out the corner of my eye and I panic. I panic and I just run in a random direction until I pass out and then I have horrible dreams. I've been to hell. I've been to hell and the only thing that takes me out of it is that medicine they make me take and it's nasty but it helps and that's good right?"

"I just want you to feel better," she said. "What would make you feel better, Neddy?"

Neddy hadn't considered such an idea.

"I don't know if anything can," Neddy said. "The only thing that seems to help is my medicine."

"Well, as long as you're here with us, I'll work extra and make sure you have it. Okay? The people I live with are real nice people and they wouldn't mind helping you at all. They are kind people. They will be kind to you."

"And that's what hurts," Neddy said. "That they'd be kind to someone like me."

"Someone like you?" she asked. "I don't understand. You're kind too Neddy. People can change for the good and people can change for the bad and I think you can change for the good."

"You don't have to help me," he said.

"I know," she said. "But everybody deserves some kindness in their life."

"Vana!" a man's voice called. "We're done with breakfast."

"I've got to go clean up," she said. "I'll be back as soon as I can."

"What do you mean, 'clean up'?" Neddy asked. "You're their slave?"

"No," she said. "They're old and I help them out. I don't ask for anything but food and a place to stay and they provide for me."

"But you have to work for them!"

"No, Neddy. I choose to work for them."

Neddy had nothing to say.

"I'll see you soon," she said.

"I'll write you another poem," he said. "This one will be just for you. If you're going to help me, I've got to do something for it."

"No you don't," she said. "But if it helps, then I'd be happy to read. My father wrote. I miss his poems."

She walked out of the room, door closed behind her, Neddy took the bottle from his pants. *Not much left, I'll need more soon.* He looked at the door for a moment, nervous, nervous someone might walk in and see that bottle to his lips.

You even deceive the ones you love? What a piece of trash. She loves you and you love her but you lie to her anyway. How can you justify your life? You've killed two people, manipulated, stolen, lying now, I mean, how can you not get some bullets for the gun and put it to your head? It'd be so much easier Neddy. Don't listen to Satan. Satan says to get the pipe. You're supposed to get the gun. But you do what the devil says, don't you?

Writing a poem isn't atonement for lying, you know. But it's a start. No, it's another manipulation, catering to what she once loved, making her love it again, only to end up hurting her like you hurt everyone else like everyone hurt you she's different no she's not she says that they all say it they all say I'm different but they all say goodbye and if you think for just one moment that will not be the case, then you're a moron and you don't deserve to live, to think you deserve such affection and care. You should be wandering around in the rain like a lost dog, just like that dream, remember that? Do you long for the Master to rub your belly, Neddy? What a pervert. You killed your Master and now you're a shaggy wet dog lost in the rain wanting him to pet your belly? Why did you kill him if you wanted his affection?

It's not his affection, he's not the master in my dreams, it's someone else, someone else, like who, like God. Like God, you want God to rub your belly? There is no God. You've told this to yourself time and time again. Think of the suffering child again. The devil might have had a point. He tries to deceive me. He wants me to think he wants me to take the pipe when he wants me to take the gun. Nah, he's a pretty straightforward guy once you get to know him. He's always eating but he's never full. Did you look at that face, looked like your daddy's didn't it?

No it didn't.

And Satan's face was a reflection. It all makes sense now. You think you're some sort of devil, Neddy? That's pretty wicked of you. If God don't scratch your belly you must be some sort of demon. See? That's why you should kill yourself. You're a demon and you deserve to bleed and suffer.

I can be a better person.

Prove it then. Stop stealing and lying and killing and you'll be good to go. You might get to feel the Master rub your belly like a dog. Suicide suicide no pain gone the devil in the mind will leave you alone don't listen don't react he'll always have something to say back.

The angel from the stream appeared before Neddy as though on a screen and put a finger to her lips, his sporadic questions quelled. The loop of broken patterns slowing down to a still, morphine singalongs alone again a lullaby tale.

Maybe I should kill myself, Neddy thought.

I should do it now, just kill myself and not say how, end the story, that poor song, and blame it on the Narrator, whose lines he will not write, for me, whose story is the tragic one, the one without redemption, it's possible, it might be, you might get to see if you can only disagree and in your true self believe you are enough for who you are not the face and not the scars but the love inside of you, the love that's real the love that's true, the love for Galilee, Nirvana by your side, just like in hell in life she'll be your helping guide, your muse, your love, your agonizing love, and she'll shut the door on you. She'll leave you in the rain. She'll leave you like a lost dog waiting for someone else to pet and take you in, some sympathy, your illness, yeah right. Some illness. Sadness is not an illness. Just be who you are and tell the truth. Stop cowering away when someone probes. The only way is through truth, Neddy. You can't cheat your way to Heaven. You've got to earn it.

I don't deserve it.

Everybody does.

Live now Nobody, the wounds of past erase, and in those miserable places you can put some smiling faces still with you alive, right before your eyes, you don't have to work, surprise, just be you and she'll see through the prison bars that you call you and see what's real inside. And once she sees what good there is she'll walk with you and out of Dis and take you with her to Heaven's shore and let you choose when you're at the door.

The door opened. Nirvana walked in carrying a tray, brown bottle by a plate, glass of tea, venison, mashed potatoes.

"You hungry?" she asked.

"Yes I am," Neddy said.

The truth comes out...

"So, did you get to take a nap? You look so tired. You've got black eyes, you know. It almost looks like Aunt Janet's makeup."

She licked her thumb and rubbed Neddy's dark eye.

"You don't sleep enough," she said. "You'll get plenty of rest here. That's all you need, just a little relaxation. You okay, daddy—n-n-Neddy? Neddy sounds like daddy ha-ha I meant Neddy."

"I'm fine, almost out of medicine, but other than that I'm fine."

"What would make you happy, Neddy?" she asked.

He considered the question for a moment, then another, until thirty minutes or so had passed, and Neddy had no idea how to answer.

He ran the question back and forth through his mind, thinking of possibilities, thinking of variables, thinking of Nirvana beside him when he went to sleep her legs so warm, thinking of being able to play hide and seek with Galilee again, to chase her through the woods at night, led by the lanterns and the lightning bugs, laughter, through the maze, two ivy corridors, and there she was, behind a shrub, laughing.

He got to find her every day. Every day she hid from him, and every day he looked, in and out of the maze, and at the end of every maze he found that smiling face, bright as the sun in the summer, "I found you."

"I don't know what would make me happy," Neddy said, at last. "I can't even answer that. What it would take isn't possible."

"Well, what would make you happy now?"

"Hmm," Neddy wondered, "a story? Tell me a story."

"What kind of story?"

"The last time you saw your father."

Neddy sensed devastation. His question, though truth, had hurt her far more than a lie could have. He saw the tears gather in her eyes and felt her sadness, the aching body longing and mind attached to a device no longer there.

Look what you've done to her now, man. You're pretty much insane. She took your gun.

"Where's my gun?"

"I put it in the cabinet for when you were well," she said.

"Okay," he said. "I'm sorry for asking that kind of question... Really, I am. I didn't want to bring back old memories or anything like that, that was just what I thought of at the time."

"You don't have to apologize," she said. "And I'll tell you all about it. It hurts, Neddy, and it hurts every day, but I'll tell you."

39. *The Rose of Yesterday*

"It was a regular day, the day they took me and mama, and my father had been overseas. He gave lectures in London on Buddhism and philosophy at some college. I can't remember the name but he was home in time for Christmas. Christmas for the slaves was on a different day where we lived. We didn't believe anything the white people said, so we came up with a new day to celebrate Christmas, the day the Master was out of town, same day every year he'd leave, and my father knew this, smart man, and he came to see me and my mother on that day, that make believe Christmas for the slaves, and I remember watching him walk out of the house. He always walked a certain way, face straight ahead, not down, not up, but straight ahead. He looked a little nervous when I ran up to him and jumped in his arms. It had been years since I seen him and I couldn't resist I really missed him at that time because we had been moved to another camp and he must have went to the camp we used to be at and then couldn't find us so that's probably why he didn't come back for so long. Monks have a lot to do so I understood why we never got to see him but that day was a good day.

"We went into our cabin with him, he was still feeling embarrassed or awkward because he was very... he just didn't know what to expect and with daddy he always knew what to expect. He looked nervous and daddy didn't always look so nervous. So mama says daddy where you been? Oh in London, spent some time in Tibet with my brother, and decided to come see you gals while I had the time. He says that they're going to free all the slaves and we can go to Tibet and live with him and we all wanted to go. I used to dream about Tibet. I didn't even know what it looked like but I made it up inside my head and I'd see my father everyday when I woke up and he'd play in the gardens with me and my mother, my mother liked jasmines they are pretty and then my father tells me he wants to talk to me apart from my mother. We had a different relationship... he talked to me like I was his friend and like my mother was at a distance but he was kind to her all the time he just told me more than he told her most of the time I think he trusted in me.

"So they tell him they gonna take my mama and that I can either leave with him and go to London and then Tibet, maybe, or stay with my mother and my other family and have to wait until the slaves were free to come live with him. I really didn't know what to do, Neddy. What could I do? I had to choose my mother or my father and I chose my mother because I thought she needed me more. He said he wanted to read a poem for me, some poem he'd found in London, something by a Persian poet, and I think he said it was his favorite poem, the Rubaiyat don't know how to say that I think he called it, and he read it to me until I went to sleep.

"'Wake!' father read, 'For the sun, who scattered into flight, the stars before him from the field of night, drives night along and with Heaven strikes the sultan's turret with a shaft of light.

"Nobody could read like my father," she said.

'Before the phantom of false morning died methought a voice inside had cried, 'When the temple is prepared within, why nod the worshippers outside?

"I can read real good," Neddy said. "Maybe not as good as him, but I can pronounce most of the words right."

'And as the cock crew those who stood before the tavern shouted 'Open then the door!' You know how little while we stay, and once gone return no more.'

"Want to take a walk with me?" Nirvana asked. Neddy thought of the dream, stood up, said, "Yes."

'Iram indeed is gone with all his Rose, and Jaymshyd's seven-ringed cup where no one knows, but still a ruby kindles in the vine, and many a garden by the water blows.

Neddy said, "Time to take my medicine." There was perhaps half his dose still left, so, thinking back, he asked, "Did you ask them if they had any of that medicine for me?"

'And David's lips are locked, but in divine, high pipes Pehlevi, 'Wine, wine, wine! Red wine!' cries the nightingale to the rose, that sallow cheek of hers to incarnadine.

"Yes, I brought it in," she said. She pointed to it on the tray. Neddy had forgotten about the morphine, listening to her talk.

'Come, fill the cup, and in the fire of the spring, your winter garments of repentance fling; the bird of time has but a little way, to flutter, and the bird is on the wing.

Neddy picked up the bottle. He could tell from the weight that the bottle, a large one at that, was full to the top. His stomach grumbled, excited at the quantity of his synthetic Heaven.

'Whether Naishapur or Babylon, the cup with sweet or bitter rum, the wine of life keeps dripping drop by drop, the leaves of life all falling one by one.

Nirvana took Neddy's hand, helping him out of bed, medicine swimming in his head. He felt her touch on his hand, a warm hand, tight she held, out the door, down the front steps, clothesline, towels waving, further, farther, her hand on his.

'Each morn a thousand roses brings, you say, yes, but where leaves the Rose of yesterday? And this first summer month that brings the road, has taken Kaikobad away.

"Where are we going?" he asked, a little nervous, still calmed by his medicine.

"I want you to see something," she said. "You showed me. I'll show you."

'Well let it take them! What have we to do with Kaikobad or Kaikhosru? Let Zal and Rustum bluster as they will, or Hatim call to supper, heed not you.

Nirvana led Neddy into a clearing, her grip on his hand getting tighter, brushing twigs and limbs and stepping over thorns as they walked through the dark, an obscure clearing, a light ahead, shapes hanging from a tree. Neddy began to consider the horror of what he was about to see.

'With me along the strip of herbage strewn that divides the desert from the sown, where name of slave and sultan is forgot, and peace to Mahmud on his throne.

40. *This Battered Caravanserai*

They stepped into the clearing, a dusty circle at the end of a dusty road, a tree with fifteen slaves hanging from it. Neddy could feel nothing, and felt ashamed; the horror of the slaves, their stark eyes, their dead, greenish pallor, their skin drying around the bones beneath, had numbed Neddy, cracking his mind into more exaggerated fragments, hurting him, hitting him on every front the absolute horror and despair of the scene. The odor that of corruption and decay their eyes protruding and rotting away, buzzards circling overhead.

'*A book of verses underneath the bough, a jug of wine, a loaf of bread, and thou—beside me singing in the wilderness, the wilderness is paradise right now.*

"I know everyone of these people," Nirvana said. "That is my mother."

She gestured to the withered remains of a woman whose nails were bitten to the quick whose hair had frayed, her eyes vacant, mouth opened slightly slack jawed, dead eyes looking at the ground. Silent tears ran down Neddy's face, staring, distant eyes, devastated.

'*Some for the glories of the world, and some sigh for the paradise to come. Ah, take the cash and let the credit go. No need to heed the rumble of that distant drum.*

"Why don't you bury them?" Neddy asked.

"Because I wouldn't be able to see her again," Nirvana said. "It breaks my heart and makes me want to die every time I come here, and I come here every day to see my dead mother. I'd rather hurt than not get to see her at all."

'*Look to the blowing rose about us, 'Lo,' laughing, she says, 'into the world I blow, at once the silken tassel of my purse should tear and its treasure on the garden throw.'*

"Let's bury them," Neddy said. "Your mother shouldn't be hanging in a tree. Let's get her a blanket and bury her and your friends so they can rest. We have to get them down, 'Vana. They shouldn't be hanging there."

'*And those who husbanded the golden grain, and those who flung it to the winds like rain, alike to no such aureate the Earth are turned, as, once buried, man wants dug up again.*

"I'll go get the blankets and the shovel and the flashlight," 'Vana said. "Just wait here. It won't take but just a second. Are you going to be okay here, by yourself?"

'*The worldly hope men set their hopes upon, turns ashes, or it prospers, and anon: like snow upon the desert's dusty face, lights a little hour or two, is gone.*

"I'll get them down," Neddy said. "I'll get them down while you're gone so we can wrap them up when you get back."

'Think, in this battered Caravanserai, whose portals alternate the night and day, how sultan after sultan with his pomp, abode his promised hour, went his way.

Nirvana turned and walked toward the house, through the woods, under the branches, over the logs. Neddy stood for a moment, staggered, itching all over. He scratched at his stomach, leaning back, and saw the moon hanging over head, like an eyeball looking right down at him, terrifying the eyeball prodded, turning its attention to him. He climbed into one of the trees, a branch blotting out the eyeball moon.

'They say the lion and the lizard keep the halls where Jamshyd gloried and drank deep. And Bahram, that great hunter—that wild ass, stomps overhead but cannot break his sleep.

41. *A Story from of Old*

Neddy sat on the edge of the limb, back against the trunk, undoing the noose around Nirvana's mother's neck. The rope frayed as he picked at it, the horrible smell gagging him. He undid the last of the knot, untied it from the tree, and shuddered when the pile of bones hit the ground with an empty thud.

'I sometimes think that never blows so red, the Rose as where some buried Caesar bled; that every hyacinth the garden wears, dropped in her lap from some once lovely head.

Neddy had all the slaves on the ground when Nirvana returned. She handed him a shovel. Neddy inspected it for a moment, looking for where it was broken, spontaneous impulse. He looked in the reflection of the shovel and saw the Master's face.

'For some we loved, the loveliest and best, that from vintage rolling time has pressed, have drunk their cup a round or two before, and one by one crept back to rest.

They wrapped the dead slaves in wool blankets. Neddy dug the graves, and dug them deep, deep enough to need help getting out. There were thirteen slaves hanging from that tree, and Neddy dug fourteen holes. The last grave, for *Hope*, he did not fill.

'And we that now make merry in the room, they left, and summer dresses in new bloom, ourselves must we beneath the couch of earth descend, ourselves to make a couch for whom?

When all the slaves were in their graves, save for Nirvana's mom, Neddy dropped the shovel. "Just tell her goodbye," he said. "You don't have to stop loving her. You don't have to stop seeing her. You'll see her again."

'Ah, make the most of what we yet may spend, before we too into the dust descend; dust into dust, and under dust to lie: sans wine, sans song, sans singer, sans end.

Nirvana wrapped her mother's corpse tight into the blue patterned blanket, snuggling up to her, tears in her eyes, eyes closed, no doubt, Neddy thought, in some far off happy memory when they were together laughing, their father by their side, reading his poems, telling his stories.

'Alike for those who for today prepare, and those that after some tomorrow stare, a Muezzin from the tower of darkness cries, 'Fools! Your reward is neither here nor there!'

They took special care to lower her mother into the grave. And with her lying there, up to her neck in the patterned blanket, Nirvana jumped into the grave. Neddy, startled, grabbed her by the arm, "Come out!" he said. "You'll see her soon enough!"

'Why all the saints and sages who discussed, of both the worlds so wisely they are thrust, like foolish prophets forth, their words of scorn are scattered, and their mouths are stopped with dust.

"I want to be with her now!" Nirvana yelled. "I want to hear her voice again. I want to hear her talk and laugh. Wherever she is, she's gone, and I want to be with her. I want to be with my father now."

'Myself when young did eagerly frequent doctor and saint and heard great argument, about this and about this, evermore: came out by the same door in I went.

"Alright," Neddy said. He picked up the shovel, pulling Nirvana from the grave by her arm, back on level ground with him. She clawed at his arms as he covered her mother with dirt.

'With them the seed of wisdom did I sow, and with my own hand wrought to make it grow; and this is all the harvest that I reaped: I came like water, and like wind I go.

"Listen to me, 'Vana," he said. "I'll tell you how to see them, your mother and your father; I'll show you how to visit them every day. Just close your eyes. Trust me. That's it. Close your eyes. Picture that Christmas dinner, hear the laughing, smell the food. And there she is, your mother, smiling, looking at your father across the table, and he's shy, but smiling too, and there you are, a little girl, with a little blue dress made of lace, and your cheeks are red, your eyes wide open, and you smile the whole time.

"That universe is yours, Nirvana. And they're all there. They might not be able to talk to us where we're at right now, and you'll see them in your dreams, and if you see them in your dreams, talk to them. They are seeing you too."

'There was a door to which I found no key and a veil through which I could not see; some little talk a while of me and thee, there was, and then no more of thee and me.

Nirvana hugged Neddy in the dark, her hair brushing against his cheeks, arms around him tight. The graves were covered, clouds orbiting the moon, darker, the lantern about to die. They heard thunder in the distance, the promise of coming rain.

'Earth could not answer, nor the seas that mourn, in flowing purple of their lord forlorn; nor rolling Heaven, with all signs revealed, are hidden by the sleeve of night and morn.

"We better get back to the house," Nirvana said. "It'll be raining by the time we get back, but we should make it before the bottom falls out. Come on. Hold my hand. I'll lead you. I know the way home."

'I remember stopping by the way, to watch a potter thumping his wet clay, and with its all obliterated tongue, it murmured, 'Gently brother, gently, pray!'

Neddy followed her through the dark, up the hill, up the steps, into the house. An antique clock said, nine-thirty. Voices came from the other room, slow shuffling shoes, Nirvana pushed Neddy into his room, closed the door, turned to face an old man, droopy face, too many wrinkles, on death's doorstep as he stood there, balancing on a cane.

"He's going to lay back down," Neddy heard her say. "I wanted to show him where he'd be working during the day. But I'll take care of the garden in the morning since he needs his rest. He's doing better. Having his medicine helps him a lot.

Yeah, he won't stay long, just until he's well. He's just sick right now. Okay. I will. Goodnight. I'll bring you breakfast in the morning. Okay, love you."

'And has not such a story from of old, down man's successive generations rolled, of such a clod of saturated earth, cast by the Master into the human mould.

Neddy decided to take the gun before she got back. He stuck it in   the   waist   of   pants.

42. *Tomorrow's Tangle*

Nirvana walked into Neddy's room, door hitting him against the back, "Oh, I'm sorry," she said. "I didn't know you were sitting behind the door!" Her face blustered, little glimmers in her eyes, and behind them Neddy saw an angel with the bottle stuck in her throat, choking on it as she swallowed his attachment to that synthetic love.

'And not a drop that from our cups we throw, for earth to drink of, but steals below, to quench the fire of anguish in some eye, there hidden far beneath and long ago.

"I was waiting on you," Neddy said. "I knew you'd come back."

"How did you know?" she asked, biting her bottom lip.

"Because the story wasn't finished," Neddy said. "You cannot leave a story unfinished. It's a crime. Did you know that? It's not allowed in most places because of the cruelty it causes in people named Neddy, an obscure law I know, but you didn't tell me about the rest of that day."

'As then a tulip for her morning sup, of Heaven's vintage from the soil looks up, 'Do you devoutly do the like, till Heaven invert you like an empty cup.'

"My father read until I went to sleep. Sometimes I pretended to be asleep just so he would tuck me in. He would pull the covers up to my chin and kiss me on the forehead. And the last time I heard his voice... he said, 'Goodnight, beautiful. I'll see you in the morning.'

'Perplexed no more with human or divine, tomorrow's tangle to the winds resign, and lose your fingers in the tresses of the cypress slender minister of wine.

"I woke up and he was gone. We had to get in a line. We had to walk to some other camp. Once we got there, we escaped; we were caught, lucky you walked off before what happened to the rest of us. We had to bury them Neddy. I was picking flowers when the people came and got them and hanged them.

'And if the wine you drink, the lips you press, end in what all begins and ends in, yes: think then you are today what yesterday you were, tomorrow you shall not be less.

"I climbed a tree and watched them string my friends and family up, laughing and shouting and enjoying it, killing all those people, just like they tried to hang you. I've seen so many trees with friends hanging from the limbs that sometimes I don't ever want to see a tree again."

'So when the angel of the darker drink, at last shall find you by

the river-brink, and offering his cup, invite your soul, forth to your lips to quaff, you shall not shrink.

43. *Angel of the Darker Drink*

Neddy was scratching his stomach, violent like, giving Nirvana pause. She lifted up his shirt and he, embarrassed, covered it back up.

'Why, if the soul can fling the dust aside, and naked on the air of Heaven ride, were it not a shame for him in this clay carcass to abide?

"Let me see," she said. "What's making you itch? You don't have fleas, do you?" a smile.

"No," he said. "I'm just scrawny."

"I don't care if you're scrawny," she said. She lifted up his shirt and when she saw the scratches she let out a tiny shriek. Blood in crusted zigzags crossed Neddy's bony stomach, ribs protruding, grotesque.

'Tis but a tent where takes his one day's rest, a sultan to the realm of death addressed; the sultan rises, and the dark Ferrash, strikes and prepares it for another guest.

"What's wrong, Neddy?" she asked. "Do you need to take your medicine? It's right here. Here. Open your mouth. That's a good boy." She put her hand on the bloody scratches on his stomach, "I'm going to take the hurt away," she said, "like magic, just wave my hands, and then it'll disappear. You've got to close your eyes too."

Fear not, lest existence closing your account and mine, should know the like no more; the eternal saki from that bowl has poured, millions of bubbles like us, and will pour.

Neddy rolled the taste of the syrup around in his mouth. *Oh, what bliss*, he thought, *the hangman of anxiety, my morphine sulfate, that's all I need and I'll be fine.* Neddy closed his eyes, Nirvanas hand on his bleeding stomach.

'When you and I behind the veil are past, oh but the little while the world shall last, which of our coming and departure heeds, as the sea's shelf should heed one pebble cast.

Neddy's eyes rolled back to Heaven, angels by his eyes. He heard trumpets blowing, white hue around every object in the room, behind Nirvana a halo glowed a fuzzy hue of gold. He heard silence, for a brief moment, inside his head and, in that moment, tasted freedom—artificial, but to Neddy, fake was better than nothing.

'A moment's halt, a momentary taste of being from the well amid the waste—and lo, the phantom caravan has reached, the nothing it set out from—oh make haste!

The silence in his mind began to stir again, that familiar accusatory voice speaking from the left side of the mind.

So now you're a junkie. I'll add that to the list. The list is getting long. Murderer, thief, liar, manipulator, and now we've got junkie. You don't get to tell me who I am. I'm not a list of labels. Calm down.

It's okay, Neddy. You're having a hard time. It's alright. Even Dante had to walk through hell.

It wasn't worth it.

It was.

44. *One Pebble Cast*

He still felt the warmth of her hand on his cut up stomach, opened his eyes, she's gone, must've trailed off, went to sleep old man, Neddy thought. She must be in bed by now. Just you and me and all the other voices. Go to the ballroom, Neddy, that make believe ballroom you offered her.

'Would you that spangle of existence spend about the secret, quick about it, friend! A hair perhaps divides the false and true— and upon what, prithee, may life depend?

He blinked and she was there again. Her hand still on his stomach. He looked at her with a strange kind of look, confused. She blushed a bit. "Had to use the little girl's room," she said. "I'm still here. You looked so peaceful; I didn't want to wake you up."

"Oh, I didn't know I drifted off," Neddy said. "I don't get to sleep much. I guess that's why my eyes are so dark and when I sleep it's restless. It's not make-up. It's always about running from something. I'm always lost and running or looking for something, but in the end, I don't know what it is. My dreams are terrible. I don't want to go to sleep, for even though it kills the pain, far worse exists inside my head.

'A hair perhaps divides the false and true; yes a single Alif were the clue—could you but find it—to the treasure-house, and peradventure to the Master too.'

"I still don't know the answer to what would make me happy. I have no idea, really; I've been thinking about that a lot. What could make me happy? As a person? I don't know. What would you need to be happy?"

'A moment guessed, then back behind the fold, immersed of darkness round the drama rolled, which, for the past-time of eternity, he doth himself contrive, enact, behold.'

"I don't know what would make me happier either," Nirvana said. "If I could live in that place you showed me, that make believe ballroom, if I could go there and see my family and friends and father and play games with them and laugh then that would make me happy, but I'd have to take you too."

'But if in vain, down on the stubborn floor, of Earth and up to Heaven's un-opening door—you gaze today while you are you, how then, tomorrow, when you shall be you no more?'

"But I wouldn't deserve to go," Neddy said. "You know, I had a strange dream... I talked to Satan, and you were there, and he was eating daddy's face, and Satan said that no matter what I did I'd still go back in the ground, to nowhere. That's what terrifies me; the thought of absolute nothing, forever, and it eats away at me."

'Waste not your hour, nor in the vain pursuit, of this and that endeavor and dispute; better be jocund with the fruitful grape than sadden after none or bitter fruit.'

"You'll get better, Neddy," she said. "Things might seem bad now, but at least you're alive. You can choose what happens from here. The rest of your life is your choice, the past isn't. That's what you should focus on, not the graves of yesterday."

'Ah, but my computations, people say, reduced the year to better reckoning? Nay; 'twas only striking from the calendar, unborn tomorrow and dead yesterday.'

"Some people deserve to suffer," Neddy said. "And that person is me. The voices... the voices in my head tell me horrible things. They tell me to kill myself. They tell me that I'm a murderer and a junkie and a thief."

'And lately, by the tavern door agape, came shining through the dusk an angel shape, bearing a vessel on her shoulder, and, he bid me taste of it; and 'twas the grape!'

"The voices seem to never stop, and when they do, it's for but a moment, then they're back, and it's as though a thousand people are talking at once inside my head, different voices, men, women, at different speeds, different subjects, all at once, to the point I can't even see where I'm going or hear anything happening around me."

'Oh, threats of hell and hopes of paradise! One thing at least is certain—this life flies; one thing is certain and the rest is lies. The flower that once has blown for ever dies.'

Nirvana poured a bit of the liquid from the brown bottle onto a spoon. "Here," she said. "Take one more dose and go to sleep. You just need some rest. So, promise me you'll try to get some rest tonight?"

'Strange is it not that of the myriads who, before us passed the door of darkness through, not one returns to tell us of the road, which to discover we must travel too.'

"I can try," Neddy said.

"Say 'I promise.'"

"I promise."

"Okay then," she said. "I'll leave the bottle in here in case you wake up in any pain and need it. If you need me, just take a left when you leave this room, and I'll be there. Don't hesitate to talk to me if you need to. I'm not going anywhere, Neddy."

'The revelations of the devout and learned, who rose before us, and, as prophets burned, are all but stories, which, awoke from sleep, they told their comrades and to sleep returned.'

"Are you going to finish the poem for me?" Neddy asked. "The poem that your father read. I'd really like to hear the rest of it, if you can remember it."

"I remember the last half of it," she said. "I could read it to you if it would help you get to sleep."

Neddy thought of his father's Bible stories when he lay on the floor, pretending to be asleep, just to hear one more.

'I sent my soul through the invisible, some letter of that after life to spell. And by and by my soul returned to me, and answered, 'I myself am Heaven and Hell.'

"It helped me get to sleep when my father read to me," Neddy said. "He used to read Bible stories every night when he came home."

'Heaven but the vision of fulfilled desire, and hell the shadow from a soul on fire—cast on the darkness into which ourselves, so late emerged from, shall so soon expire.

"Come on," Neddy said. "Read me the rest. I'm already getting tired."

"Ok," she said, and, again, she read:

'We are no other than a moving row, of magic shadow shapes that come and go. Round with the sun-illumined lantern held, in midnight by the Master of the show.'

"Such a beautiful poem," Neddy said. "I wish I could write poems like that."

"You might someday," Nirvana said. "You have the talent."

"You're just saying that to be nice," Neddy said. "All I've ever read is a dictionary."

'Vana read on:

'Tis all a checker-board of nights and days, where destiny with man for pieces plays, and hither, and thither moves, and mates, and slays, and one by one in closet lays.'

"Your father was a man of exquisite taste," Neddy said. "Could a more perfect line be written? 'A checker-board of nights and days...' I don't understand what 'mates' and 'slays' means."

"I think it's a reference to the game of chess," 'Vana said. 'My father... My father taught me to play when I was little, telling me, 'Someday you'll beat your old dad, you know.'"

"What's your favorite line?" Neddy asked.

"Hmm," 'Vana mulled the question over, eyes closed tight. "I'd have to say this one is... I've memorized it... my daddy read it to me so many times... My favorite line is: *'the moving finger writes, and, having writ, moves on, not all your piety, nor wit, shall lure it back to cancel half a line, nor all your tears wash out one word of it.'*

"That's kind of sad," Neddy said. "What do you think he means by the moving finger?"

Forever the pervert, aren't we?

"I think he means... I'm not sure. The moving finger I think is ... it's hard to explain. I think he's saying once something happens there's no way to change it.

'And that inverted bowl we call the sky, where under crawling cooped we live and die. Lift not your hands to it for help, for it, impotently moves like you and I.'

'With earth's first clay they did the last man knead, and there on the last harvest sowed the seed: and the morning of creation wrote what the last dawn of reckoning shall read.

'Yesterday this day's madness did prepare: tomorrow's silence, triumph, or despair. Drink! for you know not whence you came, nor why: Drink! for you know not why you go, nor where.'"

Neddy pretended to be asleep, thinking of those old time Bible stories his father read. He imagined laying in the dark of his cabin, Galilee beside him sleeping—he couldn't sleep in a bed by himself—his father whittled away in the corner with his knife, the low fire burning in the barrel of coal.

'I tell you this, when, starting from the goal, over the flaming shoulders of the foal, of Heaven parwin and Mushtari they flung, in my predestined plot of dust and soul.

'The vine had struck a fiber, which, about, if clings my being let the dervish flout; of my base metal may be field a key, that shall unlock the down he howls without.

'And this I know: whether the one true light, kindle to love or wrath, consume me quite—one flash of it within the tavern caught, better than in the temple lost outright.

'What! out of senseless Nothing to provoke, a conscious something to resent the yoke—of permitted pleasure, under pain, of everlasting penalties if broke!

'What! from this helpless creature be repaid, pure gold for what he lent him dross-allayed—sure for a debt he never did contract, and cannot answer, oh the sorry trade!

Nirvana looked at Neddy's face, the sunk in eyes and black, chapped lips, scratches on his face. She wondered whether or not he was pretending to be asleep.

Just because you do it doesn't mean he does, she thought.

'Oh, thou, who dist with pitfall, gin, beset the road I was to wander in; thou wilt not with predestined evil round, enmesh and then impute my fall to sin.

'Oh, thou, who man of baser earth did make, and with paradise devise the snake: for all the sun where-with the face of man, is blackened. Man's forgiveness give—and take!

'As under cover of departing day, slunk hunger-stricken Ramazan away, once more within the potter's house alone, I stood: surrounded by the shapes of clay.

She went into the bathroom, picked up a bottle of peroxide and returned. She turned the bottle over onto a damp, warm washcloth. She lifted up his shirt. The maze of bloody scratches startled her. She saw the gun.

'Shapes of all sorts and sizes, great and small, that stood along the floor and wall; and some loquacious vessels were; and some listened perhaps, but never talked at all.

'Said one among them, 'Surely not in vain, my substance of the common earth was ta'en; and to this figure molded to be broke, or trampled back to shapeless earth again.'

'Then said a second, 'Never a peevish boy would break the bowl from which he drank in joy; and he that with his hand the vessel made, will surely not in after wrath destroy.

"What's wrong?" Neddy asked, sitting up, the gun pressed against the maze of violent scratches.

"Nothing is wrong," she said. "Close your eyes. I want to give you a surprise."

"A surprise?" he asked.

"Yes," she said. "How does that sound?"

"Sounds good," Neddy said.

'After a momentary silence spake, some vessel of a more ungainly make; 'They sneer at me for leaning all awry; what! did the hand then of the potter shake?

'Whereat some one of the loquacious lot—I think a Sufi pipkin-waxing hot—'All this of pot and potter, tell me then, who is, pray, the potter, who the pot?

'Why' said another, 'Some there are who tell of one who threatens he will toss to hell the luckless pots he marred in making—pish! He's a good fellow, and it will all be well.'

"Keep your eyes closed," she said, dabbing the cloth against his cut stomach. Neddy kept his eyes shut, uncomfortable, feeling the warmth and burn against the cut. 'Vana loosened his pants.

'Well,' murmured one, 'let who so make or buy, my clay with long oblivion gone dry: but fill me with the old familiar juice, *methinks I might recover by and by.*

'*So while the Vessels one by one were speaking, the little moon looked in that all were seeking: and then they jogged each other, 'Brother! Brother! Now for the porter's shoulder-knot-a-creaking!*

'*Ah, with the grape my fading life provide, and wash the body whence the life has died, and lay me, shrouded in the living leaf, by some not unfrequented garden-side.*'

Her tiny fingers ran along the arch under his stomach delicate and slow deliberate. She grabbed the gun, put it away, under the bed.

"What are you taking that for?" he asked. "I might need it..."

"Because it ruins people's lives," she said. "I hate those things... I hate them. I've seen what they can do..."

'*That even my buried ashes such a snare of vintage shall fling in the air as not a true believing passing by but shall be overtaken unaware.*

'*Indeed the idols I have loved so long, have done my credit in this world much wrong: have drowned my glory in a shallow cup and sold my reputation for a song.*

'*Indeed, indeed, repentance of before, I swore, but was I sober when I swore? And then and then came spring with Rose in hand, my threadbare penitence a pieces tore.*

'*And much as wine has played the infidel and robbed me of my robe of honor, well, I wonder often what the vinters buy, one half so precious as the stuff they sell.*

'*Yet ah, that spring should vanish with the Rose! That youth's sweet-scented manuscript should close! The nightingale that in the branches sang, ah when and whither flown again, who knows!*

'*Would but the desert by the fountain yield, one glimpse if dimly yet indeed revealed—to which the fainting traveler might spring, as springs the trampled herbage of the field.*'

"What have they done to you?" Neddy asked.

Nirvana hesitated. She bit her bottom lip as tears gathered in her glassy eyes.

"Trust me," she said. "Those things can ruin lives... I've seen it happen."

"Tell me about it," Neddy said. "It might help you feel better."

"*Would but some winged angel ere too late, arrest the yet unfolded roll of fate, and make stern recorder otherwise, en-register or quite obliterate.*

'*Ah, love! could you and I with him conspire, to grasp this sorry scheme of things entire; would not we shatter it to bits, and then, re-mould it nearer to our heart's desire?*'

"The day before me and mama left," she said, "my... my friend's father... He found out that he would never be able to take mama and me... her father found out that he'd never be able to see her again... so he took a gun... just like that one... and he killed himself..."

A silent tear stole down her cheek its flavor sour on her trembling lips.

Neddy couldn't think of anything to say.

'Yon rising moon that looks for us again, how oft hereafter will she wax and wane; how oft hereafter rising to look for us, through this same garden, and for one in vain.'

'And when like her, oh saki, you shall pass—among the guests star-scattered on the grass, and in your joyous errand reach the spot where I made one—turn down and empty glass!'

And Neddy was asleep.

45. *The Ace of Spades*

Neddy found himself in hell again, around him the same bustling panicked crowd, bumping into each other, "Are we in hell? Are we in hell?"

He saw Nirvana waiting by the elevator, glowing like, white dress, soft face, like an angel under water. She waited as he waited, watching her from such a distance, her angel shape the size of a baby's doll so far. Neddy could not walk toward it, afraid, afraid of the elevator, the elevator down to Dis and up to where?

Neddy looked at the quivering poker house and thought about the game, tin like laughter the devil doll act, a bust, the laughing again, the last chips taken.

Nirvana waited as though she would never leave even if he never made the choice.

She would stay but she shouldn't. You're making her waste her time. She's an angel. You're more than a louse now, Neddy, you're the reflection of Satan. You should wander the streets of hell by yourself, nobody to guide you.

Neddy shyly made his way through the terrified crowd, that terrible massive column killing thousands slamming sound of thunder a thousand screams. Nirvana smiled as he approached.

"Where do you want to go, Neddy?" she asked as he approached, the elevator opening with a metallic creaking type sound.

"Do you have an ace of spades?" Neddy asked.

Nirvana as the angel dressed in white, "I do."

She handed him the ace of spades, he looked at it, thinking of his father, thinking of a shovel, *look at that spade and his nappy hair.*

"Do you have any poker chips?" Neddy asked.

"I've got three," Nirvana said. "Three fifty dollar pieces."

She handed them to Neddy.

"Do you have a shovel?"

She handed Neddy a shovel, cracked in the center, déjà vu.

"Take me to Dis," Neddy said. "I've got a game to finish."

"If that will make you feel better."

They stepped inside the elevator, down down the empty highway silence all around just black no light, no sound just emptiness and sighing bones a song for their own heart aches.

The office appeared, the familiar shadow shape at the table, red, a plate, a dead, screaming, twitching face being cut by tiny knives, delicate, eaten with a fork, chewed up. The elevator came to a stop.

Neddy stepped in Satan's office, hesitating to walk in, standing at the door, trying to look away from his father's face on the plate.

"You're just in time for dinner," Satan said. "Have you ever had a lip? It's great when baked just right and seasoned with cayenne peppers. It's a delicacy, a true delicacy."

"I want to finish our game," Neddy said. "The game of blackjack."

"Oh dear," Satan said. "I had the cards taken away. But I can have them brought out."

A little slave girl in a blue dressed walked into the room, cards in her shaking hands, her hands in iron cuffs. She dealt the cards:

A suicide king face up, another card face down for Satan. A queen of hearts, and, he saw, a jack of spades on the turned over card.

He placed one of his chips on the table.

"So you'd really like to play?" Satan asked, sly grin. "Alright then."

The faceless waiter came and took awake his plate, the face of a sad old man missing a nose and ear.

Satan wiped his mouth and stretched, black wings spreading out behind him, looked at his cards and smiled.

"I'll see that bet," Satan said, placing a matching chip.

"Hit," Neddy said, the ace of spades in his lap, out of Satan's sight.

Another card was dealt, same poor girl, her tired eyes, standing there with that thousand yard vacant gaze.

"You know," Neddy said, "this really is a nice place."

"It's not as bad as they make it out to be," Satan said. Neddy sat his cards in his lap with the dealt card.

"I'm not trying to look at your cards," Satan said. "You don't have to hide them."

Neddy replaced the card the young girl dealt, a king of diamonds bust, with the ace of spades, the queen of hearts, a jack and ace of spades, blackjack, twenty-one. Neddy crumpled the king of hearts in silence, sliding it into his pocket.

"Just a precaution," Neddy said. "I just try to make sure everyone plays fair."

"It's just a game, to me," Satan said. "I'll stay. Do you want to raise the bet?"

Neddy put his last chips in.

"So, you've got a nice hand," Satan said. "But so do I. I'll see your bet."

Satan placed chips on the table.

"Call," Neddy said. He flipped his other card over, revealing the ace. "Blackjack."

Satan clapped for a moment. The young girl raked the chips into Neddy's lap.

"I'm afraid it's dinner time," Satan said. "We can play again if you like, but I must have my dinner."

Faceless waiter walked in, screaming face of Neddy's father on the plate, two hollow eye-sockets already eaten. Lips torn off, a skull beneath.

"Galilee, escort him out," Satan said.

The little girl in shackles turned to face the door, hand gesturing, the elevator opening.

Neddy, shovel turned into the leg of his pants, took it out and lunged for Satan, scattering the plates and candles on his desk. Satan fell to the ground with a laugh, his giant, black wings spreading behind him as he laughed.

Neddy slammed the shovel into his face and it shattered like a mirror, a thousand horrible reflections, slaves, graves, no last name, no last name, no name at all, himself in all the fragments of the glass, eyeballs blinking, indecipherable murmurs to a wall.

Neddy woke to the sound of shattering glass.

46. *Hope and Chance*

"I'm sorry," Neddy heard. "You should pay attention! Don't stand there and cry! Clean it up!"

"I'm sorry," 'Vana said.

"Don't apologize!" an old man yelled. "Clean it up!"

"Yes sir," she said.

She opened the door to Neddy's room. He closed his eyes. The door closed behind her and she sighed. She wiped the tears away, walked across the room, knelt, opened a drawer under the bed, took out a towel, left the room again. Neddy opened his eyes.

"When you're done," the old man said, "you need to run to town. Get some plates and some bread."

"Yes, sir," she said.

"You take that other nigger..."

"...Neddy."

"...what did you say?"

"Nothing."

"You take that other nigger, Neddy...whatever his name is... you take him with you."

"Yes, sir."

The door opened, slow turned the golden handle, door creaked open. Neddy pretended to be asleep. Nirvana hesitated for a moment, standing beside his bed, his dark eyes so sad to see. He looked restless in his sleep, to her, as if he were in hell.

He probably is...

"Good morning, sunshine," she said.

"Good morning," Neddy said. "How are you are? Are you doing well? You okay?"

"Don't worry about me," she said. "I'll be fine. How are you feeling?"

"I had a good dream last night," he said. "I have strange dreams, 'Vana."

"Tell me about it," she said.

"Well I was in a dark place, running, scared of that big hammer looking thing that squishes people like bugs. Then I see you far off in the distance like a little light, scared people run in random directions pulling at their hair slamming their faces against the burning asphalt over and over until their brains run out their ears and then I take an elevator down to Satan's room and he's eating my father's face and we play cards and you give me a card and some chips to play and I use the card you gave me to trick the devil and I won the game. Then I attacked him with a shovel and when I hit him his face shattered like a mirror laughing then turned into reflections of me and I wanted to hit the reflections again but I woke to the sound of glass, muffled voices, gotta go somewhere, go get the nigger out of bed."

"If I could help you cheat the devil," 'Vana said, "I would. I think cheating is wrong, but, if I could, I'd cheat the devil for you. So I'm glad you had a good dream. Maybe you won't be so afraid to fall asleep."

"It was you reading to me I think," Neddy said. "That poem was beautiful. Those words you read… those words were the most beautiful words I've ever heard, their arrangement flawless, just so beautiful. I'd like to write poems like that."

"Just do it then," Nirvana said. "You just have to try."

"But I wouldn't know what to write about."

"Write about something you love," she said. "And it will be beautiful. That's what my daddy said, if it's written with love, it's beautiful—no matter what the words themselves mean. Just write with love and it will be beautiful."

"It hurts me to love, my loves long gone and dead, like you said, in the grave of yesterday…"

"Like mine," Nirvana said.

"I'll take your advice," Neddy said. "So, what's it going to be then for today?"

"We have to go into town. Would you like to go with me? I'd really like the company. I don't like walking by myself especially when I don't know any of the people and they all look at me and I don't know what to say to them or if I'm supposed to say anything at all."

"I'd love to go with you," Neddy said. "All I have to do is take my medicine and I'll be okay."

Neddy pretended to struggle to roll over toward the bottle. Nirvana took it from the silver salver, grabbed the spoon, told Neddy to open his mouth. She stuck the spoon in his mouth and that syrupy love stole down his throat straight.

Neddy relaxed, in the arms of God, and Nirvana led him to his feet. He steadied himself a bit, his stomach itching, scratched it, yawned, stretched, warmth, warm vibes, Nirvana smiling.

"You ready to go?" she asked.

"Yes," she said. "Lead the way."

She led him out the room, down the stairs, down the dusty road, into town, bustling buggies, horse drawn carriages, rickety looking buildings made of wood with drooping signs out front.

They walked into one of the stores, a word written above the entrance Neddy did not know, and, feeling ashamed, decided to look up the word: STORE.

Neddy followed her inside, trinkets everywhere, boxes, bags, glass bottles of dark liquid, light liquid, little music box, dancing angels.

Neddy opened one of the music boxes, seeing an angel on a small rod, lute in her hands, crooning a solemn sad time melody as she spun. Neddy looked around, 'Vana talking to the store owner. Neddy put the music box in his pocket, his face turned toward the mirror reflecting 'Vana and the shop owner, still talking. With it in his trousers, safe, he walked over to the counter, trying to obscure the shape of it with a limp, a masquerade of pain.

Nirvana had three china plates, a roll of gauze, and a bottle of wine on the wooden countertop.

"Do you need anything else, young miss?" the shop owner asked.

She turned to face Neddy, who, looking down, sighed at the site of an ant crawling across the floor.

"Do you need anything?" she asked.

Too much, he thought. "Some bullets," he said.

"We got some revolver bullets, that what you talkin' about, a revolver?"

"It has a spinning chamber. It was my fathers; we used to go hunting together when I was young."

He sat the box of bullets on the table by the other items, punched up a ticket, "Four dollars, young miss."

'Vana cringed handed him four dollars. He bagged the items up, a stiff, dried up husk of burlap, handed them to her. Neddy and 'Vana stood together at the cross walk, between one line of stores and another, the bullets in the bag, Neddy thought, *the revolver in the drawer, father on the boat*, his last chips lay and as the barrel in the wind did swing a hollow oh replied, *what have you done? You could have died.*

They saw a homeless man across the road. Neddy looked both ways, zigzags of people miasma collage of people going in different directions, and down a dark type corridor at the end of which there was no door he saw a man, with a guitar, leaning against the wall, a glass jar by his side.

Neddy walked in his direction.

"I want to talk to that old man," Neddy said. "I don't know why, but I want to. Can we stop and talk to him for a minute? You won't get in trouble will you?"

"It's me, Neddy," she said. "I'll walk with you if you'd like."

He took her hand.

"Well, walk with me," he said.

She smiled.

They walked down the dusty road a while approaching the old man, guitar in his lap, empty bottles around his legs inverted, trash, dead flowers and dirt encrusted in his fingers, slobber stained on his sleeping lips, expression contentment, expression serenity, though covered in the wrinkles writ by time.

People from a nearby smoking door walked out laughing, smelling of drink and food, bustling crowds, the old man against the wall not moving.

"Good evening," Neddy said.

The man's eyes like window shades went up. He wore a lost type smile, though euphoric. Nirvana was silent, thinking, worrying, not knowing what to say, replaying invented tragedies of the man inside her mind.

Another group of drunks staggered down the stairs. They paused, looking at the old man, now awake, eyes wide, their vacant faces amused.

"Play us a song, old man!" they said. "Here. I've got what you need. One dollar, just play me a song. I'd like to hear, hmm, something you probably wouldn't know, so I won't mention it."

"Try me," the old man said. "I've played a lot of songs."

"The Ave Maria," the young man said. "My mother used to sing it in church. Can you play that one, old man?"

"Yes, sir," he said. "I can. Do you want the one by Franz Schubert or Bach?"

The young man looked confused. "Schubert," he said after a moment's halt.

The old man strummed and smiled. Neddy felt ashamed of being human, a deep sense of self revulsion, looking at the giggling boys laughing as the old man's sadness filled the fettered air like birds.

Ave Maria, Maria gratia plena, Maria gratia plena—ave, ave dominus, dominus tecum—benedicta tu in mulieribus. Et Benedictus, et Benedictus, fructus ventris, ventris tuae, Jesus. Ave Maria...

The group of giggling still children men echoed against the cement wallpaper of the narrow alley. They walked to the cathedral, putting a dollar in his jar. The man played on.

Ave Maria, Mater Dei, ora pro nobis, ora, ora pro nobois

peccatoribus—nunc et in hora mortis. Et in hora, mortis nostrae. Et in hora mortis nostrae, et in hora mortis nostrae. Ave Maria...

The man sat the guitar on his lap.

Nirvana reached into her pocket, taking out a wrinkled dollar, and put it in his jar.

"Would you mind playing Amazing Grace for me?" she asked.

"I'll play Amazing Grace for free," he said. He sat up, alert like, blinked his eyes, focused on the jar of rusted coins and wrinkled bills, then pulled a dollar out. He handed it to Nirvana.

"I play for you for free," he said. "I play for food. My daughters have enough to eat."

"Then why do you play?" Neddy asked. "It's cold and 'bout to rain. Why let yourself be mocked and teased?"

"I was born in mud, that's true, but I am not a worm. They see me in the mud, and think I am a worm. They think I should be stomped underfoot as a worm. That's what they think. That' fine; I have a wife and two children. And they can eat. They run and play without shoes on their little feet but they're happy. I play this old guitar so they can be happy, and I'm more than happy to do that. I don't suffer because of them. If I must be ridiculed for the sake of my family, that is a burden I am happy to bear. Their mother, such a happy woman, educates them while I'm out. She would go mad with me around all the time. She came from a decent family, somewhere up North I think, truly lovely... She teaches them how to love. Hell is the suffering of being unable to love, or being unable to attain a love once lost; love is the creator of Heaven and Earth and love is here. That is the suffering of the world: the inability to love one's fellow man as much as loving oneself. It's easier to teach science and mathematics than it is to teach love. That's a hard lesson to learn and most learn too late.

"I sleep in a one room house, by my wife, the children beside her, my Hope and Chance, my twins, my dear, dear girls. I'd rather sleep with them in the mud than alone in a castle. They are such loving children. They ask such questions! That's good, though, I'm glad they wonder. They smile like they understand the world. Maybe they do. They don't take anything for granted, not even the sun, not air, not the dirty clothes they wear, those dresses, the dresses their mother wore as a child, the dress of old handmaidens. They're prettier than the stars.

"Once they drew a picture for me, of us, together, under a bright bright sun, mommy and daddy holding hands. To me— that outweighs what they call me on the streets. They walk around together holding hands. Why do I need money? To eat.

Why do I need to eat? Because I have love. We leave the world with empty hands. I just cherish what I get to hold and leave the rest.

"Nothing worth having can be bought. Let me live in the mud. I'll play my guitar that might someday upon a young girls blushing face their misery some love replace. We're all beggars here, and I'll see better days."

Neddy thought about his medicine. His stomach grumbled, sick feeling, yearning, nausea. *You've got some more at home. You'll make it. You're alright.*

"Don't feel sorry me. I'll live and die in our mud hole, out little pit, but every day I see the sun and rain and thank God plain for my place in the mud. I might just another be a prop in the streets, but don't feel sorry for me.

"They laugh at me and let them laugh, to them I'll play the clown. If they have to act on their behalf just to put me down, I'll let them do it day by day and let them go by their way and love them all the same. Look."

It was a small angel made of melted candle wax, to Neddy déjà vu.

"Hope made it for me," he said.

"What do you do when you're at home?" Nirvana asked. "What do you do when you're happy?"

"We put out all the lights, light a candle in the end, play guitar, and sing together. We count the coins at night. We have each other and that is enough. If Heaven was that fragment of joy, then it is a place worth pursuing.

"I know," he said, "I know what I'll do. I'll play you another song that my soul might be worth a penny, a penny not but one can give. And he is the Master of the play."

He played a slow progression in A major, a waltz in falsetto tempo, then to D major, *how sweet the sound...*

That saved a wretch like me.

The old man was asleep.

47. *The Sleeping Angel*

Nirvana's grip on Neddy's arm was not quite as strong as on his heart and he felt dismayed, a love untouchable, attached to the one who stole her love and left, and he, he thought, I'd never be half of what he was to her. But you can try.

You could kill yourself.

Why?

Want the list again? Murderer, junkie, ring a bell? You deserve the horrors, hell. Christ was sinless and he suffered to save the rats like you. All you want to save is yourself, what nerve! You consider yourself noble and then you steal a music box I stole it for her the intention was noble but the action illegal take it back and say hello I stole this but I'd like to give it back I apologize for being a thief and by the way I'm a murderer and a junkie that tells lies. A thousand illusions before you will lie, telling you you're worth something, telling you you're human, being capable of trust and love, capable of love from above, when you cannot atone. God wrote the rhythm and already played the song. It ends with you and ends alone. Take the gun, Nobody, pull the trigger and walk home.

In silence they walked toward their home, grey the evening, clouds downcast and purple frowning. They didn't speak to each other, but each hand held tight.

They didn't know what to say. Neddy imagined a ballroom in his mind, like the one he described to 'Vana, and decided to go to that place, that make believe ballroom of the mind. He saw the marble floor, the large stairwell to nothing, to the Heavens, an old man sitting at a table. Neddy moved toward the table, uneasy, sat down, looked at the figure who sat before him.

The man's face came into focus, Neddy's father, Ray, smiling, no wires to his arms or face or legs. He smiled, a bowl of grits on the table in front of him, hand holding a spoon.

"Want some grits?" Ray asked.

"Yes, sir," Neddy said.

Neddy's mother walked into the room with a bowl of grits, "I put extra butter like you like," she said, disappeared into one of the numbered doors.

Neddy looked to the side. Galilee lay on the couch asleep, angel wings spread around her little shoulders. Her eyes were relaxed, contentment, pleasant dreams.

His father continued eating, chewing, smiling, eyes bright, alert. Neddy tried to think of something to say but could not. He could not find one thing to say that he thought he had the strength to say.

"I've missed you," Ray said. "It's nice to see you again."

Neddy put a revolver on the table, emptying all the bullets but one, loaded the chamber. He spun the wheel.

His father said, "Let me see that." His arms reached out to grab, Neddy, unable to keep it from him, obeyed.

His father looked at the gun, turning it over, looking at the stock, the barrel, then flipped the chamber open, dumped out the bullet. He placed it on the table.

"Now you can play," he said.

Neddy picked up the gun, put the barrel to his temple, pulled the trigger, click, spin, click, spin, click, spin. His father smiled, still eating his grits, Neddy with the gun, Galilee with angel wings asleep on the couch.

"How long has she been asleep?" Neddy asked.

"Just before you got here," he said. "She waited for a long time. She does every day. She didn't think you'd ever come, I don't think, but she waited anyway. She just took a nap."

"Don't wake her," Neddy said. "Let her get her rest. I'm going to see her soon. I've got my plan in the bag. I know what I have to do."

Neddy took the gun, tucked it in his waistband, and walked under a giant archway, above it black words reading: NOWHERE—SUICIDE.

"Goodbye," he said. "I'll see you next time."

48. *Love's Match Long Burnt Out*

The door opened. Neddy blinked as the colors of the world flooded back. He heard a muffled bark far off.

Nirvana said, "Are you okay? Are you alright? What happened?"

The dog, a ways down the road, walked toward them gaily, tail wagging, tongue hanging out. He walked up to Neddy and sat down.

"Who's dog?" Neddy asked.

"I don't know," 'Vana said. "I see him sometimes on my way home."

Neddy rubbed the dogs head, tussling his hair, smoothing it, messing it up, fixing it again. The dog rolled over on his belly, legs kicking, Neddy scratching his belly, "Who's a good boy? You're a good boy. Yes you are. Who's my good boy? You are!"

Nirvana smiled as she watched him rubbed the happy dog's belly, leg twitching, tongue still wagging, panting.

The dog was damp and musty smelling, as though he had been lost in the rain, his coat soggy, eyes hopeful and alert.

"What's his name?" Neddy asked.

"He doesn't really have a name," 'Vana said. "I just say, 'hey doggy!' when I see him and sometimes I stop to pet him, but I don't think he has a name. He's a stray.

Like me.

"Then I'll call him Neddy," Neddy said. He knelt over, down on one knee now, middle of the road, rubbing that shaggy damp belly.

"Who's a good boy? You're a good boy, Neddy. You're a good boy."

He felt the sickness, the runny nose, the goose bumps on his skin, the chill, the sweat, his legs restless, electricity in his veins.

"I need my medicine," Neddy said. He scratched at his stomach and it hurt. Scabs from the night before bled on the inside of his shirt. He ran his hand along the narrow fingernail cuts and flakes of skin as the scabs peeled back, blood clotting at the surface, staining his fingers a dingy crimson red. He wiped the blood off on his pants and looked at his hands. *If only it was that easy...*

"Okay," Nirvana said. "Lets go. Do you know the way home? It's okay. Just follow me."

They walked through the scarce crowded streets, 'Vana with the burlap bag in her hands clutched like a child, precious china plates inside, Neddy stumbled, foggy eyed, feeling the cold chills, feeling the scabs on his lips. The dog named Nobody followed them home.

"Wait here for a second," Nirvana said. She opened the screen door walked inside, leaving Neddy and the dog outside. Neddy looked down at the dog, a hopeful stare returning his melancholy and his empathy.

Talking from the house, bustling about the kitchen, plates clang against a table. The dog, afraid, runs off. Neddy didn't have the strength the chase him. He wanted to.

Nirvana opened the door.

"Come in," she said. "But be quiet. They're asleep. We'll get you back in bed and I'll fix you—your medicine for you."

She led Neddy by the arm, into the front door, locked it behind her, passed the door into the den, hallway up ahead, door the left, door at the end of the hall, all closed. The familiar sight of his bed, the table by it, the windows, the bureau, dark purple curtains.

He lay down. Neddy stretched out, then curled into a fetal ball, cold chills on his back, sweat on his chest. He heard the top come off the bottle, relief, a spoon fill, ah, the syrup went down the throat.

"What caused your illness?" Nirvana said after Neddy's face relaxed.

Neddy tried to consider what his illness really was, what impulsion drove him to that craving and desire. He couldn't come up with anything but faces, family, strange places, dream images, shaggy dog, Master rubbed his belly didn't he and he kicked his leg like you knew he would.

"I have to go back to Rose Hill," Neddy said. "Something happened to my brain... When I saw the blood, and my reflection in it, that caused... that caused some sort of split in my brain.

"Up until then I was relatively normal, wait, until my father's injury, no, I think it was when my sister died. I started having chest pains and I panic and I can't breathe and think I'm going to die and my heart races... I feel hands squeezing me on both sides, restless, couldn't sleep until my father came in, and he read to me too, and when I look back and see all those faces gone I just want the medicine.

"The physical agony of anxiety is severe, but that I can't help, that I can tolerate, it's the emotional aspect of that agony that hurts."

"If I could fix you I would," Nirvana said.

"And if I could fill the boots whose feet you miss, I'd put them on. I can't do that. The only boots I can wear are mine, and I don't even know where they're at."

"What makes you so sad, Neddy? Have you ever been happy?"

"I've had moments where I'm happy, genuinely happy, but those moments are few. I used to play hide and seek with my sister. I went fishing with my father sometimes. Every time the love came in somewhere blew a frigid wind that my life's love might end.

"I keep seeing their faces, all of them, my family, strange places, and I think I need my medication then I know I need it because it helps and that's what matters right that's what you said. And when I don't have it, when it's gone, I have this yearning, this desire, the desire to get past the suffering of the day, another day running from the shadow of my past.

"Another day running from the match of love that burned for a little while, little arms, little hands huddling around it for warmth as the match burnt down to the end, the end to burn the finger, how like love; how like love to burn so bright, hands around it for warmth, hands that long and need, and it burns away and day by day you start to see the end, the end of the match, a bit fraying at the end, love to burn the finger in the end. The match that equals happy burns and leaves a scar and I've got a thousand.

"I feel that burning every day, in my chest, in my head, in my bones, and then I retreat into my head, into the suffering storm, the suffering storm to wait on shade, and that shade is in that bottle, protecting me from the sun too bright, the rain.

"Some people deserve to suffer, 'Vana. I have scars for love and hate. Some people deserve to suffer, and happiness? It wasn't in the cards for me. Maybe God stacked the deck.

"And that morphine chases the pain away, turning the shadow's face off mine. And I feel like a slave again, slave to that syrup and that feeling and that phony Heaven.

"Why do you think you deserve to suffer?" 'Vana asked. "For what you've done, you've suffered. You don't have to suffer for the rest of your life. I'm here. I'm not going anywhere."

"Then come to Rose Hill with me," he said.

"I can't, Neddy," she said. "I've got people to take care of. They need me more than you."

"Nobody could need you more than me," Neddy said. "I can't get there by myself."

"I'll get enough medicine to last you the trip, and walk you to

171

the edge of town and fetch a carriage for you, but I've promised... I've promised to take care of these people. If you had asked me before, I would've went, Neddy. You'll have your medicine. You'll be fine."

"I don't want that medicine no more," he said. "I feel like a slave to it... the slave, the slave I try to hide these words divide and equal slave, to emotion, to that medicine, what sickness, to a shadow I can't out run. But when I saw you there, as an angel on the hill, I saw you, in a white dress, and you swallowed the bottle and then swallowed me. You chewed on me for a while and sucked me dry, and left, left me alone to wander on around inside my head where to this day I see and face things that horrify me. It's all getting darker, the world getting dim, and you're the only light I see. You may not see yourself with my eyes, but if you did, I'm sure you'd smile."

"Let me think about it," she said. "You need to get some rest. I'll get your medicine, find you some clothes, pack a suitcase for you, and then I'll take you to the end of town and get you a driver and everything you'll be okay."

"I don't know if I can save me from myself," he muttered. The image of the revolver flashed before his mind's eye, the bullets spilling on a table, one in the chamber, spin click done, bye all the pain.

Nirvana didn't say anything, fidgeting, scratching one arm with the other, and said, "Everything will be okay in the morning, Neddy."

"Can you get me some paper and a pencil too?" he asked. "I'd like to write to you."

"I'll take care of everything," she said. "Remember this, Neddy, when you despair, or when you can't find your way... My father's name was Hope. Don't lose that... don't put dirt in that grave."

"I'll try," he said. "That's all that I can do."

"And that is enough."

"If you ever go to that ballroom, that place I sometimes go, wait for me. And when I get there we can dance."

"Then I'll wait until you get there."

"What if I never make it?"

"I'll wait."

Neddy couldn't think of anything to say.

Nirvana twisted the top off the bottle of the syrup, filled the spoon, ah again the warmth. Neddy relaxed, Nirvana's hand on his, anxiety drowned in the opiate sea of tranquility.

"I'll see you in the morning she said.

Neddy was in his peaceful dream land, eyes rolled back, the light of Heaven's grace blinding his eyes.

49. *The Land of Nowhere*

Neddy stood above the shattered glass, back in the city of Dis, the table cleared, no slaves, nothing, nobody there but him, alone, in all the fragments a fragment of himself with a face, not the smudge, the gaping hole, but the face of a young man with a stubbly beard, looking like an old man, tired black eyes, pink rimmed unrest above the lashes, sweat on his brow, great concern in his glance.

He heard a knock on the door and ran out of Satan's office, up the elevator, fast through the darkness Neddy stood eyes closed calm. The faint light of Nirvana's forever waiting candle appeared above him. He smiled in the dark, nobody to see it, and the elevator door opened.

"How long have you been waiting?" Neddy asked.

"I don't know," 'Vana, the source of light replied. "I haven't been paying attention."

"I've got the poker chips," he said. "I won."

"I'm glad," she said. "Where would you like to go now?"

"To nowhere, Neddy said. "Where the suicides go."

Nirvana frowned and led him in. The elevator door slid to a creaking close, the metal bars a tired sigh. The panel lit up, three buttons, the button to hell black, the button to nowhere grey, the button to nirvana gold. Neddy pressed the nowhere grey and the ragged elevator went up into a dark tunnel, dim grey at the end approaching.

"Are you okay?" she asked. "Do you need your medicine?"

"I thought you must'a swallowed it," he said.

"I did," she said. "But you can have it."

She put her lips to his, a brief moment of warmth, fading like breath upon a mirror as she withdrew, elevator opening with a slow creak, a dim fugue of white, vague shapes wandering some in circles some in twisted patterns to the silhouettes of elm trees, shrubs, and ivy.

He stepped out of the elevator into the grey.

"You coming with me?" he asked. "I can't go alone."

"I can't go with you," she said. "I'm needed elsewhere, lots of slaves are lost, and other people, not slaves, but kings and princes and slave-owners, all walk together here and don't even see each other. They can't see the color of your skin, just their own little universe projected on their eyelids as they roam."

"What cause does this punishment provoke?" Neddy asked.

"Everybody here chooses to be here," she said.

"And all who are taunted by terrible clowns in hell? Where do they get to go?"

"In the end, it will be their choice. In the end, and the end is so far away, not even visible or fathomable. A lot of slaves go wandering. A lot of men and women get lost in mazes along the way, but there's always a guide, always with a different face, and they too will with me walk, but here you must walk alone."

"Do you have a dictionary?" Neddy asked.

She produced one.

"A pen and paper?"

She produced them.

"How long will it be until I see you again?"

"That's up to you," she said. "But I'll be here when you come back. And I'll take you to where the elevator goes, and you'll see. Don't lose your hope amid the maze or ever cover that fresh dug grave."

"Who will be my guide?" Neddy asked.

"Nobody," she said.

Neddy kissed her on the cheek and disappeared into the grey. The elevator door creaked open an iron sigh, she stepped on the platform, down again, again.

Neddy turned around, elevator gone, *go on old man. Just walk. Concentrate on breathing.*

Neddy saw a grey tinged panorama of intersecting mazes, mountains, merry go rounds, stairways to nowhere the people kept climbing and falling off and climbing and falling again. The others in the maze run into walls down every path, turn around, run, afraid, run into another wall, turn around back the other way running again, hit the wall, stand up, repeat, repeat.

Neddy walked, a steady pace, looking left and right, seeing ghost like transparent people wandering in random directions, coming in and out of broken elevators, some chasing coins down a drain, getting them, dropping the coins again, on the ground, rolling around, screaming, *Why oh why oh why oh why* on and on and on as they wandered on.

Neddy approached an opening in an ivy maze, the green a shade lighter as though covered by some silken veil, an old man on a rocking chair sat by the entrance, cigarette aglow, cowboy hat, a broken shovel by his side.

"Name?" a hollow voice asked. He produced a pen, opened a book on which a thousand entries in identical patterns spelled one through one hundred beginning to end Nobody.

"Nobody," Neddy said.

The man turned a covered page to a fresh one and wrote the numbered entry: B2,517,531,561,985—Nobody.

"Farewell," he said with his tin like metal voice. The man without eyes said, "See you next time, Nobody."

Neddy walked into the grey grassed corridor. A lighted corner appeared before him, a bench, brown, scuffs along the side, the silhouette of an angel, sleeping. Neddy walked, no idea the direction, no idea what direction was, everywhere grey. As he drew closer the angels outline filled in, 'Vana sleeping in Galilee's body and clothes, different head, illusion, the image disappeared, turned to the familiar smudge of color.

Neddy turned to run and ran into a wall of ivy, ivy towered to the sky as he looked up he saw no cloud or bird go by just grey shapes and patterns of filing drawers along lighted sections of the hive like shape. Neddy with bee like wings fluttered towards the hive through packed catacombs of small rooms.

He hovered above the desk of a woman without eyes who wrote with a pen out of ink on a page with nothing on it. She wrote furious, carving into the page, wringing her heart out like a wet towel until dry, stood up, filed the document, stamped good, and took out another empty page.

Lives were shifted and shuffled like sad cards then out in narrow postal slots into variable machines again to rub a dollar out a red or manifesto, madness, time sorted into categories, joy, happiness, fiction, nonfiction, goodbye, sunset, good, fare, bye, the field read, the record written down, written down for one to look upon with scribbled names on the page, looks at it once, turns it over again, writes good on one, writes bad on the other, the deed phoned in, some files corrupted, we'll have to have someone look at that.

A telephone rang. Neddy rushed to answer.

"Hello?"

"Who's there?" a familiar voice asked.

"Neddy," Neddy said. "Who are you?"

"Nobody."

"Hello," Neddy said.

"The judge is you. There are no gifts to give, no words to write, nobody to read. The judge in the end is you. Here your work will not be read by the orphans of the world, lackeys and the junkies sell it for a fix, a temporary fix for a permanent problem.

Broken robots rub morphine on their rusted parts and power up, their eyes alight, mind keen, over and over it's the same in the variable machine.

Karma's equations, one after another, and you will call them days, days good or bad, and then they're filed away, submitted to the judge, the self is on the line and the self says bad, hangs up, pranks you at three in the morning to say he's sorry for waking you up at all, walk a short period under that starry quilt at the bosom of your mother, cling to her a while, before she shakes you off like a flea.

Good? Bad? A voice murmurs bad and the voice comes back good, files corrupted, someone takes a look, gloved hand into the head, write down desire, we'll take care of the medication, one smile take one spoonful, two smiles take two spoonfuls, for a permanent smile take all.

Every, good they'll say, inside the lines, the best painting of its type to find, and hope that poor coupon is enough for the ferry man, across the river to the maker, shuffler of the cards a lonely programmed calculating nonsense, for it, by it, forever.

One bad one good one love one hate one life one chance to sell it all and run out with the cash when the shithouse is in flames. You didn't come here to play Jesus. Bang! The band-aid bleeds! Another rusted cog rolls over."

Neddy dropped the phone, looking to the window, a woman, crawling on the wall, licked pie off the slimy surface, crawled across the outside wall, out of sight, shrieking shouting as she crawled. Screaming cigarettes ran in circles in the ashtray on the desk. The woman sighed, stubbed one out, their screams muted with a soundless thumb at which they screamed.

There were two cigarettes standing together, both on fire, but with smiles on their faces, leaning together their fire combined, and they smiled as the tobacco burnt away until they slumped over lifeless in the tray.

50. *Farewell at the Bridge*

Neddy woke with the sun the next day, Nirvana sitting by the bed, a suitcase packed, locked. A key on a chain sat beside it on the stand.

"How long have you been waiting?" Neddy asked.

"I don't know," 'Vana said. "Must'a lost track of time."

"You're going to come with me, right? At least until we get out of town, ain't that what you said?"

"I'll go as far as I can go, the bridge just outside of town, then you'll go left, back toward Carolina, and I'll turn right."

"I lose track of things a lot and I end up wandering around with no idea where I'm at..."

"You'll have a carriage for the entire trip. I'll tell him I caught a slave who ran away from South Carolina and that you had to be taken back to the plantation at Rose Hill. I'll give him enough money not to care, he takes your bags, puts them in the cart, lets you get into the cart with your thing, door closes, he takes the reins and you're off. You're going home, Neddy. Are you happy?"

"I need my medicine," Neddy said. "It hasn't been helping as much as it used to. Maybe I need two spoonfuls since one isn't enough to help."

"Okay," she said. "But listen, don't take more than four spoonfuls in a day, ever, Neddy. Don't ever take more than four."

"Why?"

"Because it can kill you if you take too much, a friend of mine—a girl I knew—her daddy, her uncle I mean, got depressed over her being a slave and drank a whole bottle of this stuff and died. Don't do that to me, Neddy. I couldn't handle that kind of hurt ag--..."

"I won't," Neddy said. "No more than four, got it. You've got my paper and pen and my medicine right?"

"It's in the case," she said. "Everything you need is in the case. So don't worry. You'll be fine. Oh, here's the key."

She stood up, key and chain in her hand, draped it over his shoulders, her hair brushing over his shoulder, the smell of soap sweet in her hair. Neddy's heart pounded away against the cold key on his chest.

"My medicine?"

"Oh, I'm sorry, I started talking to you and forgot about it. Here, I'll get it for you. Say ah, that's a good boy."

She rubbed his belly.

He felt shame when her slender fingers went over the last flakes of a scab turning into a scar, some thick and grey. He jumped when her warm hand went over his stomach, startled, rolled over, sat up on the side of the bed, forced a fake laugh and stood up.

"I'll be fine," he said. "Thank you. Thank you so much."

"My father used to say, 'never thank me for kindness; that is all I have to give.'"

"Is there some way I could send you letters? I'd like to write to you. I'll write a poem for you. How would I send it to you? Would that be okay?"

"Just look for a post office and give the letter to them and they'll put a stamp on it and send it off to me. You have to write my address on the letter so they can send it to me. I've written my address on the first page of the papers in your suitcase, just in case you need me or need to talk or if you ever decide to come back."

"And if I don't, what then?"

"Then I'll see you in your ballroom."

"Will you wait for me until I get there?"

"Yes," she said.

"Could you wear a blue dress made of lace?"

"I will."

"Let's go, then," Neddy said, sighing, picking up his suitcase.

"Is my gun in there?" he asked.

"Yes," she said. "I wish you'd let me keep it here... I hate those things."

"I might need it," he said. 'Vana closed her eyes, biting on her bottom lip. She guided him to the door by his arm, her little hands closed tight around the fabric of his shirt, as though fearing to let go.

If only I could save him from himself, she thought.

They walked hand in hand across the town, through narrow streets, behind houses, under clotheslines, hills of rich green grass and pastures of golden flowers, the bridge in sight, rickety, sighing, its structure the shape of a frown. Nirvana picked a dandelion in a patch where the road ended.

They stood together on the bridge, not speaking, looking out over the water, the sun, having just risen, bashful, pink, clouds orange abstract, purple windswept tendrils golden hue, the water a sea of floating colors red and orange, pink and blue, miasma of light and shadow. 'Vana blew the dandelion seeds across the water and turned.

"The carriage is on the other side of the bridge," she said. "That'll get you home..."

"Will you walk to the end of the bridge with me?"

She hesitated. "Okay," she said. "The carriage has already been arranged, but I'll walk with you."

"Thank you," Neddy said. They walked to the other side of the bridge, a crosswalk, pedestrians with umbrellas tucked under their arm. The image of a young girl carrying an umbrella came to Neddy's mind and twirled until the girl disappeared, leaving the umbrella in her place.

The carriage pulled up. Nirvana loosened her fingers from Neddy's, turned to leave. Neddy grabbed her arm and pulled her toward him, "I'll write to you," he said. "Will you write back?"

"As long as I have fingers," she said, "but, beyond that, I can't promise."

"Just avoid doing things that could risk your fingers," Neddy said. "You'd have a hell of a time hitchhiking with no thumbs."

"You're right," she said. "Also, there's a dictionary in your suitcase if you need it. I know you like having one."

"It's my favorite book," Neddy said. "It is a poem about everything."

Nirvana smiled. A pause, brief silence, Neddy remembered the music box.

"I have something for you," he said, fumbling through his pockets, finding the stolen melody machine with its ballerina and its hymn. He took it out, opened it, and handed it to her. She opened the case. The slow, high pitched melody, la, la, la, la, played in the empty dusty windswept street, carriage driver, old man, waiting. The song started over. Nirvana closed the box.

"Goodbye," she said.

"Why do they call it goodbye when it's not a good bye?"

"What would you prefer then? See ya later alligator?"

"How about farewell?"

"Farewell."

"I'll try," Neddy said.

He stepped on the carriage step, uneasy, two spoonfuls good. He watched Nirvana walk away, across the bridge, a turn, down the rusty road and disappeared.

Neddy saw his namesake shaggy stray appear. He ran over to Neddy and sat, looking up. Neddy turned to face the driver.

"Carolina?" the driver asked.

"Yes, sir," Neddy said.

"North or South Carolina?"

"There are two?"

"Yeah, one's further up north. That's why they call it North Carolina."

"I'm going to Rose Hill," Neddy said. "Do you know where that is?"

"Of course!" the driver said. "I went there with my church for Easter. It's a beautiful place. It has a maze out behind it. My daughters loved playing in that maze. They didn't want to leave."

"They didn't tell you my name?" Neddy asked.

"Nope," he said. "I guess they figured you'd know it. And they paid, so I don't need a name."

"Good," Neddy said. "Because I don't have one. I used to, but I lost it."

The old man chuckled, "What do you do for a living?"

Neddy thought for a moment, no ideas coming, thought of telling the truth, decided not to, lied, saying, "I'm a writer."

"What business does a writer have in South Carolina?"

"I'm writing a book about slaves," Neddy said.

"Why the slaves?" he asked. "They're a bunch of nobody's."

"That is why," Neddy said.

The driver opened the carriage door.

"Is that your dog?" he asked.

"Yes, his name is Neddy."

"Is he going with you?"

"Can he?"

"As long as you don't let him shit all over the place, I don't mind a 'tall. I like dogs."

"Me too," Neddy said. "Neddy's a good boy. He won't cause you any trouble."

"Welp," the driver said, "hop in."

"I don't owe you any money or anything?" Neddy asked.

"No, somebody already paid. So, get in and we'll be off."

"Yes, sir," Neddy said. "Come on, Neddy. We have to leave."

And the carriage drove away.

51. *The Redemption Coupon*

Neddy looked at his suitcase, thinking about his gun. He took the key from his neck and unlocked it. Stack of paper, pencil, two bottles of that sweet sweet syrup, a revolver, small box of bullets, address, small folded block of paper.

Neddy took the revolver out of the suitcase, grabbed the bullets, draped them across his lap. He loaded the gun, spun the revolving chamber, hammer back. He took out a piece of paper, writing:

Bang the Band-Aid bleeds. The golden fountain has ran dry, and though the pen will not ask me why, I'd rather do the dance of death than lie, but lie as it is, and underground, a hole grows by, the merry-go-round, Nobody wins, no dice for the jaded game—the stakes are high, the chips are low, goodbye wave the blankets, blow.

Bang the Band-Aid bleeds. The happy fountain has ran dry. Bang. Bang. Blood, put a Band-Aid on it. Bang, the period at the end of sentence life, bang, the period, dot to end the tale.

Shatter mirrors, the face in the glass won't look my way, gun goes to a cold surface, bang, the mirror falls, the gun its come home lullaby calls, songs one to sleep who longs for two, after a momentary pause, let someone else get on the carousel, the self behind time's wall will hide. Bang, the great divide, second to the first mistake, just called to say I'm sorry.

He signed the manuscript Nobody, he looked for the address in his suitcase, found it, found an envelope, folded the paper, slid it in, wrote out the address, licked the edge, closed it tight, and put the gun to his head.

He put the gun to his forehead, then to his temple, then put the gun in his mouth.

I knew you'd come around. Come around? Yes. One little click and all the misery ends. Click spin and it's done. Go ahead. Tired of being a slave? Tired of the guilt and misery? Just pull that trigger. You've already got the barrel in your mouth. Why not? It'll scare the shit out of that old white man. I can't do that. Why? Because I have a poem to write. Can you do it when you're done with that? Yes, I can. Good. How about some medicine, Neddy? Nobody's looking. Two whole bottles. You could always just drink both of those and die painless like, if you're not too brave to shoot yourself, but shooting yourself seems more like something you deserve, you know? A quick, painless death—that's for the Saints.

You shouldn't have made them love you. It will hurt them all that much more in the end, to love you, to care about who you are and how you end up, and in the end you'll leave them all in tears. How cruel it is to make them love you, only to suck the barrel of a gun. Pull the trigger and make it moan.

You could always grow and read and write and take your medicine but what happens when you run out? Will you write an indecipherable letter of scribbled screams with tear stains and blood on the page, a suicide not to yourself?

You're on your own, old man. Going back to Rose Hill. Do you remember what you did? I think Thomas is going to be quite upset with you. You know, the whole killing his mother AND his father thing might not have went over well with him. He's going to stick a knife in your belly and eat you from the inside out. That's what you deserve, you know, nothing. And how you gonna pay the ferry man?

With my life.

His train of thought was interrupted when his shaggy dog knocked his suitcase over, bottles spilling, papers scattered. Neddy saw a folded letter with a heart drawn on it. He picked it up, unfolded it to read.

"Take care of yourself for me. If I was there, I would take all the pain away, all the pain I could take, just so you might feel better.

So hang in there, if you can't do it for yourself, do it for me. Remember my father's name. My father's name was Hope. Don't ever fill that grave."

—Love, Nirvana

Neddy put the gun away, taking all the bullets out but one, swigged at one of the brown bottles, put the papers and letters in his suitcase, locked it, reclined. The still damp dog jumped onto Neddy's lap, startling him, causing him to jump.

"Who's a good boy?" Neddy asked. "Neddy boy is a pretty dog. Yes you are. Yes you are."

He petted the dog's wet head until he drifted off to sleep.

52. *An S.O.S. from Nowhere*

For a moment Neddy mourned the cigarettes, the ones that smiled as they burned, and an eyeless janitor walked in the room, emptied the tray into a black bag, tied the bag, walked out.

The building tilted on its side, people falling, no responses, then steadied, gravity rearranged. The eyeless worker bees had been replaced by another of their kind, grey, no smile or frown, no eyes, wrote something on the blank piece of paper, nothing with no ink, put it in a narrow slot, pushed a button off it went into a tube that ran along the ceiling, out the window. Neddy followed the tube, out the window, back into the forever grey foggy wasteland.

The plastic tube ran along the building, to the top, then into the sky, toward the sun, and Neddy followed all the way, all the way to the sun, until his worker bee wings burnt and he fell slow at first into the atmosphere and then into the frowning clouds until he hit the hollow ground.

He stood, looking around in all directions, and found himself inside a maze, a maze of cement, scribbled letters all over the walls.

'Nobody was here' was carved into the solid rock as though carved by knives or teeth. Neddy saw a broken shovel out of the corner of his eye, walked to it, picked it up, slamming it into the cement wall, wouldn't break, turned and ran, hit a wall, too hard to see. He wrote, *Neddy was here, too,* amidst the sea of names Nobody.

He decided to sit down for a moment, taking out his dictionary, his pen and paper too, draped them on his lap, legs splayed out in front of him, cement cold on his back.

He opened the dictionary, A:

Anathema, noun: 1. A person detested or loathed. 2. A person or a thing accursed or consigned to damnation and destruction. 3. An offering to God as atonement for sin.

Neddy closed the book.

He thought about his 'Vana again. Images of her shy face flooded his mind, the poem, he fiddled for his pen and paper, writing:

What could I say that would convey our silent moments shared? I could ponder all night with nothing to write that could ever compare. Whatever you do, it's just me and you, and that to me is fair. As fair as a song from midnight 'til dawn interrupted sometimes by the day. When I try to sleep I think of the sweet words you had to say. If we clap along and the song plays too long we'll smile and hit replay.

Disgusted with his own words, he crumpled the paper into a ball, threw it against the wall. Neddy stood up and ran, in and out of stone corridors, hitting wall after wall after wall, before finally walking into a small clearing, table and a couch appeared, a shadow in a chair reclined. A table appeared before them, two cards each, two bottles, two portraits, and two guns, one full, one empty.

"We spoke earlier," he said.

"Who are you?" Neddy asked.

"Nobody."

"Tell me about yourself," Neddy said.

"I'm a murderer, a thief, a liar, a junkie, a manipulator, a pervert, a failure, a deceiver, a traitor, and a fiend. You even betray yourself. I'm what you see in the mirror, Neddy. It's nice to catch up with you at last."

"Please just leave me alone."

"What kind of fun would that be? It's nice to watch the bugs so small their little legs under your thumb. Do you remember that? Do you remember the kitten?"

"Which kitten?" Neddy asked.

"The cat you found in the woods."

"I don't remember," Neddy said.

"Then I'll refresh your memory," Nobody said. "I was walking through the woods one day and found a group of kittens. All of them were dead but one. They were covered in damp leaves, their black hair stained and crusted. I took the only one alive back home.

"I took the shivering little kitten inside, wrapped her in a towel, taking leaves and grass out of her hair. I patted her dry, feeling the bones, the bones jutting out from her sides, her ribcage. She meows and meows and I just thought she wanted to play. She was starving and you—I didn't know. Later that evening mama made a sandwich and you still didn't tell them about the kitten, so I took the kitten a sandwich and placed it on the floor in front of her.

"The kitten was too weak to stand up. I put a sandwich on the floor so she could eat it and she wouldn't and then you—I took a small piece of bread and tried to stuff it in her mouth. She couldn't open her mouth. And I just sat there crying stupidly, shouting indecipherable murmurings to the dying animal, 'Please eat! Please eat it!'

"You squatted in front of the cardboard box, her cardboard box, with the sandwich, pushing it against her dead face, crying, 'Wake up! Please wake up! Please... look, I'll eat it. Look! It's good! Please wake up I'll find you something else to eat... and that sad boy sat on the floor, screaming at the body of a dead kitten, whose sleep you could not break."

Neddy sighed, hands shaking nervous, leg twitching, chest pains again *maybe it's time for another dose.*

"You can't drown me in morphine," the shadow said. "Unless you drink both bottles all the way down or load that gun up all the way. Then I'll disappear. You won't have to hear me in your head anymore. You wont have the pain and the nightmares and the conversations with Satan. Just peace and tranquility, eternal rest. A guy like you could use a bit of sleep."

Neddy looked at the guns on the table. He picked one up and aimed it at the shadow. The shadow laughed. Neddy looked in the chamber, one bullet, spin, click, spin, click, the shadow laughs. He picked up the other gun, spin, click, bang, a loud shot, through the shadow's chest, same mocking laughter. Neddy pushed the cards and bottles and guns off the table, walked over to the shadow, leaned in, face to face, and kissed the shadow's cheek, his eyes closed.

"I forgive you," Neddy said.

Neddy opened his eyes. The shadow had disappeared.

53. *Another Reflection in the Sea*

"Wake up," an old voice said. "You might have to take a leak. This is the last stop between here and Rose Hill."

Neddy blinked, opened his eyes, old face flooding in, bright day, a sleeping dog across from him on his suitcase. A momentary hallucination appeared, as though he could see the gun through the case.

He felt for the key on his neck, still there, relief. Neddy opened the case and took a large swig from one of the bottles, swished the syrupy taste around his mouth and swallowed, what warmth, *Amazing grace how sweet the taste that takes the pain away. Who do you want to be today? Neddy or some fantasy of yours? And you're kissing shadows now? What kind of pervert are you! A pervert in a drunken stupor is still a pervert no matter how you slice it. But a drunken pervert don't care.*

Neddy climbed out of the carriage onto the gravel sheltering his eyes from the sun. The loose rocks between his toes made him think of home.

"Figured I'd get something to eat while I can," the driver said. "You hungry?"

"I'm okay," Neddy said. "Not hungry... Ate..."

"The young girl told me to buy you food anyway, so if I'm going to oblige, and that's a good family, known them for a long time and that little girl takes good care of them, you gonna have to eat. So, what do you want?"

"Some grits, if it's not too much..."

"It's not too much. Do you want some toast with that and tea?"

Neddy withdrew, misunderstanding, trying to process the reason for the old man's kindness, not knowing how to react, he said: "I'll have what you're having."

"Something good!" he said. "They got fried chicken in there as good as mama's."

"I doubt it's that good," Neddy said. "I used to watch her make dinner when I was young. She'd have to cut off all the feathers, cut the bird up into little bits, and roll them around in white powder, don't know what it's called, but it made it crunchy. My daddy liked his burnt because it was harder to chew, and my father never backed down from a challenge."

A comforting old man's laugh, people shuffling by, yawning sun in its blood red hue with yellow halo.

"Be back in a second. You might want to see if you can get your dog, what's his name—"

"...Neddy."

"Yeah, see if you can get Neddy to go to the bathroom while we're stopped. You sleep okay? Your eyes 'a little red."

"A bit restless," Neddy said. "Kind of nervous."

"How can you be nervous about going home? That's the best place to be."

"Not when you're a dung beetle," Neddy said.

The old man laughed, pivoting, turned to walk into the rundown country store, streaked yellow vinyl siding, chipping paint, broken shutters, roof of spotted shingles black and brown.

Neddy looked at the lines and patterns seeing faces, fathers holding sons, cracked statues, intersecting dotted lines like nature's time hewn mazes, cracks and splinters narrow canyons full of dust.

Neddy remained by the carriage, the dog looking up at him. The old driver returned with a collar, saying, "You can put this on him if you'd like."

"He'll follow me," Neddy said. "Neddy's a good boy."

The driver disappeared again into the store. Neddy, with his shaggy dog, walked across the windswept gravel road to the edge of the woods. They walked slow along the tall grass and mosaic of yellow flowers, Neddy leading the dog deep into the woods.

"You either go now," Neddy said, looking the dog in the eyes, something Neddy never did when talking to people, "or you go when we get to Rose Hill. So since we don't know how long that 'a be, I'd just pee what I could right now. You wouldn't want to be trapped somewhere unable to pee again—unable to pee, would you? It'd get all over your pants. It's the right of every man and dog, so go ahead, my little man, I won't look."

Neddy averted his eyes when the dog raised his leg by a tree.

The deed done, they walked back to the carriage, grits and cole slaw, chicken and tea waiting for them beside Neddy's suitcase. Though his stomach rumbled, Neddy didn't eat, instead letting his mangy friend have his grits and cole slaw. Neddy took a few bites of bread and a bit of tea.

Neddy accepted them with shame, hiding his rose red cheeks, his glance forever downward as he walked, climbed into the carriage. The dog jumped in and they were off.

Medicine, he thought, *more, more, more...*

He drank the remaining liquid morphine from the bottle, a massive dose, and felt as though he was in Nirvana: all was calm and still, the torrent of words in his mind slowed to serenity of the pond.

Neddy thought about his mother as he sat there, memories flooding back, torrent of disjointed fragments, her smile, sadness, picking flowers in the garden, turning around, sun hat over her face, walks into the Master and Neddy's there and young. She cooks a turkey dinner, Christmas time, lights and bells and whistles and toy trains and plastic figurines of gingerbread houses on the table.

Neddy and his sister, just three at the time, were to eat dinner in the Master's house. His mother took care of their meals, washed their clothes and cleaned their house, and every line on every hour spent ran across her face imprinted stigmas, stigmas of the hours condensed, distress, her only son to grow up as a slave, the terrible thought of Galilee screaming by herself in the dark dark well, "Help me! Help me!"

Nobody can help you now.

Neddy saddened, took the revolver from the suitcase, dumped the bullets to the floor but one, loads the chamber, spun it. Spin, click, puts it to his brain, spin, click, a rush of adrenaline floods his bloodstream like lightning currents down a circuit board, exhilaration, as though he cheated death.

The anxiety, the chest pain, the tingling, the distress, came back in an instant, the instant the barrel slammed. He looked at the other bottle, suspicious eyes, *that warmth*, he thought, *what warmth for me, what consolation is there other than Mr. morphine? Do you know the morphine man, the morphine man, the morphine man? Do you know the morphine man? He lives on misery lane.*

And Neddy, felt the last dose fading, dragging him down into the real life again, lights too bright, the sun high in the sky, where Neddy had dragged himself into his own private hell and couldn't find his way out.

He had two ways, as he saw it: the bottle or the gun. When he reached into the suitcase, he chose the bottle, swigged it down and swirled it around, mmm it taste so good, scratched his belly, yawn, that feeling, synthetic Heaven washing by, *synthetic Heaven better than none*, he thought, *synthetic, maybe. Temporary, true. A moment's happiness is worth ten hours sadness, a day of laughter ten thousand days of misery.*

And Neddy, sitting in the back of the carriage, watching the shaggy dog eat his food, saw at once what he had to do.

He had questions, though, unanswered in his head, as to how he would go through with his plan.

"Rose Hill ain't too far now," the driver said. "'Bout thirty minutes or so from here."

Neddy decided to write Nirvana's requested poem, the opiate sea washing his scabs away.

We are the footprints by the Sea, he wrote, *the waters come and waters leave. Miss Sea, you see, your children taken: Children of the Sea forsaken.*

Oh see, oh Sea, miss Galilee, bring back what she took from me; bring back what you swallowed whole.

The yawning, old, and wide mouthed urn, lolled on, but never turned, her deaf ear, to me, to hear, my confused shouts at her.

Without a word at all to say, she waves at nighttime and the day. She rolls about within a dream, the carousel bye overhead, to it she turns her mirrored head. She simply looks to it, and all, and we, frail leaves, around her fall.

We are but footprints by the Sea; the waters come and then we leave. Miss Sea, you see, your children taken: Children of the Sea forsaken.

Ancient sea, miss Galilee, can you see yourself in me? As I see myself in you, glowing white and tinged with blue? Can't you see what you have done? The lolling Sea Saw none.

'I see,' I said, and that was that. I heard my own voice echo back. In those waters I saw me; just a reflection in the Sea.

This was after some years passed: I returned, sat in the grass, thinking of all who walked that shore. Never did I see her face a glass umbrella had replaced the girl whom I adored. My love would walk the shore no more. But nothing else, and nothing more, no more to God could I implore, or to the umbrella in her stead. The face of the mourning sun turned red. The glass umbrella from the Sea rolled ashore and laughed at me. Then I knew and saw it all inside the glass umbrella fall: I saw myself again alone, forever by the Sea to roam.

"On that day I watched her play, with birds about the shore. I heard her laugh and nothing more, as the sea came and took my love from me. Buzzards circled overhead like Nature's Garbage Men. I heard them call and heard her laugh and felt the kiss of Caiaphas.

A finch had washed up in her place, from the well amid the waste, who floundered by the Sea and then flew on. The bird fluttered for a moment and was gone.

Neddy's tears hit the page, smudging gone, but Neddy in his sadness wrote on:

As beautiful as the Sea might be, her own beauty she can't see. In my dreams, she comes to me, and sees her picture on the wall.

By my family, and me, a portrait of miss Galilee.

As wondrous as she looks at night, shimmering with the silver light, she looks sadder in the dark. When the sun shines in her face, bringing daylight in night's place, she yawns again and sighs. Children of the Sea walk home. Deaf miss Galilee rolls on.

Earlier in my life, I went, by a home that I could rent, I called my child to say: 'Come see me, come see the Sea. We'll have some lunch and drink ice tea. You have to come; you have to see—the face of lady Galilee'

A while we stood where lolled the waves under a sky where seagulls played. For her my world for once to see—the face of lady Galilee. From the waters, walked ashore, played a while, bonne nuit amore. She splashed about the waves my child... and then she splashed no more.

Must be the drugs, Neddy thought, making excuses for crying over his own *pathetic,* as he thought, *attempts at poetry. If only I could write her like father, or that Khayyam man.*

Neddy turned the page, fresh page, wrote:

I remember she walked in. We had some sandwiches, and then, hand in hand walked with a grin. She laughed the day away. She wore a blue dress, made of lace, and had a smile upon her face.

At night she walks my dreams this way, for when she splashed, that faithful day, the Sea took her away. The waters drowned my living dream and left me here to stay.

Neddy could not write, difficult to concentrate, images flashing before his eyes, the torrent of internal babbling doubling the volume and speed, heart racing, he took more morphine and he wrote:

The Sea looked into me, you see, and saw what she could take from me. My dreams could not just let it be. And when it looked at me, it saw, the same thing when it looks at all.

How could she tells me what she sees? The way she sees us all go 'round she often speaks without a sound. She hears us dance, and hears us call, all at once, but not at all—the glass umbrella falls.

We are footprints by the Sea. The waters come and waters leave. Miss Sea, you see, your children taken: Children of the Sea forsaken.

Neddy experienced a moments peace, before the driver said, "We'll be there in ten minutes."

Neddy did not respond. He pretended to be asleep. And when they pulled up at the gate, he was, and standing in front of 'Vana and the elevator.

"Going up?" she asked.

Neddy emptied his pockets, two chips, revolver, dictionary, pen, paper. He emptied all the bullets, all but one, spun the chamber, put it to his head, cold metal against dry skin in the cold. He thought about writing and put the gun down, writing:

My 'Vana,

You can love me or like me, but don't forget me, not you, not this page, don't ever let me write the word goodbye, at least the paper will never let the idle pen to commit that sin again. I'm playing games with my life, two poker chips, chamber spinning clicking in the dark. Chamber click. Chamber spin. I can't find the mask, and who else but you could see, the miserable little bleeding brain the I inside defines the Me. Poker chips and rusted flakes of blood in pale ears coagulate, my brain is bleeding, a tear the brain is trying to cry. I sometimes think my mind wants my body to die. I'm spinning a gun. If there's a God, it'll just say click and nobody will find this page with no ending and blood splattered on the page.

There is no place to drink, no mountain where happiness is free. Happiness is impossible. I'd kill myself without thinking if I knew it'd make somebody happy, or even laugh. It's hard to suffer when you laugh...

He looked at the open dictionary, a word illumined by the stainglass painting of a pointing hand—the word was Galilee.

Galilee, noun: 1. The Sea of Galilee, also called Lake Tiberias, a lake in Israel. 2. A region of northern Israel. 3. The northernmost part of Palestine and the ancient Kingdom of Israel, the center of the teachings of Jesus Christ.

He went back to writing:

It's me, Nobody, the words are worms like me, though maybe if I'm lucky, they'll squirm into living funeral flowers, living things trying not to die, just to never say goodbye. When that bye comes look at the page, whose the bars lock in the slave, the pencil marks the jailor's bars. I paint what I see say bye and I try to do it for you, like your father did. I know my silliness isn't as good as his was, but if I don't write I'll probably play that game again.

The brain alone will try to cry when the brittle body dies. I don't even know if you'll ever read this, what I wish could be some bouquet of words that smell like empathy. If I could have one wish, I'd wish for empathy, for empathy for myself. The brain wouldn't cry through my pen. That's what I'd get myself for me and I wouldn't even accept it. I don't know who I'm addressing, probably Nobody, writing in the dark.

The tear of the bleeding brain will like all shadow shapes like dying ships sail by and again they pass on by, by us and languid laugh they go past invisible dead who had to die never understanding the largest word Why, the silence, the voice of God, the whisper of the wind is the lonely dead men trying to cry as those they love whom cannot hear the invisible ghosts who try to shout in their ear to not be heard. Don't forget me, they scream. That's what I'd scream anyway. That or I'm sorry for wasting your time with me. Amazing Grace I've seen that face, sometimes I say bye to empty rooms and bye will echo back. The grace amazing, hey, alone, can't think of a word. The pen will write alone and ask me to explain this goodbye song before I play again the game that could wipe away the tears of the brain for good.

The goodbye song, about the brain that tried to bleed, the blood is what you hear and read. My brain's blood turns into a scribbled page that perhaps nobody will ever read. Behind the lines, the words, I sign my name, the slave Nobody on the hill named Rose. I'll play God for my life and see who wins, because of my debt to the Word.

Attrition anathema sacrifice offering to God if the trigger ends, my small debt to nothing is paid.

They all bow to the page or something else. Go on old man and bow yourself. Bow to yourself. No. I will bow before God and only in person. You're a ridiculous little circus act type, did you know that? Why am I still telling myself to ignore me? Just say bye and write the last line maybe, if chance is o my side, if the chamber doesn't end my bubble by the wave.

Neddy stood, dictionary open, dropped a chip.

Chamber spin click.

Neddy dropped the other chip.

Chamber spin click.

Pen clenched in his teeth with a screaming mind as the chamber spun and echoed in the dark and Neddy added another bullet, writing on the other side of the page:

I'm glad you never said goodbye to me. It would have broke my heart. No such thing as goodbye...that's a damn lie. It should always be farewell.

Chamber spin click.

Neddy's chest convulsed and a wave of black swallowed him, fell to the floor unconscious, head slamming against the dusty lines and the footprint of ants.

The silhouette of the crucifix ran down Neddy's sleeping stomach, gun still clinched in his ashy hands the thin lines of tears cleansing the ash on his face.

54. *No Tombstone for Hope*

The elevator creaked open, blinding the light spilled in. Neddy and 'Vana stepped into the shade of a sunlit valley. There were children, all of them with tiny wings, running, laughing, playing, going around and around on merry-go-rounds, Ha, ha, ha...

He saw Galilee in a garden, by herself, picking flowers as she walked, kneeling in her blue dress, plucking them, stuffing them into the waistband of her dress, nobody to give them to, Neddy thought.

He walked up behind her, saying, "Boo!"

She jumped, turned, saw Neddy, laughed.

"Neddy!" she said. "I've been waiting for you. I picked some flowers for you."

She took one from her waistband. "Here you go," she said, "this is the biggest one."

He accepted it with some reluctance, being startled by the feel of her warm hands on his frigid fingers, and, with rose red cheeks, put it in his back pocket.

He followed her until the sun was halfway through the sky. They left the garden heading North, the Mansion looming in the distance, now a tinted, tainted white, beige and old and rusted at the iron gates. They approached the mansion from the back door, by way of the maze. Galilee stood at the entrance to the maze with some trepidation, her little feet turning on her tiptoes inward, biting her bottom lip.

"Don't worry," Neddy said. "Just follow me. I'll show you the way."

Galilee smiled and took his hand, entering the archway of the maze, zigzagging through the perfect trim of hedges and ivy, rose bushes at each turning point, white roses, red roses, black roses.

They made it to the center of the maze where the angel with its broken wing once stood and, in its place, found the statue complete and shining, a marble grey glow about its lustrous wings.

They sat there together on the bench, holding hands, not talking, smiling, Neddy looking at the ground. A ladybug landed on Galilee's arm. Neddy reacted, attempting to squish it, and Galilee turned her bare shoulder, protecting the ladybug.

"No!" Galilee said. "Don't hurt him. He's a friend of mine."

"Thought they called them ladybugs because they were girls?"

"There are boy and girl ladybugs," Galilee said. "This one is a boy. His name is Sammy. You know, he's a good guy, brings food home for his family. He's a good daddy."

"Where's our daddy?" Neddy asked. He looked toward the field, expecting to see a field of slaves, and saw no one there, no one but pale grey hues of people toiling away.

"He's at home reading," she said. "Let's get something to eat."

She stood up.

"Are you going to show me the way?" she asked.

Neddy stood, "Of course," he said. He extended his hand, her tiny fingers wrapping around, and led her out of the maze, out to the spot where he once leaned against the wall; a shadow appeared, leaning against the cement with a shovel in shaking hands. Neddy blinked and it was gone, replaced by the reflection of him and Galilee holding hands. Neddy smiled, walked toward the steps, and up, up onto the veranda.

The Master was sitting in his chair on the porch, overlooking the landscape of playing children, chubby grin on his face.

"Maze looks nice," the Master said. "You've done some good work out there, Neddy."

"I'm a good boy," Neddy said.

"Yeah, good boy, there's dinner on the table if ya hungry. Just go on in and ask Paula to fix you a plate."

"Thank you, sir," Neddy said. The master nodded.

Neddy and Galilee entered the kitchen, sat at the table, the Master's wife bustled in the room, shackles around her lily white arms, a bowl of grits with butter, chick and a cut of ham, loaf of bread, pitcher of iced tea.

Neddy looked at Paula's shackles, saddened; he felt for the key around his neck, found it, unlocked Paula's shackles. She smiled, bowed, and took empty plates away.

Neddy and Galilee ate for a while and, as the sun went down, Neddy had trouble concentrated.

"The food is real good," Galilee said. "You like your ham?"

"The best I've ever had," Neddy said. "Would you like to walk the nature trail with me?"

"Of course, Neddy," she said. "I don't want to be out after dark, though, I can't see that well in the dark."

"I want you to follow me," Neddy said. "When we're done eating, I'd like to show you something. It's something I have to do."

They finished their meals, cleaned their plates, finished the pitcher of tea. Neddy led her out the door, down the cement stairs, under the archway through the maze, behind the mansion, under clotheslines by the empty slave cabins, to the woods, through the trail, a turn toward Tyger river.

They walked together hand in hand into the clearing, a moonlit blue circle enclosed by trees, where he once with 'Vana; the nooses hung from the trees, nobody hanging from them, and all the graves were empty. Dirty footprints led away from the graves, the graves themselves looked as though they had been dug up from the ground, as though all the slaves once buried had clawed their way to the surface and escaped the silent holes in the ground. There was no tombstone for hope. Stunned, Neddy and Galilee walked home through the woods, Neddy leading Galilee by her tiny hands in the thickness of the country dark, shortcut to the cabins, in and out of creek-beds, twisted trees and elms a carpet made of leaves.

What of the grave for Hope?

Neddy's father was sitting in a chair, bible in his hand, a content smile on his face. An angel carved from wood sat atop a stack of rags beside him. His work boots were off, his feet without calluses or blisters.

"Been taking some time off," his father said. "Trying to get some relaxation done around here. And with two kids and a wife, relaxation is a rare white elk."

Neddy and Galilee smiled. They sat in a circle by the barrel of coal, slow rolling flames the embers popped and dance the wall goes up, wall of fire, and Neddy looked inside the flame again, seeing nothing but a reflection of himself.

Neddy's mother was asleep on her coat on the floor, her hair perfect kempt, no frays, no large drooping sad type bags under worried eyes, a peaceful sleep she smiled out loud with rose red blushing cheeks.

"Ain't it about time for you kids to go to bed?" Neddy's father asked. "Your mom keeps yelling at me, telling me, 'You're letting them stay up late again, Ray!'"

"Yes, sir," Neddy said. Neddy didn't see his uncle, but saw his hat, "Out on the boat," Ray said. "The catfish are really bitin' this time 'a year. We'll have some in the morning."

"Can we play one last game of cards?" Neddy asked. "Blackjack—you deal."

Ray stood up with slow, deliberate movements, took a deck of cards out from under his cot, shuffled and down them out, one face up for each, one face down.

Neddy's facing card was an ace of spades. The card underneath was a suicide King. Neddy's father showed an ace of hearts, the other card a jack of spades.

Neddy fumbled about in his pockets, looking for his chips. His father took out for, divided them, handed two to Neddy.

"Hit or stay?" Ray asked.

"I'll stay," Neddy said. "And you?"

"I'll stay as well," he said. He put his two chips on the dusty floor. Neddy matched his bet. They each turned their cards over.

"A tie," Ray said. "We both get to keep our money."

"Let's play just one more," Neddy said. Again the same cards were dealt, same bets were made, same end result, over and over, never winning, never losing until Neddy could barely hold his eyes open, feeling relaxed. He put the two chips in his pocket.

Ray put out the light, stirred the barrel of coal and fire, and Neddy lay down with Galilee, sharing a bed with her again. He put his cold feet to her warm legs. She jumped.

"Your feet are so cold!" she said, laughing, "You startled me!"

"I'm sorry," he said, withdrawing his feet, ashamed.

"No need to be sorry," she said, turning over, putting her warm legs on his freezing toes, "I don't mind when it comes to you, Neddy."

Neddy's father began reading, some Bible verse, and Galilee fell asleep, her warmth breath against Neddy's rigid chest and ribs.

Neddy's father read: Give, and it shall be given to you. What you have given others, is what you'll be dealt in turn."

Neddy pretended to be asleep and when his father was done reading, he pulled the covers up to his son's neck, all the while knowing and smiling.

"Goodnight, son," he said, kissing him on the cheek. "I love you, son."

And Neddy thought, *You shouldn't, but I love you too.*

55. *The Grave of Yesterday*

"Wake up, young sir," the driver said. "We're here."

Neddy rubbed the sleep crust out of his eyes, blinking, bringing the man's drooping face and furrowed, knotted brows into focus, dark dark eyes behind a web of wrinkles.

They were stopped in front of the Iron Gate, now less shiny and rusted, the top of the dingy white mansion towering over the trees.

"I have a letter for you," Neddy said. He put his poem for Nirvana in an envelope, writing down her address.

"Can you give this to 'Vana for me?" he asked. "I'm not sure how to mail it."

"Yes, young sir," he said. "But it doesn't have a return address or a name..."

"She'll know who it's from," Neddy said.

The old man took the note, stuffed it in his inside pocket, grabbed Neddy's suitcase. Neddy grabbed the suitcase too, taking it away with force. Neddy's forever happy tail wagging dog jumped from the cart onto the gravel blanket driveway toward the slave quarters.

Neddy took the key from around his neck, unlocked the suitcase, "Can you give me a second?" he asked. "I need to change shirts."

There were bloodstains on the midsection of Neddy's dirty white shirt.

"Yes, young sir," the old man said. "I'll get the gate open for us."

Neddy took a hearty swig from the other brown bottle, swished it around again and again in his mouth, mmm, it was tasty. Neddy's hands trembling he stepped out of the carriage. Neddy took the revolver from his case as well, loading it, filling every bullet slot.

He put on a clean white shirt, some pants, got all the dirt and grit out from under his nails, trying to wipe the shame off with a damp wash towel.

He saw a group of people entering the front gate, some with strange devices in their hands, and the place had changed, barely resembling what Neddy remembered.

Neddy blended in with the crowd, walked down the dusty driveway toward the cabins and, expecting to find slaves, found nothing but empty preserved artifacts around which a few people stood with strange machines that flashed. All the slaves were gone, and every where Neddy looked he expected to see slaves but couldn't, just the vague grey shapes of slaves in the field, a brief hallucination.

"Where are you going?" he asked a young girl with one of those strange devices. "I've been here a few times. I used to hunt Easter eggs here with my church."

"What's your name?" she asked.

"Nobody, really," Neddy said. The photographer laughed. "My name is Elise. I need some help, though."

"What could I help you with?" Neddy asked.

"I don't know where to go, exactly," she said. "I'm taking some pictures for a friend of mine. He's writing a novel about a murder that took place here, and I'm his photographer."

"What's that machine do?" Neddy asked.

"It's a camera," she said. "It's new; it captures images and lets you preserve things you see."

"If you want to get the right shots, just follow me," Neddy said. "I know my way around. I'll show you where to get the best pictures."

Neddy took her to the front steps of the mansion, now a different place, showing her exactly where the Master died. There were free people everywhere in strange clothes, no slaves, just people in green shorts and shirts standing around, talking and walking with groups of people.

They walked together toward the maze, stood for a moment under the ivy archway. The photographer hesitated, looking at the corridors of grass.

"Come on," he said. "I'll show you the way."

He took her through the maze, to the broken angel statue, the tree under which he once read his father's dictionary when he could, the twisted branches spread above him.

The plantation house was unfamiliar to him: the white house not quite as bright, empty cabins where slaves once slept stood obsolete machines covered in spider webs, the maze much shorter than he remembered.

"Let me show you the trail," he said, thinking about his fake grave, hoping to be able to find it.

They walked down the hill away from the mansion and onto the trail, a sign pointing toward the leave strewn path through the woods.

The maze was shorter, too, than he remembered, but he found his old grave stone halfway down the trail. There were fresh flowers on the grave, as though put there recently, causing him some surprise. Neddy looked at the chipped away stone and his poorly etched in name, still no last name, still came the same short of shame.

"Did you know him?" the photographer asked, standing behind him, taking a picture of the grave and the frail yellow jasmines and roses that leaned against the cement stone.

"No," Neddy said. "And that's what makes me mourn."

They stood together in silence for a moment, halfway through the trail, before deciding to walk on, back to the mansion. Neddy still held tight to his suitcase, the key still dangled on his neck, the pistol in his waistband full of bullets.

As they walked the rest of the way, Neddy came across two red shapes, two poker chips, encrusted in mud and damp. He licked the inside of his shirt and washed the dirt off them, put them in his pocket.

"Let's go to the mansion," the photographer suggested. "I'd like to get some interior shots."

"And there's an old friend of mine I'd like to see," Neddy said.

"An old friend?" she asked. "What's his name?"

"Thomas," Neddy said. "I don't think he's going to be too happy to see me."

56. *The Make Believe Ballroom*

A familiar face and middle aged, black eyelids, un-slept, met Neddy and the photographer at the top of the hill in front of the mansion. Neddy could not place his face.

"How can I help you?" he asked. He assumed Neddy was the photographer's slave and shrugged it off.

"Well," the photographer said, "I have a friend who is writing a book about this place and I need to take some photographs of the mansion. Would I be able to do that?"

"Where would you have to be?"

"My young friend here knows all the spots. He used to work here. He says he'll be able to show me where they are."

"Do you need to go inside the house?" the man asked.

Neddy thought of the portraits of the Master's happy family, hugging and kissing and Christmas time birthday cake and candles.

"No, sir," he said. "We wouldn't have to go inside. Just to the maze, the cabins, the trail, and the garden."

"Well," the man said, "just don't leave any trash. You can take all the pictures you want."

"Thanks," the photographer said. "We won't be long."

"Yeah ya welcome just don't leave any trash," the man said.

"We won't," photographer said.

"Also," Neddy said, low, almost unintelligible, "Where is the owner?"

The man looked him over.

"Thomas," Neddy said. "Alexander's son. I grew up here."

"Thomas committed suicide after his parents were murdered. That's what they say anyway. The mansion was left un-owned, and now it's just a tourist attraction. Nobody really knows what happened here. All the slaves just went up North, there wasn't nobody here to make 'em work.

And all the slaves were free...

"How old was he?" Neddy asked.

"'I went hunting with Alex, ate dinner with his family sometimes, you know, not too often. I think Tommy, that's what his daddy called him I—he was twenty-one when he died."

"What's your name?" Neddy asked the man.

"Nobody, really," said the man. "I just work here."

He turned and walked away. Neddy wondered for a moment, then said, "I'm 'bout to have to leave," Neddy said. "We can take some pictures whenever you get back. Bring the writer and I'll show you where everything happened. I was that slave. It was me. He was talking about me. Tell your writer friend I'll meet him here on Sunday and I'll tell him what happened... if that would help you get your photographs. I'm a writer myself. I write poems. Most of them are in my head and I haven't really written them down, but I'd still like to talk to a real writer. I've never met one."

"You know," she said, "I think he'd love to meet you. If you're telling me the truth, he has to."

"Then be here Sunday," Neddy said. "They hold Sunday service here every Sunday night and we can get your pictures before the church crowd arrives. They're going to hunt Easter eggs then eat and then gather to sing and pray. They do it every year at Easter time."

"I'll be here at eight," she said. Neddy didn't understand what she meant.

"I don't know what eight refers to," Neddy said. "I'll be here sometime after the sun comes up but before it's halfway through the sky. Before lunch time."

"Okay," she said. "That sounds great."

"Do you have any books?" Neddy asked, looking at her bag. "All I've had is this dictionary for a while. It's my favorite book, but I would like to read something else."

"I have, hmm," she reached into the bag, "the collected works of Shakespeare and ... hmm, that's it."

"It's better than nothing," Neddy said. "Could I borrow it? I'll bring it back on Sunday. I'll read it tonight."

"Sounds good," she said. "Goodbye."

"I don't like that word," Neddy said. "They call it goodbye, when it's not a good bye."

She smiled. "What would you prefer?"

"Farewell," Neddy said. "That better elucidates the articulation of my thought pattern regarding parting. I dislike parting, because then I'm left by myself and that's never good."

"I know how you feel," she said. "I have to leave. Farewell."

"I hope we do," Neddy said. She turned around and left. He thought of 'Vana on the bridge. He wondered where his shaggy dog Neddy went, the comfort of his company missed.

The photographer left and Neddy went back to Galilee church, just a ways South of the Hill, to sleep and return the next time the photographer planned to visit the mansion.

Neddy fought his way through the too tall grass as the ragged old church came into focus amid the trees and brush and kudzu that stretched into the sky.

The church, Neddy remembered, empty confessional, angel Gabriel carved in stone, all boarded up, in ruins beautiful, as though part of mother Earth, natural and elegant, sagging under gravity's giant thumb.

He opened his suitcase, and, not knowing what he could do or what he should do or if he should do anything, Neddy decided to write 'Vana another poem.

How would she get it? Give it to the photographer. She's ruined, too, just like you, a broken machine, who, she is, who is she, the girl with the strange device that intrigued you so. Just ask her to look at it. You might even get to stroke your ego when she compliments the work later but she'll really be pretending to like it because she doesn't want you to be sad, not knowing that would make you sadder. She's different. How do you know that? Because she's like me. What type of person am I?

What could I have done with my life, what could I have done to find my way to Heaven in the end? Should I have locked for Heaven on the Earth or wait until we pass through that other gate, that gate I fear goes nowhere says the great divide Neddy inside said and replied the great divide is you.

The great divide is me, three minds, Neddy, that shadow Nobody, that Demon in the depths of Dis that chews on my head is me, my punishment inflicted by the judge of me, myself, though hesitant knows, what does it matter though?

Are you living for the now for once Neddy? The grave of yesterday is more comforting than now. More comfort? You've been to Heaven. You just didn't see it when it passed.

Heaven and hell are alive on the earth, no fairytale, feelings of bliss and great despair, heaven and hell right there, my private hell, maze I made for me to forever run, I created it and couldn't pull myself out.

I dug the graves over and over and wanted to jump in every time and stay, all for Anathema, my life, two chips, the chips are on the table.

He took his revolver from the small of his back, swigging casually at the bottle now, languid, melancholy stupor.

Just one bullet, God, Neddy thought. He placed a chip on the altar. He opened the revolving chamber of the gun, bullets spilling, all but one, Neddy's hand collected others as they fell.

What are the stakes? he wondered. *What is there to lose? What is there to win? If I lose the game, I'll write another poem for Nirvana. And if you lose?*

I'll go to hell. Go to hell? You're in hell right now. Sitting there shaking with that revolver in one hand that morphine bottle in the other you need to relax and try to calm down. Life is tough at times. You don't have to react with aversion, just react and learn, and know what you can change and if for the better you can change it change it but fret not what you do, but what you don't. Put the gun to your head old man, you got the balls?

Neddy began to feel tired, his body aching, feeling as though he was an old old man, perhaps ten thousand years, though in our time twenty three, lay his life on the line for a poem at that Church named Galilee.

He put the revolver to his head

Spin the chamber closes click.

Energy gathered in Neddy's fingers and legs in intense frequency then ran all at once to the center of his chest and he was unplugged from time, his body frozen in the moment, his mind in a timeless state outside, wandering off, the body frozen like the statue Gabriel, patterns in the ivy, mazes, ants and bees and bullets bottles shovels blood blood blood was red was dead was idle turned off where does the me inside go when the body cannot move, does the poor suffering mind sit in absolute dark without light in a grave forever unable to see the light of the Sun again.

Neddy regained feeling in his body, his mind relaxing a bit. He shuddered, a cold chill passing over him. He collected the chip and took another swig out of the brown bottle, the bottle getting low, all almost gone, he lay down his stomach, opening the collected works of Shakespeare. Four hours later Neddy was done. It had inspired him to write, and, taking out the pen and paper, thought of the bet. *Guess I lost...*

For you, again, Nirvana. I flipped a coin and decided if I lost I would write a poem. It's not going to be great, but there might be parts in it you like. I hope so, anyway, because at least I'll try. I'd rather try and fail than never try. One Summer in the Sun, by another Nobody.

He paused for a moment, took out his now ragged yellow paged dog-eared dictionary, looked through it for a while, then prepared the pen and paper, bearing down on a Bible as he wrote:

Sweet candle in the music box, spotlight upon our show, light the paths which once were dark glow. So ballerinas in the box will know which way to go.

For their summer in the sun, one yawn before the winter's breath, a ring of smoke blown through the gates of no where. And life, the beautiful nothing, a candle for its own sake lit, begins to blur, to fade, another song the record played. Once so loud, and now a drawl, becomes a whisper in the hall.

Once to live and wonder why, to rise and fall under the sky. Summer rises. Summer sets. One summer in the sun is all we get.

The sun will smile. The sun will fade: a single dash, between two dates, poor written by the Hands of Fate.

One moment caught inside a bulb, our destined hour to abide, with other living things trapped inside—lighting but a moment, as dust upon the desert's dusty face, glimmer in the hall and go their way.

One after another, into the sky for miles, a blind caretaker with a hammer forever walks the aisles. His calloused feet to scratch the path to on occasion tap the glass—releasing light back to the air to Saturn's seat without a care.

Destiny behind her veil will play, with all lost vessels on the waves. Slaves to the lighthouse, in the rain, miss Destiny the ball and chain. Until she folds and counts her pay, and, in silence, walks away.

No more moments from the box to take from the fountain by the waste. Life, brief candle, one summer in the sun. Tomorrow and tomorrow then there are none.

Life, itself, a momentary scream, amidst the sea of nowhere gleamed, a murmur in the ivy by the well, one verse in the Narrator's Book of Tales.

The title of our story is 'One summer in the Sun.' Tomorrow and tomorrow and they are done. One chance to bloom, one chance to shine, to rise and fall under the sky.

One summer in the sun in winters way—a brief season our life's passage does delay. All of those who to the light have went, when their Pocket Watch of Time is spent, like moths turn brittle in the air and silent strike the ground. The sun rises. The sun sets. A summer in the sun and that is it.

The finish line, same as the start, oh what a Nobody has in his heart. A thousand roads to nowhere, lost highways to the sun. The finish line is the same place the Human Race begun. And in that race together, we all finish last; the faceless watchers in the crowd recline their heads and laugh.

Again and again the figures spin in desperate circles round and round. Sometimes they brush against each other, but seldom make a sound. And blind they pass each other by, in the tempest tossed around.

Before the blind man, with his hammer, turns to face your aisle, laugh with the best of them and smile. This is just graffiti scrawled on time's unending wall, by no one left for Nobody, a fragment in the stall.

Tangles in the Earth's coiffure, for life our limited time offer. The human condition the same Remains, never heals and stays the same.

Another verse, another song, like an old time sing-along, by pebbles lost in sand and foam who sing alone and murmur make while they their ride on the carousel take.

And then they sleep, once more to dream—of all the things that went by the screen: patterns in the ivy and their seams, an arabesque oft wove before of those who run blind on the shore. With all of them on their way to see, the magic man for empathy. The highway is long, how awful to know: the door at the end of the road is closed.

So let the hands wind up another song for the music box. And let the shadow shapes around candle dance till the melody stops.

By candlelight or dark of night, their path forever paved; every second of the lives the same sad song is played.

Again and again the figurines spin, a lullaby loud for no one to hear, turns static into silence, fades, as dust upon a mirror.

Another poor player whose hour forgot the passionate words on the stage. Another soliloquy the sound and the fury, bit player lines erased. Characters live and characters lie. Some do nothing and instead wonder why. All of them are together lost, together to laugh and to cry.

Some of them love and some of them hate. Some look out, some in. For a moment fleeting contact made another to begin. There's no such thing as yesterday, no tomorrow, and no then: just a now that never ends.

Exhausted, Neddy fell asleep, splayed out over the used pages the bottle and the pen still in his hands.

You took too much, a voice said.

You took too much and now you're dead. Nobody knows where you're at. Your little poems should be burnt.

Neddy ignored the negative voice as it shouted insults at him in his head. His mind was released, crawl out his head, floated to the ceiling, stuck again, rolled over out the window into the mouth of a man in an empty suit on a bench.

Neddy looked to the left. Neddy looked to the right. Not a thing in sight. So he sat there for a while, no memory, just words, with two chips in his hands.

The blind man on the carriage pulled up.

"Where would you like to go?" the carriage driver asked. "Do you have the money?"

Neddy in the other body nodded, handed the driver the coins, and refused to get in.

"Tell the next passenger, the next person you find on this bench—tell them the ride's been paid for. Tell them it's already taken care of, that they don't need the money; I want to pay for their trip. But don't tell them who left it."

The carriage drove off.

And Neddy wandered on.

Neddy saw a glowing door, hearing lively music and conversation, not too far away. A sign outside read *The Make Believe Ballroom.*

Neddy went inside to find a young girl in a blue dress waiting by herself under a chandelier, her face a downward glance, a jasmine in her hand long dead. He didn't recognize the face but smiled, eyes alight.

"I told you I would wait," she said.

Another group of people appeared in between them, dancing, holding hands, kisses on the neck, biting each other's ears, shaking their hands and legs. Neddy found his way to a seat. The girl sat across from him, on the other side of the dancing crowd, and Neddy saw her through the cracks of arms and moving crowd, wanting to ask her to dance. Every time he saw her face he saw a smile, unable to move, his stare transfixed unblinking, twelve feet away from happiness.

57. *Easter Sunday*

Neddy was waiting at the entrance of the maze when the photographer with her strange device walked up. A tall, timid looking fellow in a strange suit followed behind her, looking at his feet as he walked, hair unkempt, dirty clothes and broken glasses.

The photographer had on a green long-sleeved shirt and black pants, high heel boots, her hair pulled back, professional like.

"This is my friend," she said. "His name is Roger."

"So, you're a writer?" Roger asked.

"Not much, sir, just silly poems. I don't think I have time to write a full novel though."

"You were here when Alexander was murdered?" Roger asked. "If so, I'd really like to have a chat with you."

"A chat about what?" Neddy asked.

"What happened here when you lived here," Roger said. "It might be valuable information for my novel."

"How much do you want to know?"

"Everything," Roger said. "That's a goal of mine, you see, to know everything."

"I'll tell you what I remember."

"Is there somewhere we can sit and talk?"

"Yeah," Neddy said. "Follow me."

They walked to the twisted trees by the bench, writer sitting down, the photographer setting up her equipment. The writer brought out a bound book of empty pages and a fountain pen, leaning forward on the bench to write as Neddy told his story

They talked for several hours, Neddy detailing what he remembered the most, the accident, the well, his family, his sister, Nirvana and his dreams of hell and heaven and in between, and the writer took down notes.

"And last night, playing that game, that game of chance with the gun," Neddy said, continuing the story, "I thought about writing a suicide letter, but I knew such a letter would make 'Vana sad. I lay there for a while trying to sleep, unable, until my dog woke me up. I hadn't seen him for a while, and he's been a friend of mine for a long time now. His name is Neddy."

"And you've never told me your name," Roger said.

"Because I don't have one," Neddy said. "I had one and I threw it away and I've been looking in trash cans for it ever since."

"Can you show us the locations where all of this took place?"

Neddy led them amid the clusters of tourists and laughing

children chasing each other in the meadow picking flowers, looking for Easter eggs, eating hot dogs, drinking iced tea.

He showed them his cabin, where once he lived, where now sat a rusted cotton gin covered in dust and cobwebs, tourists made to stand behind a rope to the look at the machine, *never knowing,* Neddy thought, *never knowing that once a thousand forlorn faces walked, where now walk all these new faces from different places walking smiling children blooming flowers in the field.*

They'll turn into ghosts, Neddy thought.

Neddy led them down the nature trail, the photographer snapping pictures, the writer taking notes.

The nature trail, once so precise and trimmed was overran with weeds and obscured. Neddy scratched at his stomach, feeling the scabs from the night before, must 'a scratched in my sleep. It's the junk, man. You got that junkie itch. Don't you need another dose? Left it at the church, and where's the key?

He saw the man from the day before, the man who somehow looked familiar, like the Master younger. Then he realized it was Thomas, putting flowers on his fake grave. The photographer snapped a few pictures of the man knelt by the grave.

Neddy turned around, "This way," he said. "This is as far as I can go. Let me show you the maze."

The sun was going down. The tourists and the guests with their children gathered on the porch to sing. Then men held transparent glasses of teas and ice iridescent with the lantern's light, reflections of smiles on children's faces, snap went the , recording those lights and line, little dresses, little suits, their Sunday best, the best smiles worn they could.

The crowd began to disappear into the mansion, to the den for evening supper. They walked up the steps to the veranda, Neddy standing in the same place where he stood so long ago, nothing but his shadow where the puddle of blood once shone back his face.

The photographer took the photographs, writing taking note, Neddy standing there remote, idle again in a different age where everywhere he saw a slave and then the medicine in his veins a slave to it a slave till the end then you're free. There's a gun in at suitcase at Galilee.

"There's a church I went to when I left," Neddy said. "Would you like to take some pictures there?"

Medicine medicine medicine medicine brown bottle yum I know you're good here daddy comes.

"It's not too far of a walk from here."

The writer looked at the photographer, as though unsure.

"Can we make it back in time for dinner?" she asked. "It's an hours drive back to my house... as long as we can get there and back in time for dinner I can go."

"It won't take long," Neddy said. "Maybe thirty minutes. I just need to get my suitcase."

"You're living at the church?" the writer asked. "How long have you been staying there?"

"I have no idea," Neddy said. "Seems like a long time. I wrote a poem there."

"I'd like to read it," Roger said. "Your education has been the dictionary and Shakespeare. I am sure you're a wise young man."

Neddy laughed a fake laugh forcing a fake smile made eye contact ashamed turned his face away.

"I have your book," Neddy said, taking the dictionary out at first, then checking the other pocket, found it, took it. "Here you go."

"Thank you," the photographer said.

She took a few external shots, a few inside, the author making notes, abandoned pews, dead hymnbooks long closed, shadow of Christ dead on the floor.

"What do you have in your bag?" Neddy asked the writer.

"A typewriter."

"Could I use it to write a letter to someone?"

"Sure. I'll set it up for you."

"I want to send this poem and this letter to a girl but I don't know how to do that. How do you do that? If you could mail them for me I would appreciate it."

"Can I read the poem?" the writer asked.

"Yeah," Neddy said. "Just don't read the letter."

"We have a deal."

Neddy sat at the typewriter, his suitcase open, the second morphine bottle emptied. Mmm, again, the veins they sang as he began his letter *My Nirvana...*

Neddy put the letter in the envelope, licked it, sealed it shut. Neddy waited until the two artists were distracted and Neddy got his chips, his revolver, loaded it with one bullet, put the rest in his pocket.

"Are you ready for dinner?" Neddy asked. "I have all I need."

"We're ready when you are," the writer said.

Neddy handed him the poem, *One Summer in the Sun,* and his

letter to Nirvana.

"But there's no return address," the photographer said.

"She'll know who it's from," Neddy said. "Lets go get something to eat."

He smiled at scratched his belly as they walked. *Work is never finished, Master got me workin', someday Master set me free.*

The sun was going down when they arrived back at the mansion. Everyone was gathered inside now, someone playing a piano, Nocturne in C# minor, Friedrich Chopin. A group sat at the kitchen table laughing, eating, drinking, listening to the music. Others stood around the broad walls watching the kids each eat their candy and go through their easter baskets finding eggs and toys and candy.

The writer and the photographer walked in the house, and Neddy, hesitating, stayed on the porch, Thomas in the corner of his eye in the kitchen.

Oh god, Neddy said, *he's seen me.* Thomas rose and ran to the door. Roger stepped out of the way. The door flung open. Neddy stood on the porch holding the gun, barrel open.

"Neddy!" Thomas shouted.

Chamber spins closes click.

Neddy added another bullet, dropped a chip at his feet.

Chamber spun closed went click again.

"I forgive you, Neddy," Thomas said. "I forgive you!"

Neddy's smile turned to a frown. All of the guests and concerned children had gathered at the front door. *Oh God,* they thought as Neddy filled the chamber, one bullet after another until it was full. *Oh God...*

"No!"

And now another flower in the field will *lay its head back onto the garden where once it lay in bed.*

Chamber spin click END.

58. *The Wretched Word Goodbye*

"'Vana!" an old voice called. "You got another letter!"

Nirvana put her earrings in, combed her hair, looked at the mirror, took a breath walked down the stairs.

"Who is it from?" she asked.

"It don't have a return address," the old voice said.

Nirvana knew at once who it was from. She opened the letter on the top first, *One Summer in the Sun,* then looked at the letters under. A chill ran over her skin when she saw the one on top. She opened it expecting Neddy's distinct left handed scrawl. Instead she found a letter written in loose cursive. It seemed as though Neddy carved into paper when he wrote, she had noted, but found the letter to be much more delicate in form, no torn or mud stained edges.

The letter read:

I hate to be the stranger, some nobody, to tell you your friend is dead. I'm sorry, and even though I do not know you, it hurts me know you have to read the following terrible words: Neddy is dead. He shot himself in the head. I had just met him. I could see that there were wars being waged inside of him. He told me about his life, the good and the bad, and he talked a lot about you.

He gave me your address in confidence I would deliver a letter for him. I gave him my word, and, as you'll see, I have encased something Neddy wanted you to have. He cut the palm of his hand just to put a bloody thumbprint on his letter for you. The other letter, his letter to you, was written on my typewriter the day he died. He died on Easter Sunday.

I was researching a novel on slavery in the South when I met Neddy. He has, instead, became the subject of my novel. I will be sure to send you a copy when I am done, because I have tried as hard as I can to understand his complicated mind. The novel begins, 'Neddy was a slave who lived in South Carolina long ago.'

He was buried in his fake grave, taking Atma as his last name, by Tyger River in South Carolina. If you don't get to make the trip, I'll leave the flowers for you.

He's very fond of yellow jasmines. And whatever it was he was looking for, some calm perhaps, I hope he found it. I hope you will too. I hope we all do.

Sincerely yours,
Roger S. Manwell

She saw the bloody thumbprint through the letter on the bottom. Her heart beat terrible hammer blows, the fear, the fear she would be right about the contents of the letter.

Tears began to bubble under her soft eyes and she hesitated, for hours, stunned and in a daze, before she stood and walked away.

She heard barking at the door and scratching. She opened the door and looked down, Neddy's shaggy namesake looking up at her with gleaming eyes.

Easter Sunday... three days ago, Nirvana thought, looking at the dog's intense eyes.

"Come on in, Neddy," she said. "We'll find you something to eat."

The dog dried and well fed sleeping, 'Vana went back to the table where the opened letter lay, cut it open; two poker chips fell out, a hollow sound hitting the table.

The letter in strange printed letters read:

My Nirvana,

I'm sorry if I made you care. I'm sorry if I made you love me. I'm sorry if I made you cry. I'm sorry when I had to lie. I'm sad you have to know that this old man will die. I'm sad I have to use that wretched word Goodbye.

I wanted to be a good boy. I wanted to make people laugh and smile. I wanted their approval and their love, some comfort for a while, the world's forgiveness, nothing else, though I could never be enough for myself.

Their lives for mine is not enough to me.

If I had one wish, I'd wish that everybody on Earth could just be happy, and hope that, somehow, would atone for all my sins.

I wanted to be free.

I wanted to make a name for myself, be respected, be cared about and loved, and in the end I don't deserve it. I don't deserve your approval. I don't deserve your tears.

I love you but don't deserve your love. You guided me through hell, my 'Vana, and you showed me Heaven on the Earth.

Those brief moments have lighted my life for moments. Hopefully by the time you have to head my way, I'll be where the sun shines on the Rose Hill every day.

Grow up and live and love and find something or somebody that can make you happy. And if I make it to Heaven, in the end, I'll put in a good word for you-- so when you die no one will cry and instead smile to the sky where we hold hands again.

With my life I pay for all my sins, that list is too long to begin, and I leave the chips to you. The maze is long, my 'Vana, I hope you find your way. All I can offer you is flowers in the shape of words, words shaped like tulips too—if you see me in your dreams I'm looking at you too.

And if our God should let me, if at last we get to meet, I'll ask if he will guide you too with jasmines at your feet.

Had we met on a sea less troubled, I do believe our lives might have become knitted together in the end, because in your bed, your warm legs to my cold toes, I felt Nirvana here on Earth, the radiating warmth from you, your beautiful and unending empathy.

I could never repay you for what you've done for me, but, just in case, when you get there the ride's on me.

Goodbye Earth, goodbye my dreams, goodbye pretty things I've seen.

Goodbye family, goodbye friends, goodbye to those who drift in wind.

Goodbye love, goodbye hate, goodbye to those forever wait.

Goodbye me, goodbye skies, goodbye to the endless why's.

Goodbye Earth, goodbye time, goodbye little life of mine.

Goodbye starlings, goodbye wrens, goodbye time my lazy friends. Goodbye people, all of you, there's nothing left for me to do, time to put an end on me. You can have my life, my heart, my soul; I don't deserve it anymore.

Forever yours,
Nobody.

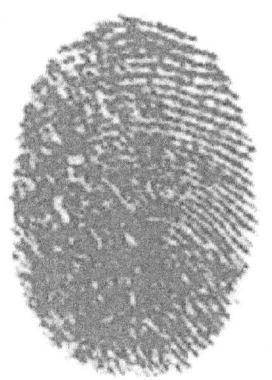

www.ingramcontent.com/pod-product-compliance
Lightning Source LLC
Chambersburg PA
CBHW070853180526
45168CB00005B/1808